THE SACK OF PANAMÁ

Also by Peter Earle

Corsairs of Malta and Barbary
Henry V
James II
Robert E. Lee
The World of Defoe
Monmouth's Rebels
The Treasure of the *Concepción*

Essays in European Economic
   History, 1500–1800 *(editor)*

PETER EARLE

The Sack of Panamá

Sir Henry Morgan's Adventures
on the Spanish Main

The Viking Press   *New York*

Copyright © 1981 by Peter Earle

Published in 1982 by The Viking Press
625 Madison Avenue, New York, N.Y. 10022

Published simultaneously in Canada by
Penguin Books Canada Limited

Library of Congress Cataloging in Publication Data
Earle, Peter, 1937 –
    The sack of Panamá.
    Bibliography: p.
    Includes index.
1. Panama (Panama) — Destruction, 1671.
2. Morgan, Henry, Sir, 1635? – 1688.
3. Privateering — Caribbean area.   I. Title.
F1576.P2E18   972.8'75   81-65267
ISBN 0-670-61425-4   AACR2

Printed in the United States of America
Set in Bembo

Contents

List of Illustrations

Maps

The decorative emblem throughout the text is derived from an illustration of a barque of the period from Père Jean-Baptiste Labat's *Nouveau voyage aux isles de l'Amérique*.

Acknowledgement is due Jane Pugh, who drew the maps, and the following institutions for the plates: The British Library, 1 & 2, 3, 4, 7, 9, 11; The Archivo General de Indias, Seville, 5, 6, 12; The Mansell Collection, 10, 13.

Introduction

'THUS was consumed the famous and antyent citty of Panamá, the greatest mart for silver and gold in the whole world. . . .' Henry Morgan's epic capture and sack of the city of Panamá is one of the most fascinating of historical stories and one that caught my attention at a very early age. It has all the ingredients of the classic adventure story with the added twist that one never really knows whether to admire or despise the brutal men who are its heroes. What I have tried to do in this book is to tell this story once again, but to give it an entirely new dimension by devoting nearly as much space to the Spaniards who were the victims as to the Jamaican privateers themselves. This has been possible through the exploitation of the massive and hitherto almost totally unstudied sources in the Archivo General de Indias in Seville. It hardly needs to be said that the capture and sack of important colonial cities by small bands of adventurers caused official concern, and it is the courts of enquiry which resulted from that concern which have provided me with most of my information. The result is, I hope, a very much more balanced, but no less exciting, retelling of an old story.

The book starts in the summer of 1666 and covers just five years in considerable detail. This period, which has a certain unity within the history of Jamaica and the West Indies, is packed with exciting incident and dramatic changes of fortune. The narrative covers four campaigns by the Jamaican privateers, culminating in the expedition to Panamá, and one successful counter-attack by the Spaniards. Altogether, we have one island captured three times by different people, two cities and three towns captured and sacked, and one of the most extraordinary fleet actions in naval history. Each of these expeditions is rather different from all the others – a fact which should give the book variety and avoid making it into merely a catalogue of the privateers' successes. Other chapters help to give the

9

book more depth by looking at the reaction in Spain and England to events in the West Indies and by examining the attempts made by the Spanish colonists in the Indies to defend themselves from their enemies in Jamaica. Consideration of the problems of defence in the Spanish colonial empire should make it clear why Henry Morgan was so consistently successful, without diminishing his own contribution. Whatever one might think of his character and his profession, there can be no denying that Morgan was a remarkable man who deserves to be remembered not just as a successful privateer, but also as a really great leader of irregular forces.

I would like to thank the staffs of the various record depositories which I have used and, in particular, the staff of the Archivo General de Indias in Seville, who were very kind to a researcher who reads Spanish much better than he speaks it. I would also like to thank Victoria Stapells-Johnson and John Hemming, who gave me much assistance in finding books and sources during the early stages of my research; David Hebb, who read and commented on the manuscript; Jane Pugh, who drew the maps; and Joan Lynas, who typed the manuscript with her usual speed and accuracy.

Translations from the Spanish are not always completely literal. I have tried instead to make quotations readable while retaining the sense of the original. Dates are New Style, which means that, from an English or Jamaican point of view, everything happened ten days earlier than appears in the text.

London and Bury St Edmunds, PETER EARLE
September 1980

CHAPTER ONE

Santa Catalina

'LAND ahead on the starboard bow!' It was noon on 25 May 1666 when the ageing privateer, Captain Edward Mansfield, heard the lookout's cry. He clambered up into the rigging to check his position. One quick look through his perspective glass and he could relax. There was no mistaking the rugged hills, over a thousand feet high, of the lonely island which the English called Providence and the Spaniards called Santa Catalina.[1] The old captain glanced back at the rest of his squadron. All four ships were still in sight, spread out across the otherwise empty sea. They all looked as though they had been a long time out of port, weather-beaten, paint faded, sails patched, but still moving well through the water, their bottoms clean after a recent careening. Three of them were very small, lateen-rigged sloops with no deck or cabin to protect their cramped crews from sun and sea and rain; and even the fourth was only about fifty tons, a small, square-rigged, half-decked frigate which, like Mansfield's own similar ship, had been recently captured from the Spaniards off the Central American coast. None of them carried many cannon, but no one who saw them would have been in any doubt that they were best to be avoided. Small, fast ships like these, crammed with men who knew from experience that four muskets could do as much execution as one cannon,[2] had terrorized the waters and coastal settlements of the Caribbean for decades. Mansfield signalled the frigate to furl her topsails to reduce visibility and crept forward towards his goal. By late afternoon he was only twelve miles from the southernmost point of the island, and the squadron hove to until nightfall. Tomorrow, with any luck, the island would be his.

Mansfield badly needed to capture something to retrieve his reputation. He had made an almost complete circuit of the Caribbean in the past six months and had virtually nothing to show for his pains.[3]

General map of the West Indies

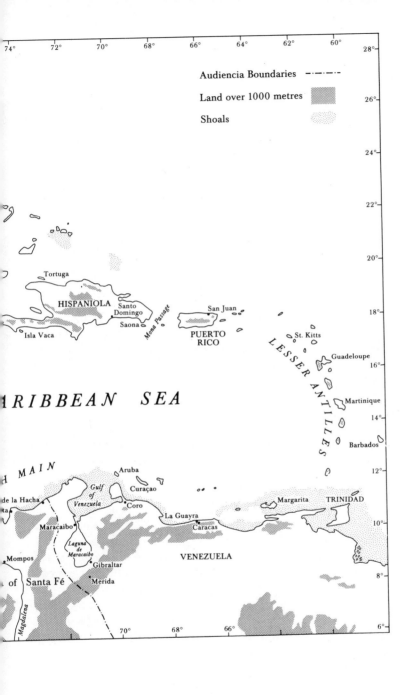

Audiencia Boundaries — · —·· —

Land over 1000 metres

Shoals

74° 72° 70° 68° 66° 64° 62° 60° 28°
26°
24°
22°
20°
18°
16°
14°
12°
10°
8°
6°

Tortuga

HISPANIOLA
Santo
Domingo
Saona
Isla Vaca

Mona Passage

San Juan

PUERTO
RICO

St. Kitts

Guadeloupe

L E S S E R   A N T I L L E S

Martinique

Barbados

RIBBEAN   SEA

MAIN

de la Hacha
ta

Aruba

Gulf
of
Venezuela

Curaçao

Coro

Maracaibo

Laguna
de
Maracaibo

Gibraltar

La Guayra

Caracas

Margarita

TRINIDAD

Mompos

Merida

of Santa Fé

VENEZUELA

Magdalena

70° 68° 66°

It was, however, rather doubtful whether the capture of a Spanish island would win him much favour with the authorities in his home port of Port Royal, Jamaica. These were the days of the Second Dutch War, and Mansfield, a professional privateer, was sailing with a commission issued by Sir Thomas Modyford, the English Governor of Jamaica, which allowed him to attack and plunder the Dutch. So far, his voyage had done little damage to that maritime nation. The privateers had rendezvoused on the south coast of Jamaica in November 1665 with the clear intention of attacking and capturing the Dutch commercial base on the island of Curaçao off the coast of Venezuela. Some six hundred privateers had turned up and were said to be 'very forward to suppression of that enemy'. Their first move had, however, been in the opposite direction. Christmas had seen them off the south coast of Cuba, demanding 'victualls for their money'. The Cubans who, like all Spanish settlers, were prohibited from trading with foreigners had refused, whereupon 'two or three hundred privateers . . . marched forty-two miles into the country, took and fired the town of Santo Spirito, routed a body of 200 horse, carried their prisoners to their ships, and for their ransom had 300 fat beeves sent down'.[4] When asked why privateers with commissions against the Dutch should attack the Spanish, they had looked rather hurt. It almost sounded as if they were being accused of piracy. The privateer captains, after a short search amongst the papers in their cabins, had produced Portuguese commissions issued by the French Governor of Tortuga. This, of course, made everything legal. Portugal had been in revolt against Spain for twenty-six years.

By the middle of January 1666, their victualling completed, the privateers were ready to sail again. They chose Captain Mansfield as their admiral and assured an emissary from the Governor of Jamaica that they 'had much zeale to his Majesty's service and a firm resolution to attack Curaçao'. But this resolution soon wilted during the long beat east straight into the prevailing trade winds. The expedition seemed all wrong. The whole tradition of privateering in the West Indies was to attack Spaniards, not Dutchmen. Ship after ship drifted off to make use of their Portuguese commissions against the Spanish settlers of Cuba and Hispaniola. Mansfield continued to beat to windward, but eventually he, too, was faced with mutiny and his crew refused to go any farther, 'averring publiquely that there was more profitt with lesse hazard to be gotten against ye Spaniard which was there onely interest'. As we shall see, this was sadly only too true, and it seems unlikely that Mansfield was particularly unhappy as he gave the order for the ships to go about and run with the wind down to the coast of the Spanish Main. One of his captains was later to make the best of it in a report to the Governor of Jamaica. They had tried to beat up to Curaçao, he said, 'as much as they could, but was so long on their way that they spent their victuall and were forced to fall down with the wind and current to Boco Tauro [Boca del Toro] to recruit'.[5]

Mansfield still had fifteen ships under his command when he arrived at Boca del Toro on the borders of Panamá and Costa Rica, a favourite haunt of the privateers. Here the original fleet split up into two squadrons. Mansfield sailed with seven ships up the coast to Costa Rica, where he landed and marched inland across the coastal lowlands and then began to ascend the Cordillera with the intention of crossing the mountains to raid the city of Cartago. He was checked by shortage of food and a vigorous resistance by the garrison of Turrialba, ninety miles inland and 2500 feet above sea level, and the invasion ended in an ignominious retreat.[6] The survivors, 'exhausted and dying of hunger', re-embarked and made their way back down the coast to Boca del Toro.

Here two more ships deserted Mansfield, and the old Admiral was left with the dreadful prospect of returning to Jamaica discredited and completely empty-handed, a failure in the eyes of the privateers and an embarrassment to the Governor. It was now that he had the idea of attacking and capturing Santa Catalina. It was true that the island was Spanish and his Jamaican commission only gave him permission to attack the Dutch; but maybe the Governor of Jamaica would look kindly on the man who captured this particular Spanish island, for it had not always been Spanish.

It had in fact been one of the very first English colonies in the New World, settled in 1630 by men sent out from Bermuda and England by the Puritan Providence Island Company.[7] The island was at that time uninhabited, and the Company's avowed intention was to develop their fertile and isolated colony as a godly plantation where pious men raised exotic crops for the greater glory of God and the profit of the London-based shareholders. It is clear, however, that

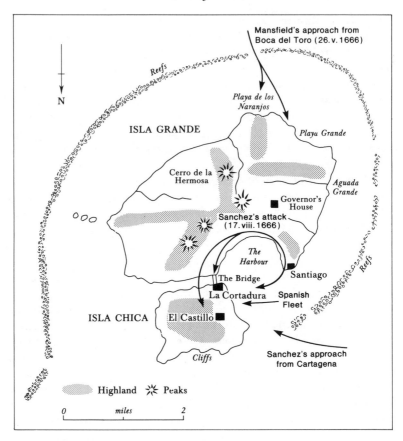

Mansfield's approach from
Boca del Toro (26.v.1666)

Reefs

N

*Playa de los
Naranjos*

ISLA GRANDE

Playa Grande

Cerro de la
Hermosa

*Aguada
Grande*

Governor's
House

Sanchez's attack
(17.viii.1666)

*The
Harbour*

The Bridge

Santiago

La Cortadura

Spanish
Fleet

ISLA CHICA

El Castillo

Reefs

Cliffs

Sanchez's approach
from Cartagena

Highland   Peaks

0   *miles*   2

The island of Santa Catalina or Providence

this was simply wishful thinking, and from the beginning the
colony's main function was 'to annoy the King of Spain in the Indies'.
Providence Island, as it was now called, was ideal for this purpose –
only 450 miles of easy sailing from Cartagena, the largest and
richest city on the Spanish Main, and even closer to Portobello, the
terminus of that maritime lifeline of the Spanish colonial empire, the
annual silver fleets. Providence was fertile enough to maintain a large
garrison and several privateering ships and, once properly gar-

risoned and fortified, extremely difficult to capture. A ring of reefs almost completely surrounded the island, and the one good port was commanded by huge rocks and cliffs. When the harbour had been fortified it was nearly impregnable, as the Governor of Cartagena was to discover when the expedition he led against the island in 1635 retired with the loss of many men, 'being much torn and battered by the ordnance from the forts'. The Spanish attack was taken as sufficient cause to issue large numbers of privateering licences, and for the next six years Providence was to be the very worst enemy of Spain in the West Indies.

A second Spanish attack was beaten off in 1640 but, in the following year, the Captain-General of the silver fleet, Francisco Diaz Pimienta, mounted an invasion force so strong that the English and Dutch defenders of the island had no chance. Pimienta's landing with an advance force of six hundred seasoned Spanish soldiers was fiercely opposed, but to no avail, and he marched across the island to the settlement at New Westminster where he laid siege to the Governor's house and the church. Resistance soon collapsed and, on 26 May 1641, High Mass was celebrated and a *Te Deum* sung in the town square of New Westminster in the presence of the Spanish troops and the four hundred heretical English and Dutch prisoners. The booty was immense – six hundred black slaves and over half a million ducats' worth of treasure, the former property of Spaniards captured by the English and Dutch corsairs. It was the greatest Spanish triumph in the West Indies for many years, and Pimienta became a famous and much-fêted man.[8] Now Edward Mansfield, anxious not to return to Jamaica 'until he had done some service to his Majesty', resolved to recover this property of the King of England and make it once again a hugely fortified advance base for the Jamaican privateers. And what better day to do it than on 26 May 1666, the twenty-fifth anniversary of the capture of the island by Pimienta?

Since 1641, Santa Catalina's garrison and fortifications had been badly run down.[9] The Spaniards had considered abandoning the island on several occasions, for it seemed to be rather a useless drain on the very scarce resources of men and money that were available for the defence of the Spanish Main; but always the thought of a second occupation by the English had changed their minds, for the

English were now even more formidable than they had been in the 1630s. The capture of Jamaica in 1655 had led to a huge increase in the scale of depredations carried out by privateers who used the island as a base. A second smaller but closer Jamaica, entirely devoted to privateering, was a nightmare. And so the small, rugged, mountainous island, once again called Santa Catalina, was retained. But now, in 1666, it was no longer the mighty fortress that had given 'the Spaniards' whole armada' such a fight in 1641. Lack of money, lack of men, indifference, corruption and apathy had all taken their toll, and the island's situation was not improved by a long-running argument between the Governor of Cartagena and the President of Panamá as to which of them had the financial responsibility for its defence. In the absence of an agreement, each man naturally spent as little as possible on the upkeep of the island, and ships from the mainland only rarely brought fresh supplies of food, weapons and comforts for the miserable garrison. The results of such neglect were only too predictable.

Many of the English guns and fortifications remained, rusty and crumbling through disuse, but only one fort was still garrisoned. This fort, known as La Cortadura, overlooked the port and stood in the few yards of sea which separated the main island from the small and fairly easily defended islet of Isla Chica at the north end of the island. The garrison of Santa Catalina was supposed to comprise 140 regular soldiers, but no garrison in the Spanish Indies was ever up to strength and, in 1666, there were only ninety soldiers on the island, twenty of whom were too old or too sick to bear arms. Many men in the garrison had come out to the island with Pimienta's invasion force in 1641 and had stayed there ever since, quietly vegetating in their lonely tropical fastness. Others had been sent there as exiles; four years in Santa Catalina was a common punishment for delinquents from the mainland. Women who lived scandalous lives in the cities of Cartagena or Panamá were also likely to find themselves removed to this convenient dumping-ground for the human trash of the Spanish Main. Such people, together with their children, 150 slaves and a few Indian herdsmen, formed the population of Santa Catalina. Contrary to all military principles, they were scattered throughout the island, living on their own small farms in huts and shacks and neglecting their military exercises for the more important tasks of raising maize and manioc, pigs and goats for their own sustenance. What else could they do if they received no food from the mainland? The men did have posts to which they were supposed to run in case of attack, and there were elaborate signalling systems to give the alarm. It is possible that many of the men would have recognized those signals if they had seen or heard them, but was there likely to be any such signal? The English had not been near the island for twenty-five years. Why should they come today?

Such, clearly, was the attitude of Pedro Perez and Luis de Aguiar, the two soldiers whose turn it was, on 25 May 1666, to serve as sentinels on the Cerro de la Hermosa at the south end of the island. Each pair of soldiers spent two days on sentry duty on this lofty peak, and no doubt it was felt to be an uncongenial duty. On a clear day it was possible to see out to sea in every direction for fifteen or twenty miles, but Perez and Aguiar saw nothing as Edward Mansfield's five ships approached the island, their masts and yards silhouetted against the setting sun. Was it clear that day? 'No', said Pedro Perez, giving evidence later. 'There was no sun and it was so cloudy that he could not see the headland of the Playa de los Naranjos at the southern end of the island.'[10] 'Yes,' said Domingo de Soza, a Portuguese captive of the English who was on Mansfield's own ship. It had been cloudy in the early afternoon, but later it cleared, and during the two hours before nightfall the sky was crystal clear. The sentinels could not possibly have failed to see the ships if they had been looking. One fears that the Portuguese was telling the truth and that the two sentries took a long siesta on that lovely afternoon. It was just bad luck that it had to be their turn to be on duty.

Captain Mansfield was no doubt well informed as to the numbers, competence and morale of the island's garrison, for as he had run with the trade wind down to the Spanish Main and along the coast to Boca del Toro he had picked up many other prisoners in addition to Domingo de Soza – merchant seamen, fishermen, herdsmen. Anyone cruising along the coast or loitering unsuspectingly on the seashore was likely to end up on the deck of a privateer. And then, as the famous travel-writer and former buccaneer, Captain Dampier, tells us, they would be examined 'concerning the country, town, or city that they belong to . . . how many families, whether most Spaniards? . . . whether rich, and what their riches do consist in? . . .

if fortified, how many great guns, and what number of small arms? Whether it is possible to come undescried on them? How many look-outs or centinels . . . and how the look-outs are placed? . . . And if they have any former discourse of such places from other prisoners, they compare one with the other; then examine again, and enquire if he or any of them are capable to be guides to conduct a party of men thither.'[11] Amongst Mansfield's prisoners on this occasion were a mestizo called Montes and a Spaniard called Roque, both of whom knew Santa Catalina well and had agreed to guide the privateers for a share of the prize. They would need good guides, because their proposed invasion of the islands would take them by a route that was dangerous enough in daytime and was believed to be impossible at night. Such, at least, was the belief of the island's Governor, Don Estevan de Ocampo, who went to bed that night in his unfortified house quite oblivious of the disaster that was to wreck his military career after serving his king in Spain and the Indies for twenty-five years.

As night fell, Mansfield signalled to his squadron to set sail towards the island, sounding continuously as they approached the reefs. At about ten o'clock they anchored just outside the one gap in the reefs which surrounded the southern end of the island and waited until the moon rose at midnight.[12] Now, as the pale light illuminated the razor-sharp rocks stretching on each side as far as the eye could see, they launched their canoes and disembarked, leaving just two or three dozen men to guard the ships. They were a wild-looking crowd, sunburned, ragged and emaciated after their long and fruitless cruise; some two hundred men – eighty Frenchmen from the island of Tortuga, a few Dutch and Portuguese, the two renegade guides and a hundred or so Englishmen from Jamaica. Each man placed his long musket carefully in the canoe, keeping his two pistols and his cutlass in his belt, and then off they paddled swiftly and silently through the gap in the reefs into the milky, lukewarm waters of the lagoon within. Here they split up into two squadrons, one paddling straight ahead to Playa de los Naranjos and the other setting off a bit farther to the west to land at Playa Grande. Once the men had landed on the two beaches, the canoes returned to the ships – a dramatic gesture worthy of a greater captain and a greater exploit. There was now no retreat. They must conquer the island or die!

The paths up from the beaches were thought to be impassable by night; but they seem to have given the privateers no problems, and soon the men were marching along in single file to where the two paths met. Here they had been told by their guides that there was a lookout post, but after a stealthy approach they found it deserted. So now all the privateers marched together, along the rough track grandly called the Royal Road, rounding up the men from the isolated farms along the way. One of these prisoners was deputed to guide them. He was pushed to the front of the column, his hands tied behind his back and a lasso round his neck whose pressure was sufficient to indicate what would happen if he made a false move. He led them to Aguada Grande, the watering-place on the west coast where one of the island's four small rivers met the sea. Here a foolhardy Spaniard tried to seize a musket from one of the invaders and was shot for his pains – the only man to resist Mansfield's invasion and the only man to die.

By this time, the sentries on Cerro de la Hermosa had woken up and, rubbing their eyes in the harsh dawn light, stared out to sea at the five ships anchored off the reef. Terrified, they ran down the hill to warn the Governor, who was still in bed. He shouted for a messenger to ride over and give the news to the Sergeant-Major* who was in charge of the fort, and then got dressed quickly and saddled a horse. But not quickly enough. Looking up from his task, he saw the enemy surrounding his house. He dashed inside to grab his sword and sell his life dearly, but there was to be no easy and noble way out for him. The enemy were already in the house, and the Governor was captured without a shot fired in his defence.

Diego Rodriguez had risen early and was supervising the building of a bridge joining the fort of La Cortadura to the two islands. He had first joined the Spanish Army as a boy of ten and had served as a groom in the garrison of Badajoz in Spain. At fourteen he had come to Santa Catalina and now, nineteen years later, he was Sergeant-Major and second-in-command of the island.[13] But, despite his rank and long service, he had probably never seen a shot fired in anger. The sun was only just over the horizon when four soldiers came

---

* A much more senior rank than its English equivalent, second-in-command to a military governor or to the castellan of a castle or to a *maestre de campo* in the field.

running and shouted to him that the enemy had landed and had captured the Governor in his house. The Sergeant-Major rushed into the fort and called to the gunner of the guard to get the guns in order. But now they had to pay the price for those twenty-five years of neglect and indiscipline. There was no powder by the guns, and the four soldiers were sent to look for it; but when they found a chest full of powder they could not find the key. And where were the cannon-balls and the grapeshot? It was so long since they had been used that no one could remember. Sergeant-Major Rodriguez was still rushing around the gun-platform, shouting at people and looking for things, when he saw the enemy approaching in the distance and realized that the bridge he had been building was likely to make the assault rather easy. He raced down and threw the loose planks into the sea, but then could not find the hammer to prise up the planks that had already been nailed down by the negroes who had been working under his supervision. The negroes themselves had, of course, fled to the hills at the first news of the enemy. So, much of the bridge was still in place when Rodriguez scampered back up to the gun-platform and looked out along the barrel of the now loaded gun at the enemy.

The English shouted at him in Spanish to surrender. If he did not, they said, they would kill every man, woman and child on the main island and then come back to kill him, too. They looked quite capable of it. Rodriguez searched desperately for something to raise as a white flag and surrendered without a shot being fired – a fact he was at some pains to explain when he was later interrogated in Portobello. What good would it have done if he had fired one charge of grapeshot at the enemy? He had only eight men to defend the fort and he would soon have been overwhelmed. As it was, everyone on the island had remained alive and so could return to recover the loss on another occasion. It was a sentiment with which most readers will no doubt sympathize, but it did not receive much favour from the authorities in Portobello. Spanish soldiers were expected to win or die.

A few minutes after Rodriguez' surrender, the English flag was flying over the fort and the Spanish prisoners in the ships outside the reef heard three cannon and a volley of musket-fire – the signal that Santa Catalina was English again. It was eight o'clock in the morning. Now it was just a question of rounding up the rest of the population and piling up the loot. Finding hidden loot was usually a major task for the privateers, but this time their approach had been so stealthy and the capture of the island so rapid that they were to have little trouble. How much they actually captured is difficult to say. The Spaniards naturally exaggerated the value of what they lost, since the greater the loss the more chance they had of remission of taxes and other favours. The English always minimized their gains to protect themselves from their creditors in Jamaica, and so we read in Sir Thomas Modyford's account of Mansfield's exploit that 'they acknowledge but very little plunder, only 150 negroes'. But this is clearly nonsense. Don Antonio Garmendia, a young Basque who was the *contador* or accountant of the island and so was fairly well placed to know the truth, said in evidence later that the English took, apart from the negroes, 5000 pesos belonging to the King and all the silver, jewels and other valuables of the inhabitants, which were worth about 50,000 pesos. Many of the negroes seized by the English were actually free; one was an officer in the garrison. Adding all this up, and estimating the negroes at the usual valuation of 100 pesos a head, makes a grand haul of 70,000 pesos or £17,500* worth of booty. Shared out equally between the 230 men who sailed with Mansfield, this comes to about £75 each – a good night's work in a world where a labourer was lucky to make £15 a year, and not what would usually be described as 'very little plunder'. It is not difficult to appreciate the attractions of the life of the privateer.

One other attraction usually enjoyed by these rough English heretics was denied them on this occasion. When they went off to wreck the church they found their way barred by their Catholic French allies, who promised the priest that they would guard him and prevent the English from getting at the images and altars. They planned to take the Holy Scriptures back for use in their own church in Tortuga. The disappointed English felt obliged to desist. It was such fun smashing up images. Whether they made up for this disappointment in other ways we do not know. The Spanish evidence makes no mention of torture or rape, but it would seem inconceiv-

---

* The exchange rate naturally varied, but I will take 4 pesos = £1 as the basis for comparison in this book. The peso is the same as the piece of eight, i.e., eight reales.

able that the privateers had no enjoyment from those scandalous ladies who had been deported from Cartagena and Panamá.

Edward Mansfield remained less than a fortnight on his conquered island. He left Captain Hatsell with a garrison of thirty-five men and fifty negro slaves to hold the island until he had reported back to Jamaica, where he hoped to persuade the Governor to recognize the justice of his action and reinforce the garrison. But, first, he had to honour the surrender terms and land the Spanish garrison on the Main. On 11 June he dropped anchor at Punta de Brujas on the coast of Panamá and bid farewell to the dejected Governor Ocampo and the 170 people, many of them women and children, who had elected to leave the island rather than remain under English rule. It must have been a rather cramped journey but, fortunately for them, a quick one. Then Mansfield set sail once again for the north and arrived in Port Royal, Jamaica, with just two ships on 22 June. Here he reported to the Governor, Sir Thomas Modyford, giving, as most privateer captains did, a somewhat exaggerated account of his action. It turned out that there were two hundred Spanish soldiers on the island, not the ninety which the muster-books declared, and that all two hundred had managed to get into the fort to defend it, not merely the eight that Sergeant-Major Rodriguez could see. This was standard stuff. There was no such thing as a humble, self-effacing privateer. Mansfield was able to emphasize the essentially English nature of the island by pointing out that several of the twenty-seven guns he had captured had the arms of Queen Elizabeth engraven on them. As Mansfield had expected, there were few recriminations for the misuse of his commission. Modyford was to confess as much four days later in a letter to Lord Arlington, the English Secretary of State:

I have yet only reproved him for doing it without order, which I should suppose would have been an acceptable service had he received command for it. . . . Neither could I without manifest imprudence but accept the tender of it in his Majestie's behalfe. And considering its good situation for ye favouring any designes his Majesty may have on that rich maine right against it . . . I hold it my duty to reinforce that garrison and to send downe some able person to command it.[14]

Such a letter was, as we shall see, rather typical of Modyford's artful approach to the governorship of Jamaica.[15] There had, however, been a radical change in the situation in Jamaica in the six months that Mansfield had been away from the island, and the Governor had found it necessary to court the privateers in every possible way. Modyford had found that his refusal to issue commissions against the Spaniards had drained Jamaica of fighting men, as privateer after privateer had drifted off to seek French or Portuguese commissions from that other great promoter of the privateering business, the Governor of the French island of Tortuga. Modyford found the situation most alarming. He had no ships of the Royal Navy to defend Jamaica, and now he had no privateers, either. Never had the island seemed more vulnerable. There was the constant threat that a huge Spanish fleet might appear over the horizon to try to repossess the island the Spaniards had lost ten years previously; for they still felt deeply the dishonour of an English Jamaica, their first big island to fall to foreigners. And then there were the Dutch, with whom England had been officially at war since February 1665. Finally, and most dangerous of all, there were the French, who, by an agreement made in 1662, were obliged to come to the aid of the Dutch against the English. So far they had not honoured this obligation but, if and when they did, a Jamaica without ships and with a depleted militia would be too tempting a target to resist. How could Modyford ensure that the privateers returned to their allegiance in Jamaica? The answer, in the lunatic world of the seventeenth-century West Indies, was simple. The only way to get men to come to Jamaica to defend the island against the French was to issue commissions against the Spaniards, since it was only against the Spaniards that the privateers liked to fight, except in self-defence. And so, on 4 March 1666, Modyford consulted with the Council of Jamaica, and it was resolved 'that it is the interest and advantage of the island of Jamaica to have letters of marque graunted against the Spaniard'.[16] In other words, Modyford had just made a unilateral declaration of war upon Spain – a fact which was proclaimed at beat of drum in the streets of Port Royal.

All this made Mansfield's capture of Santa Catalina on 26 May almost legal in retrospect, although it might prove convenient to tell the truth and say that 'the old fellow' had done it on his own initiative if there were any awkward Spanish reactions. Not that Modyford had any intention of handing the island back to Spain. It was English and had always been English, except for that short, illegal, unprovoked Spanish occupation of twenty-five years. At the moment, there were few men available to reinforce the garrison, but Modyford did his best. Just eight days after Mansfield's return, on 30 June 1666, Major Samuel Smith was commissioned as commander of 'all the forces made and to be made in Jamaica and other parts for the guard and defence of Providence Island . . . and also Governor of all the inhabitants'.[17] He left almost immediately to 'take the same into his charge' with a few reinforcements and the promise of many more as they became available. Amongst his papers were a bundle of blank privateering commissions authorizing him to appoint captains 'to attaque, fight with or surprise any vessell or vessells whatsoever belonging to the King of Spain or any of his subjects which you shall meet with to the southward of the Tropic of Cancer; and also if you finde it prudential to invade any of their lands, colonys, or plantations in America'.[18]

The English occupation of Providence, or Santa Catalina, was not to last for long, but a new phase in the long-running privateering war against Spain had begun. It was to end four and a half years later with the sack of Panamá. But first we have to record a Spanish triumph.

CHAPTER TWO

A Spanish Triumph

DON ESTEVAN DE OCAMPO, the dishonoured Governor of Santa Catalina,[1] led his miserable band of exiles along the north coast of the province of Panamá until he arrived at the great castle of San Lorenzo at the mouth of the River Chagres. Here he reported to the Castellan, and a messenger was sent across the isthmus to the city of Panamá to give the sad news of the loss of the island to the most important official on the Spanish Main, Don Juan Perez de Guzmán, President of the Audiencia of Panamá and Governor and Captain-General of the province of Tierra Firme.

Don Juan, who plays an important part in our story, was a loyal and intensely religious servant of the Spanish Crown, 'a man of much courage and good will, but very little fortune'.[2] He had been born in Seville in 1618, and had seen a considerable variety of military service in Milan and in the royal fleet before becoming interim Governor of Cartagena in the late 1650s and Governor of Puerto Rico from 1661 to 1664. He had arrived in Panamá to take up his present post eighteen months previously in January 1665. The Audiencia of Panamá was the smallest and least populated jurisdiction in the Spanish colonial empire, but its defence was absolutely vital to the maintenance of that empire and, indeed, of Spain herself. For it was here, at the narrowest part of the isthmus of Central America, that the immense wealth of the silver mines of Peru was exchanged for the much coveted manufactured goods of Europe. On the Caribbean side of the isthmus stood the small city of Portobello, whose magnificent harbour was the terminus of the fleets of galleons which sailed out from Seville laden with all those things which the Spanish colonists in South and Central America needed to maintain themselves – tapestries, rich textiles and glass for the fine ladies of Lima; reams and reams of paper to be filled up with the endless reports and correspondence of the colonial bureaucrats; weapons

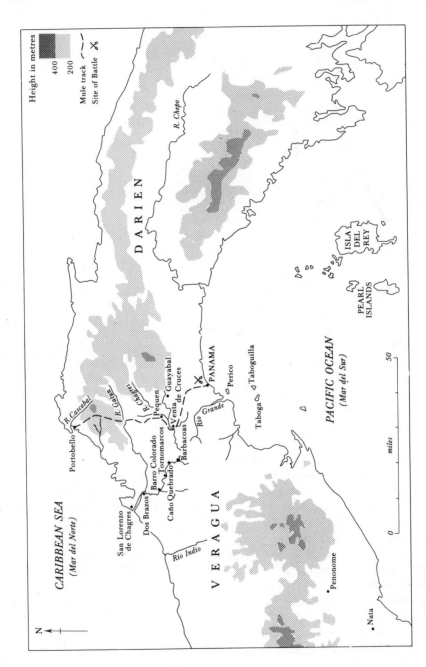

The Isthmus of Panamá

and ammunition to enable the garrisons to resist the numerous enemies of Spain. Such goods were transported across the isthmus by river-boat and mule-train to the great city of Panamá on the Pacific, itself the terminus for a smaller fleet which sailed up from Peru laden mainly with silver, which was transferred to the backs of the mules who took it back to Portobello where it was stowed away in the galleons ready for the long voyage to Spain.[3] Some of this silver naturally stuck to the fingers of the citizens of Panamá and Portobello, who arranged for its exchange and transportation, and both cities were wealthy, though not quite as wealthy as covetous minds in Jamaica and Tortuga and farther afield thought that they were.

It was the duty of Don Juan Perez de Guzmán as Captain-General of this Kingdom of Tierra Firme to protect the two cities and the dozen or so smaller places under his command and to ensure that there should not be the slightest hitch in that process by which the silver of Peru was transported to fill the coffers of the King of Spain. To help him do this he had two fortified castles and a garrison in Portobello, a fortified castle at the mouth of the River Chagres, a garrison in Panamá, about five hundred regular soldiers altogether, and the services of all able-bodied citizens in a none too dependable militia. No man who served as Captain-General ever thought that this was enough. Nearly all letters to Spain bemoaned the state of the defences and begged – almost always unsuccessfully – for more men, more money, more and better weapons. But, for all this, there had been no serious attempt to penetrate the defences of the Audiencia of Panamá since the days of Drake, sixty or seventy years previously. Until now, that is; until the loss of Santa Catalina. Don Juan was rightly alarmed at the thought of an English corsair base so near his jurisdiction, while his good Spanish heart was shattered by the pathetic surrender of the island without a shot fired in its defence and by the reports of the mocking English comments on the sad state of modern Spanish valour.

His first reactions were routine. He sent a report to Spain and ordered a court of enquiry to be set up in Portobello to interrogate the refugees and to determine who was responsible for the loss of the island.[4] He then reflected on the disaster. What a marvellous boost to his reputation it would be if he could recover the island and return it to his royal master almost before he had realized that he had lost it. His resolve was strengthened by a report from his friend and protégé, Francisco Gonzalez Salado, Castellan of the castle of Santiago in Portobello. The enemy had left only sixty men on the island, but they planned to reinforce them from Jamaica. If he acted now, he could easily recover it.

Don Juan now began to show remarkable enterprise and initiative for a Spanish colonial governor. No important decision could be made without first seeking the advice of the other senior officials in Panamá and so, on 27 June, less than a fortnight after his first knowledge of the loss of the island, Don Juan summoned a *junta de guerra y hazienda*, a council of war and business. Here were assembled the leading figures in the three main branches of colonial administration – legal, represented by the *oydores* or senior magistrates and the *fiscal*; financial, represented by the four *oficiales reales*, the royal officers, whose agreement would be necessary for the King's money to be spent; and finally, since this was a military matter, the senior officers of the Panamá garrison. Don Juan quickly set forth the main facts of the matter and then proposed that an invasion force be quickly assembled and the island retaken.

He drew attention to the great advances made daily by the pirates, saying they would make themselves masters of the West Indies, to the great disgrace and injury of the Spanish nation. Now they had the island of Santa Catalina under their dominion, they would undertake still more enterprises. . . . It was essential, while the corsairs were still not yet established in full strength, that forces should be sent to recapture this island.[5]

But, since Santa Catalina was a joint responsibility, he proposed that these forces should be jointly provided from the resources of Panamá and Cartagena. Don Juan's eloquence was successful. There was only one voice raised in dissent, and he was a well-known enemy of the President. The other members appreciated that it was unusual to take such action without royal authority, but realized that this was a case where promptness was essential.

Don Juan chose as leader of the expedition a colleague whom he had brought from Puerto Rico, José Sanchez Ximenez, now Sergeant-Major of the Portobello garrison, a man who had served twenty-four years in the Spanish army in Flanders, 'a soldier of experience and courage'.[6] The rather motley party assembled from the forces of Panamá comprised 34 men from the two regular companies of the Panamá garrison, 29 mulattoes from the city's militia companies, 5 gunners, 12 Indian archers and 45 refugees from Santa Catalina itself, 'going back like lions to regain their honour and show they were valiant soldiers' – 125 men in all. Transport was provided by requisitioning an English ship which was lying in the harbour of Portobello on charter to the Grillos, the Genoese company who had the monopoly of supplying slaves to the Spanish colonies. Her master, Henry Wassey of Stepney, was released from prison, where he had been put in irons 'under pretence that he came for a spy', and ordered to sail his ship to Cartagena, where Sanchez hoped to persuade the Governor to match his men with as many more.[7]

The reaction in Cartagena was rather more typical of Spanish colonial bureaucracy. When Sanchez arrived, he called on the Governor, Don Benito de Figueroa, and handed over the letters which he had brought from Panamá. Next day, 19 July, Figueroa held a *junta*, but this time there was little of the enthusiasm for the venture which had been shown in Panamá.[8] Most people felt that the proposed expedition was foolhardy and were, as they usually were, in favour of procrastination. More information was needed about the defences of Santa Catalina. The Queen* should be informed before action was taken. There was not enough money for such a project. Only a few of the speakers felt that, as Perez had already resolved to recover the island, it was their duty to do what he asked and help him.

The Governor was himself quite opposed to the expedition. It was against all precedent to act in such an independent manner without first advising the Queen and getting instructions from the Council of the Indies in Madrid – a process which was likely to take at least a year and probably more. He demanded to see Sanchez' instructions. His face fell as he read them and realized that his hand had been forced. The instructions stated that, if the Governor of Cartagena

---

* The King of Spain at this time was Carlos II, a sickly infant, and his mother, the Austrian Queen Maria Anna, was Regent.

refused to help him, Sanchez was to attempt to recover the island on his own and to take testimony before a notary of the fact of the Governor's refusal. The same course was to be taken if the Governor refused to supply him with food and weapons. So, whether the expedition was successful or not, the Governor was bound to be shown to have behaved in a dishonourable way. His face fell even farther when he read an inventory of Sanchez' equipment which he had demanded to be brought to him. It was clear that the President of Panamá had deliberately planned to equip the expedition so poorly as to make it obvious that success was impossible without Figueroa's assistance. The twelve Indians, 'very skilful at shooting arrows', had at least brought their bows, but the other 113 men in Sanchez' party had only forty-eight muskets and eight hatchets between them. There was very little food, powder or ammunition. Figueroa was not only going to have to support an expedition which he thought ill-conceived, he was also going to have to provide considerably more than half the food and equipment which were needed. But there seemed no way out of it, and he was forced to agree to support Sanchez, 'inspired by zeal for His Majesty's service' as he reluctantly put it. Sixty Spaniards and sixty mulattoes from the city's large garrison were ordered to join the expedition under their captain, Don José Ramirez de Leyba; food and weapons were supplied, and two ships and three barques which were lying in the port were chartered as transport.

In the midst of these preparations, three sailors who had been robbed by pirates arrived in Cartagena and reported that they had heard that the English had peopled Santa Catalina with a thousand men. One suspects that Figueroa was quite pleased with this information as he went up to Sanchez and asked him what he planned to do now. Did he intend to sail with 250 men to fight a thousand? Sanchez was unmoved. He said that he would continue his voyage according to his orders. He still believed his own information that there were only fifty or sixty Englishmen on the island to be correct, but he would, of course, send spies ashore to check before he landed. Figueroa stormed off and vented his anger in a long letter to the President of Panamá.[9] He detailed the assistance he had given, but completely exonerated himself from any responsibility for such a foolhardy expedition, 'done without any order from Her Majesty . . . You alone are the author of it.' He then went on to describe at length, and with a wealth of historical example, just how terrible were the punishments meted out in the past to generals who acted without orders and then compounded their offence by failing to achieve what they had intended.

Sanchez seems to have been completely indifferent to the hostility he met in Cartagena. He was probably used to it. Rivalry between colonial officials and arguments about the use of scarce resources were a commonplace in the Spanish colonial empire. On 2 August his small armada set sail, but he was not to have the easy passage to the island enjoyed by Mansfield.[10] Contrary winds and stormy weather delayed his progress and spoiled his English master's navigation. The first they knew of their position was when one of the barques was wrecked on a shoal and they realized that they were right on top of the terrible reef appropriately known as Quita Sueño ('Quit Sleep'), a long way to the north of Santa Catalina. Sanchez was later to praise the Englishman's dexterity in getting them off the reef and saving the men from the barque – 'without his help we would never have arrived' – praise which Henry Wassey must have received with mixed feelings, considering the object of the expedition.

On 10 August, eight days out from Cartagena, the island could be seen to leeward. Sanchez, disdaining any such deceitful English tactics as creeping ashore at night, ordered his fleet to anchor in front of the port but some way out to sea. Next day, he came in closer and, after an exchange of cannon-fire with one of the forts, sent his *ayudante** to instruct the English 'to surrender the island, which they had occupied contrary to the articles of peace between the crowns of England and Spain, saying that should they prove intransigent they should all be put to the sword'.[11]

Major Smith, the Governor, whose orders were to defend the island until further orders from Jamaica, viewed the armada with some alarm.[12] He had not been fooled for a moment by the English flag which Sanchez was flying and, at the first sight of the ships, had ordered everyone to occupy the forts on Isla Chica, leaving no one on the main island except a few men to man the gun-platform of

---

* Assistant to a sergeant-major and senior to a captain.

Santiago, which commanded the other side of the port. But 'everyone' was only fifty-one men and, although it was an article of faith that one Englishman was a match for several Spaniards, he was not too happy about the situation. No one had expected the Spaniards to act so quickly. However, his reply gave no signs of his nervousness. 'The island had formerly belonged to the English Crown,' he said, 'and they would rather die than give it up again now.'

That same night, three mulattoes who had escaped from the English arrived in a canoe and reported to Sanchez. There were only seventy-two men on the island, who were 'full of fear on seeing such a powerful invasion force' – a slight exaggeration of the English numbers which was confirmed by a captain whom Sanchez had sent ashore to gather information. The pirates' story of a thousand men was, as he had guessed, pure fantasy. Sanchez landed most of his men on the unoccupied larger island and raised the flag of the King of Spain on a fort from which, after an armourer had unspiked the guns, he was able to open fire on the main English position in the fort of La Cortadura between the two islands. Apart from the small detachment still on the main island at the gun-platform of Santiago, the rest of the English were in a fort known as El Castillo in the middle of Isla Chica. They had plenty of guns and ammunition, but very few men.

Sanchez made a second attempt to demand the surrender of the English in La Cortadura, but his heralds were fired on. It was, therefore, a question of assault and, like a good Spaniard, Sanchez determined to wait for an auspicious day – in this case, Sunday, 17 August, the Feast of the Assumption. The attack was planned to start at ten in the evening. Ramirez with the sixty Spaniards from Cartagena was given the position of honour and marched up to La Cortadura to engage the defenders. A party of ninety-two Indians and mulattoes was sent to wade up to their waists across a ford above La Cortadura to invest El Castillo from the landward side. A third party of fifty sailors from the ships landed from a longboat on the seaward side of the castle, where they were shortly joined by Sanchez himself with the rest of the men, who had first captured the enemy's isolated garrison at Santiago. Now, 'everyone having arrived in good time, we captured El Castillo with the loss of one man' – a remarkable piece of logistics and leadership with Spanish colonial troops operating at night on terrain which was unfamiliar to most of them. There was now just La Cortadura to capture. Here Smith had been able to concentrate enough fire to hold back the Spanish soldiers from Cartagena. He had made up for his lack of men with ingenuity, 'firing off batteries of sixty muskets fastened like organ pipes and fired simultaneously'. But, once El Castillo and Santiago had been captured, his position was hopeless, since daylight would see La Cortadura under fire from the cannon in both forts and from the ships in the harbour.

Smith bowed to the inevitable and sent to seek quarter. Sanchez, one suspects, was reluctant to forgo the bloody and glorious pleasures of an assault, but felt bound to grant quarter lest he lose too many men to the now desperate English. And so, at midnight, Major Smith surrendered the whole island to that 'soldier of experience and courage', José Sanchez Ximenez. The forts were garnished with the Spanish royal arms and 'prayers of thanks were also made to the Divine Majesty, who had been pleased to grant such a great and happy victory on the Feast of the Assumption of the Blessed Virgin'. The second English occupation of the island of Santa Catalina had lasted just eighty-three days.

No formal articles of capitulation exist. In Sanchez' report to the President of Panamá he stated that Smith surrendered on condition of 'el quartel de la vida'; in other words, the English were granted their lives and nothing else. But this was not the impression of the English, who stated that 'they surrendered on condition of having a small barque to transport them to Jamaica'[13] – a condition very similar to that granted by Mansfield in the previous May. The Spaniards certainly did not comply with this condition, and the harsh treatment of Smith and his men after they had been granted quarter was to be an important factor in the increase in hostilities on the Spanish Main, where revenge was to become a motive of aggression in addition to the usual one of profit. Some of the defenders did not even retain their lives, according to Henry Wassey, who must by now have been very unhappy that he had ever got Sanchez off the reef. 'He saw Englishmen lyeing on the ground being, as it was there reported, put to death in cold blood.'[14] But no one else mentions this, and he might merely have seen the corpses of the six Englishmen who were killed in the actual fighting or, possibly, those of the two Spanish spies who had introduced the English to the island and were formally shot by arquebus on the morning after the surrender.

Such matters as the death of a few heretics who, without a commission from their King, had seized a Spanish possession were probably of small consequence to Sanchez. He wrote later that all the English would have died 'if the Spanish soldiers had not had so much *piedad*'. His main task now was to reorganize the defences of the island, which was still extremely vulnerable to the threatened reinforcements from Jamaica. Examination of the prisoners had indicated that two big ships with men, food and military equipment were shortly expected, and this was confirmed from letters found in an English ship which was captured when it sailed unsuspecting into the harbour.[15] A letter from Sir Thomas Modyford to Smith reported that he had '150 men ready to goe on board as soone as the ships are ready'. He also said that he was expecting to hear of 'your defeate of ye enymy which wee were informed were intended your way' – a piece of information which arrived rather too late to be of value.

Sanchez ordered a complete inventory of all the stores on the island and then sat down to make out a huge list of things which he needed from the Main. At the top, as usual, were men – soldiers for the garrison, slaves to work on the forts and in the fields. Then there were food, weapons, ammunition and, on a more human level, things necessary for the church and the celebration of Mass and the equipment needed to stock a small barber's shop – eight razors from Seville and a stone to sharpen them, scissors, mirror, comb, brushes, shaving-bowl, two dozen cupping-glasses and two pairs of dental forceps. By 23 August, Sanchez was ready to send most of his ships back to the Main with his reports, letters and requisitions. Also on board under close guard were his thirty-seven English prisoners. One Englishman was retained on the island as a carpenter, while the six Frenchmen who had remained after Mansfield's capture of the island had managed to win Sanchez' confidence by claiming that they had been forced to join in the illegal English invasion. Their leader, a Monsieur Simon, seems to have had an exceptionally silver tongue. He was described by Sanchez as an 'hombre de bien' who was very keen to serve the King of Spain.

On arrival in Portobello, the majority of the English prisoners were thrust into a dungeon from which they were taken out each morning to work through all the hours of daylight on a new fortress which the Spaniards were building in the port.[16] To make a European work as a slave in the West Indies was hardly playing the game and when, a few months later, some of the prisoners escaped to bring the news of their fate and that of Providence to Jamaica, Sir Thomas Modyford was profoundly upset. They 'make our men slave it at their forts, which is their constant usage to us when we fall into their hands, while we use them more like friends than enemies'.[17] The three most important English captives from Providence were saved from this indignity and sent under escort to Panamá. These were Major Smith, the former governor and the only one of the three who seems to have survived; Captain Stanley, an 'honest old souldier' in his mid-sixties; and, most important of all, Sir Thomas Whetstone, a royalist nephew of Oliver Cromwell, a famous privateer and former Speaker of the Jamaican House of Assembly. Sanchez emphasized the distinction of Whetstone in his report – 'a man of much importance' who was responsible for the planning of 'all the damage done on these coasts'. Stanley later declared under interrogation that it was Whetstone's ambition to arrange with 'his friends and wealthy merchants' in London to fit out four frigates to attack the Spanish South Sea fleet which was based on Peru.[18] Such prisoners were rarely seen on the Spanish Main, and their passage to Panamá was an ungentlemanly progress as the people took this rare opportunity to throw stones and dirt at their English tormentors. Once in Panamá, they were all three cast into a dungeon and clapped in irons, and seemed likely to stay there for ever. 'I have the intention that they should never leave prison, because of the damage that one or other of them might do to us,' wrote the President, Don Juan Perez, to his Queen.[19]

Don Juan was naturally delighted with the happy outcome of the expedition, whose success was seen by the officials of Panamá as due to divine favour as a first cause, 'but also to the promptness with which the President had acted, the result of his great experience in military matters'.[20] A great fiesta was held in Panamá. The bells rang, the nuns sang a *Te Deum* in the streets, and a statue of the Virgin was miraculously adorned in stars from head to foot in grateful recognition of the first Spanish triumph in the Indies for many years. Then there were letters to write, amongst them a long letter to the Governor of Cartagena which must have given Don Juan much amusement.[21] '*Amigo* . . . it is with great pleasure that I send you the happy news of the recovery of Santa Catalina. Although it is a time for rejoicing and not for showing ill feeling, I find it necessary to reply point by point to the charges in your letter of 31 July.' There follow several pages of tongue-in-cheek self-justification replete with historical references to other men who had served Spain well by acting promptly.

Sergeant-Major Sanchez also received a letter – the sort of letter which all soldiers like to get from their commanding officer.[22] Don Juan was quite lost for words. 'You have done so singularly well in everything which I delivered to your care that words fail me to express my congratulations.' He promised that neither he nor his gallant men would have to spend long in lonely Santa Catalina. The men would be replaced by a new draft which he hoped to get from the Queen. For Sanchez there would be promotion; he would make him Castellan of Santiago Castle in Portobello or, if that was not possible, Sergeant-Major of Panamá. But, alas, this was never to happen. José Sanchez Ximenez was to be stabbed to death in his bed by one of his own soldiers from the Santa Catalina garrison after an argument about pay.[23]

Don Juan was also to suffer a setback to his career in this hour of triumph. In 1667 the fleet of galleons arrived in Portobello, and the Prince of Montesarcho, Captain-General of the Armada, may well have been rather disappointed to hear of the recovery of Santa Catalina. He had orders to lead the infantry of the fleet in a massive expedition to retake the island.[24] No soldier liked to lose a chance for glory. More serious for Perez was the arrival in the fleet of the new Viceroy of Peru, the Conde de Lemos. The two men took an instant dislike to each other and were soon arguing about the extent of the Viceroy's jurisdiction over the President of Panamá.[25] Lemos was to get plenty of ammunition to use against Perez. No one ever held the position of President without making enemies, and Perez, hero or not, was no exception. The *oydores* of the Audiencia accused him of taking some bars of silver belonging to the King. The details of this incredibly complicated case need not concern us, except to note that to use royal money for royal services was not always an acceptable action in the Spanish Empire. The immediate upshot was that, in July 1667, Perez was suspended from his post as President of Panamá, placed under arrest and taken off to Peru, where he was to remain a prisoner of the Viceroy for the next two years. In the end his release was ordered by the Queen and the Viceroy commanded to pay his lost salary and all his expenses but, for all that, a prison in Peru was a sad fate for the man who had played such a prominent part in the reconquest of Santa Catalina.

CHAPTER THREE

The Privateers

THE PAPERS captured by Sanchez from the English in Santa Catalina made interesting, if rather alarming, reading for the President of Panamá and they make interesting reading for the historian today.[1] Between them they provide a full picture of the theoretical relationship between the government of Jamaica and the privateers, and of the way in which the privateers were supposed to behave. While it is clear that privateers very often disobeyed their instructions, it will still be useful at this stage to get some idea of the somewhat wishful thinking that lay behind their actual activities.

First, there were the blank commissions which Major Smith was authorized to issue to privateer captains. The Governor of Jamaica was also 'Vice Admirall to his Royal Highness the Duke of York in the American Seas', and it was by virtue of powers delegated by the Duke of York, Lord High Admiral of England and King Charles II's younger brother, that he was entitled to issue privateering commissions or letters of marque.[2] Whether he in turn was entitled to delegate this power to Major Smith as Governor of Providence Island is rather doubtful; but this is what he had certainly done, and the blank commissions gave privateers very considerable scope for their activity. They were allowed 'to attaque, fight with or surprise any vessell or vessells whatsoever belonging to the King of Spain or any of his subjects which you shall meet with to the southward of the Tropic of Cancer'. This was fairly standard; but the commission also allowed the privateer to invade Spanish territory, 'if you finde it prudential'. Privateers often did invade Spanish territory and, while they were there, sack and rob and pull people from their beds, but their commissions rarely gave them quite such sweeping powers to do so. Usually they only had permission to land in order to supply themselves with wood, water or provisions, or to capture prisoners from whom they might acquire information. In return for this open invitation to attack and rob the Spaniards in the Indies, quite legally under English law, the commission merely required that the captain bring his prizes back to Port Royal to be proceeded against by the Jamaican Court of Admiralty and that he 'observe and follow the instructions herewith given you, and all such other orders and directions as you shall from time to time receive from his Royall Highness or myselfe for his Majesty's service'.

These 'instructions for privateers' were also captured by Sanchez. The first two clauses remind us, if we need reminding, that privateers were not always too choosy which ships they captured or what people they robbed. They were therefore instructed to do no injury to any of His Majesty's subjects or anyone carrying a pass issued by the English authorities, 'upon pain of death without mercy'. Another way in which they could do injury indirectly to His Majesty's subjects was to deprive them of their labour force. Privateering was more fun and more profitable than working. '*Item,* you are not to entertaine any planter under your command, or any other inhabitant of this island, nor any servant nor slave belonging unto them, unless they bring you a ticket under the Governor's hand for the time being, thereby permitting you to doe the same.' Then there was a section which reflected the fact that, in the absence of any formal naval protection, the privateers were the eyes and ears as well as the main defence of Jamaica. If necessary, they were to cruise as instructed by Governor Modyford in order to acquire information of possible Spanish reprisals against Jamaica, and all ships were supposed to return immediately to Port Royal if they should 'meet with any intelligence by letters or prisoners . . . which may any way concern the good or evil of his Majesty's affairs'.

Finally, there were a number of clauses in the instructions which dealt with the way in which privateers were supposed to proceed when they made a prize. Such matters were also governed by custom. When a ship was taken – usually a fairly easy task for the well-armed privateers – some goods were divided immediately and legally among the crew. These were usually things of small value, such as seamen's clothes, bedding and small arms, and were known as 'free enterrance and plunder'. It is clear that more valuable goods were also divided on board in order to defraud the owners of the privateer ship and the authorities in Jamaica, but it should be remembered that the privateers had a clear interest in seeing that no individual benefited at the expense of his mates – a fact which may well have reduced the size of this unofficial share-out. The official procedure was for an inventory of the prize-ship's cargo to be prepared. Then the hatches were sealed to prevent depredation by the privateer's crew. The inventory, the bills of lading and all other papers aboard were to be delivered to the Court of Admiralty in Jamaica. The officers of the prize were to be interrogated 'touching the design of their voyage, from whence they came and whither they are bound, with such other questions as you shall thinck fitt to demand', and their examination in writing was to be handed in with the other papers. Prisoners, it was noted with a certain irony, should be treated 'in the same manner as his Majesty's subjects are used when they are prisoners to the enemy'.

When a prize returned to Jamaica elaborate precautions were taken that it should not be ransacked before it had been adjudged by the Admiralty Court and that it was shared out according to law.[3] Notice should be given to the authorities immediately on arrival in Jamaica, and a guard was then supposed to be placed on board by the Marshal of the Admiralty Court. Then followed the process of adjudication by the Court. Witnesses were called and evidence taken to check that the ship really belonged to the nation against which the commission was granted. The ship's papers and the prisoners were again examined. If the Court adjudged that the ship was good prize, which it usually did, then a fresh inventory was drawn up and the process of division could take place. Some prize-goods, such as coin and bullion, could be divided straight away. Others were sold at auction and the proceeds then split up amongst the many people with a claim to a share.

First to put his hand in the pot was the Governor, who took one-tenth on behalf of the Duke of York, as Lord High Admiral, and one-fifteenth for the King – a fact which gave the Court, the Governor and the privateers themselves immediate official recognition, since neither of these two needy royal brothers ever refused to accept his rights. The Governor also received fees due for the privateer's commission – £20 a time, according to Sir Thomas Modyford's son[4] – and there were more fees to be paid to the officers of the Admiralty Court before the rest could 'be divided among the ship's company, owners, and victuallers according to the usuall custome of private menn of war or their own agreement, putting the same into such honest hands, as there may arise no abuse to the officers, private souldiers nor seamen'. The procedure of the Court was extremely rapid compared with most courts in the seventeenth century – a practice which the Governor was keen to continue 'for their encouragement who are so beneficiall to His Majesty, this countrey and yourselves'.

It can be seen that many people stood to gain from the activities of the Jamaican privateers, from the King himself to the very lowest cabin-boy. Ship-owners, arms-dealers and victuallers fitted out ships on credit and usually received a quarter of the prize as their return. Merchants bought the prize-goods at well below their market value and circulated them again in return for the food, drink, slaves and manufactured goods which Jamaica imported. Tavern-keepers and whores relieved the privateer crews of their money, while some of the more successful and level-headed of the captains invested their shares in plantations and slaves, ready to retire from the sea and become honest and respectable planters. This widespread commercial interest in the privateers was a very important factor in their continued existence. Jamaica could not afford peace against Spain.

When President Perez sent these captured documents home to Spain for perusal by the Queen and the Council of the Indies, he noted, with some surprise, 'that it seems that the English have declared war against the Spaniards in the Indies, since they have to pay admiralty fees [*almirantazgo*] in Jamaica for the prizes and the King of England takes a fifteenth of them and the Duke of York a tenth'.[5] One suspects that this naïvety was deliberate. Spain might have much to gain by playing the injured innocent. Perez, who had been Governor of Cartagena and Puerto Rico before moving to Panamá, was certainly aware that for the English there was nearly always war against Spain in the Indies, although it is true that great bursts of privateering activity were punctuated by lulls in which only a few ships operated on semi-legal and often out-of-date letters of marque.

Privateering and piracy in the Indies were almost as old as Spanish colonization in the area.[6] It had not taken long for the news of the fabulous wealth acquired by the Spaniards to reach the ears of the sea rovers of the Atlantic coast of Europe. Most of the early rovers were French who had no problem in acquiring letters of marque during the long wars between their country and Spain in the first half of the sixteenth century. The English began to move into the area before, during and after the war against Spain in the reign of Queen Elizabeth I. These corsairs, of whom Drake was only the most famous, operated from England although their knowledge of West Indian waters already enabled them to maintain themselves in the Indies for two or three years at a time. It was now that such names as Panamá and Portobello began to acquire that magic in English ears which they have retained almost to this day. Peace in 1604 forced the rovers to seek commissions from the Dutch and, after 1609, to engage in out-and-out piracy, but the tradition of hostility and plunder in the Spanish Indies remained, a tradition based mainly on greed but given a certain ideological underpinning by enmity to the Catholic Church and the Inquisition.

During the 1620s, Englishmen and Frenchmen began to move into the long chain of the Antilles and the beginnings of permanent settlements were laid down. These small islands had never been settled by the Spaniards, but they considered them all to be their property and from time to time made efforts to drive the illegal immigrants out. But Spain had not sufficient resources to stem this flood of English, French, Dutch and Irish adventurers who, together with their servants, were so determined to seek their fortune in the Indies. Barbados, St Kitts, Martinique, Guadeloupe – one after the other, the islands were settled, the land cleared and planted with tobacco or some other crop which could find a ready market in faraway Europe. The profits of planting were supplemented by illegal trading with the Spanish colonists or by occasional raiding. This, however, was on a small scale compared with the activities carried on farther to the west, nearer to the main centres of Spanish settlement.

From an early stage, foreign corsairs and smugglers began to use the many ports on the sparsely populated north coast of the island of Hispaniola, and later this area became a general haven for lawless men and adventurers from all over the West Indies. Petty raiding in canoes and other small craft was supplemented by living off the wild herds and flocks that roamed the mountains and dense forests of the large and nearly empty island. Such men, of whom the majority were French, began to acquire the name of *boucanier* from the *boucan*, the place where they dried strips of meat in the Indian fashion. The word was soon adopted by the English and the Spaniards as 'buccaneer', 'buckaner' or 'bocanero', but it is worth noting that only the men from northern Hispaniola were described as buccaneers in contemporary documents, be they English or Spanish. The more general use of the word to mean a West Indian privateer or pirate comes later[7] and would have been strongly resented by, for instance, the Jamaican privateers who considered themselves a cut above the evil-smelling men in crudely tanned skins from Hispaniola. Smelly or not, these half-wild men were superb shots, supremely hardy and brave, and totally disdainful of death. As such, they made marvellous crews for the corsair ships which were beginning to use the island of Tortuga, a few miles off the north-west coast of Hispaniola, as a base. Tortuga, sometimes under French control, sometimes under English, was for several years the only major centre of privateering activity against the Spaniards, but in 1630, as we have seen, it was joined by Providence or Santa Catalina. The next decade was to see a considerable increase in privateering in the West Indies, as English, French and Dutch all sought to take advantage of the now wilting Spanish Empire.[8] This period drew to an end with the recapture of Santa Catalina by Pimienta in 1641, although there was to be one last terrifying raid made by Captain William Jackson operating on letters of reprisal issued to the Providence Island Company. The later 1640s was a time of relative quiet in the Spanish West Indies, as English and French martial spirits were kept at home by civil wars and the Dutch brought to a successful close their eighty-year bid for independence from Spain. The Treaty of Munster in 1648 gave the Dutch most of the immediate commercial privileges which they desired in the Indies and they officially withdrew from privateering, although individual Dutchmen continued to seek foreign commissions or to sail under French and English captains.

The lull did not last for long. In 1654, Cromwell went to war with Spain, and this opened the last and most serious period of English privateering activity against the Spaniards in the West Indies. The main feature of this war was the 'Western Design', a plan to carve out for England a great Protestant empire in the Indies and to transfer to London the flow of treasure which now went to Seville and Madrid.[9] This reversion to a rabidly anti-Catholic, Elizabethan approach to foreign policy was by no means uniformly popular in England, where Spanish trade and Spanish friends were seen by many to be more important than the short-term gains of plunder in the Caribbean, while the slightest knowledge of Spanish royal finances indicated that the maintenance of long-term conquest in the Indies would be an insupportable burden to the English taxpayer. But, for the moment, aggression was in the ascendant and a powerful expeditionary force was fitted out to sail to the Indies and capture, as its first target, the great island of Hispaniola. Much of the promotion of the venture seems to have been due to lobbying by members of the Providence Island Company who saw that England's new-found military and naval power might avenge them for their losses at Spanish hands and, incidentally, return to them their property in the Indies.

The implementation of the Western Design was a dismal setback for the Commonwealth government. The expedition set out from England late in 1654 under the command of Admiral Penn and General Venables and, after recruiting in Barbados, sailed for Hispaniola with an army of nearly seven thousand men – a colossal concentration of power by West Indian standards. But, twenty days after landing near Santo Domingo in April 1655, what was left of the army was back in the ships, defeated by disease, a handful of Spaniards and their own cowardice and incompetence. Terrified at the thought of what Cromwell might say if they returned empty-handed, the leaders decided to attack Jamaica, an island practically deserted by the Spaniards. What Spaniards there were put up a sturdy defence, but this time the overwhelming numbers of the English were sufficient to win the island, although guerrilla resistance was to continue for several years.

Jamaica, once conquered, was seen to be even more suitable than Hispaniola for the sort of policy envisaged in the Western Design. The island was large, fertile and nearly empty, offering great potential both for the planting of tropical staples and for large-scale herding to provide skins and meat. Even more to the point was the island's position athwart the main Spanish shipping routes and within easy sailing distance of all the Spanish settlements on the west coast of the Main and Central America. Jamaica would be a new and larger Providence Island. Settlers were encouraged from the other American colonies and from the British Isles, and a beginning was made in the development of the magnificent harbour in the southeast of the island. This had been used only as a careening-place by the Spaniards, but now was provided with a Fort Cromwell and the first of the houses which would become Port Royal after the King's restoration in 1660.[10] Meanwhile, the war against Spain went on, and the soldiers and sailors of the fleet amused themselves by some not particularly spectacular raids on the Spanish Main.

Slowly, the great invasion fleet which had carried the expeditionary force began to disappear, summoned to other stations by the English Government, and Edward D'Oyley, governor of the island from 1657, began to be alarmed at the weakness of Jamaica's defences against the ever-present threat of Spanish reprisals. An easy solution to the problem was to issue privateering commissions to the corsairs of Tortuga and their buccaneer crews. Tortuga was now under French dominion, but the corsairs had no compunction about accepting English commissions, attracted as they were by the developing port and by the growing commercial facilities in which to dispose of their prizes. They were soon joined by other privateer ships, manned by former regular soldiers and sailors from the invasion fleet, by settlers or by adventurers from England who came out specifically to join in the hunt for Spanish prizes. The identification of Jamaica as a privateering station, which was to last throughout the 1660s, had begun.

This, however, was by no means clear in 1660 when Charles II was restored to the throne of England.[11] Charles had no reason to continue a war against a Spanish government which had befriended him during his exile, and in September proclamations in Spain and England declared a cessation of arms. No mention of the Indies or Jamaica was made in these proclamations, but it was clear that Spain expected Charles to honour a previous promise and hand back his illegally acquired possession in the Indies. There were many in England who thought that Jamaica was a worthless and potentially troublesome possession and would have been glad to see it Spanish again, but Charles seemed oddly reluctant to listen to them and more attentive to those merchants, slave-traders and aggressive imperialists who painted a rosy picture of Jamaica's future under English rule.

They emphasized the potential development of the island as a plantation, but also pointed out the possibilities that the island's position offered for the development of trade with the Spanish colonies. This was the great prize which stirred the minds of ambitious men in England. Spain had always prohibited foreigners from trading directly with her colonists, who were forced to buy their European goods, most of which originated from outside Spain, at irregular intervals and at very high prices from the merchants who travelled in the official fleets. Slaves, too, could only be bought from the official monopolists. The result was that smugglers were very welcome in the colonies and their presence was often connived at by colonial officials, but smuggling, although very profitable, was a dangerous trade which often ended with the smuggler in a Spanish colonial gaol. It was the ambition of merchants in England and the West Indies to make this trade legal, either by amicable agreement with Spain or, if this failed, as seemed only too likely, by making life so unpleasant for the Spaniards in the Indies that the metropolitan government would open up the trade for the sake of peace. There was never any problem in finding a justification for this sort of behaviour. The imprisonment of an English smuggler without trial and the sale of his ship at public auction were quite sufficient grounds for reprisals and, in any case, no one thought that peace in Europe meant peace in the Indies.

The result of these conflicting pressures on King Charles and the English Government was a very considerable ambiguity in actual English policy towards Jamaica. Sometimes, the friends of Spain were in the ascendant; privateering in the Indies was prohibited, and it seemed that at any moment Jamaica was about to be restored to Spain. Sometimes the policy of the imperialists and the West Indian traders was in the ascendant; privateering was encouraged and Spanish protests received polite or not so polite dismissal. All of which made life rather difficult for those settlers and planters who were now beginning to think of themselves as Jamaicans. Was it worth investing money in plantations which might at any moment have to be abandoned to the Spaniards? It seemed better to make hay while the sun shone and invest in the privateers. Ships were at least mobile. In any case, planting was not a particularly profitable occupation. Too many new colonies all producing a similar range of tropical staples had led to over-production, and prices were very low – a fact which made privateering and illegal trade seem very attractive alternatives, but which also gave strength to those people in London who thought Jamaica was worthless. The situation was succinctly summed up in a report made by the Irish double-agent, Sir Richard White, to the Spanish Council of the Indies. 'In general, there is no other way of making a fortune but by robbing Spaniards since, in Jamaica, it is impossible to make money. On the coasts of the Indies there is much money to be lost, whose owners are unprepared and have a great lack of courage with which to defend themselves, while amongst the aggressors there is an insatiable desire of riches, great courage and total disdain of risk.'[12]

Such was the situation at the time of the appointment of the last great privateering governor of Jamaica, Sir Thomas Modyford, who arrived on the island on 11 June 1664. Modyford had been a planter in Barbados since 1650 and was keen to develop the plantations in Jamaica, despite the difficult economic climate. He brought with him many settlers from Barbados and was to continue to encourage the economic and demographic development of his new home. He was also keen to build up the defences of the island against the continuing danger of a Spanish reconquest and the new threat of French and Dutch aggression during the wars of the late 1660s.

Modyford's attitude towards privateering was more ambiguous. The friends of Spain were in the ascendant at the time of his appointment and his instructions required him to call in the privateers and to prohibit the granting of letters of marque in the future. The first letter that he received as Governor emphasized the King's continuing belief in this policy. 'His Majesty cannot sufficiently express his dissatisfaction at the daily complaints of violence and depredations done by ships, said to belong to Jamaica, upon the King of Spain's subjects.' Modyford was therefore 'strictly commanded not only to forbid the prosecution of such violences for the future, but to inflict condign punishment on offenders'.[13] Modyford himself claimed to disapprove of privateering, and his first move as Governor was to honour his instructions. On 25 June 1664 he issued a proclamation 'charging all his Majesty's loving subjects to treat all the subjects of his Catholic Majesty as friends and allies, and not make prize of any of their ships or goods by virtue of any commission'.[14] But, only a fortnight later, he admitted in a letter to Sir Henry Bennet (later Lord Arlington), the English Secretary of State, that he was worried that his proclamation might drive the privateers to Tortuga and leave Jamaica defenceless. He therefore 'thought it more prudent to do by degrees and moderation what he had resolved to execute suddenly and severely'.[15]

Indeed, no proclamation unbacked by naval power was ever likely to suppress the privateers. There were said to be 1500 of them at this time, operating from twelve ships – 'brave men', 'lusty fellows', who were unlikely to turn to unprofitable and boring planting as an employment. If they did not go to Tortuga, they were quite likely to turn pirate and attack the shipping of Jamaica herself. A prudent policy was the only policy if these brave men were not to be lost to the island for ever, and Modyford was given 'much contentment' when he read that Bennet approved of his 'gentle usage' of the privateers.[16]

This gentle usage continued for the rest of 1664 and 1665, a period during which Jamaican privateering against the Spaniards declined but did not cease. Modyford's general practice was to condone prizes taken on commissions issued by his predecessors but, once these commissions had expired, he was prepared to treat their holders as pirates and even, in exceptional circumstances, to hang them. But he was always reluctant to take this final step and so deprive Jamaica of her fighting men, for a pirate today might well become a patriot tomorrow. In February 1665 we find him pardoning all but three of fourteen pirates who had been condemned to death, at the same time declaring in public that he would grant commissions against the Dutch, with whom England was now at war.[17] But, as we have seen, the privateers were not too keen on fighting the Dutch, and such commissions were often little more than a cloak for aggression against Spain.

It is easy to dismiss Modyford as a cynic who never had the slightest intention of stopping privateering in Jamaica and simply made a few gestures to satisfy his masters in England, confident that time would shortly change English policy on the subject. Since

Modyford was himself a dealer in prize-goods who bought a ship illegally condemned by his own Court of Admiralty,[18] one suspects that such a viewpoint is only too accurate. There is, however, another side to the picture. It really was rather alarming to see the defences of Jamaica slipping away to serve a potential French enemy in Tortuga. It was also rather annoying for Modyford to receive no answers to his letters to England. Lord Arlington wrote quite regularly to Modyford during his first nine months as Governor, but from March 1665 to November 1666 he seems to have sent him only one letter.[19] Since Arlington was known to have strong sympathies with Spain, this may have been caused by a general distaste for West Indian business or, more likely, by a reluctance to commit the King and himself to any policy at all in those troubled waters. Arlington's silence was to be unfortunate for Spain, for he referred Modyford to an alternative and more congenial source of orders.[20]

This was George Monck, first Duke of Albemarle, the architect of the Restoration and now Lord General, a man of great influence and power in England. Albemarle was Modyford's cousin, and his influence had got Modyford the job of Governor of Jamaica. He was also a hawkish imperialist who enjoyed receiving racy accounts of privateer activity in the Indies, even if it was illegal, and no doubt fully approved of Modyford's sentiments 'that every action gives new encouragement to attempt the Spaniard, finding them in all places very weak and very wealthy'.[21] Modyford's correspondence with his cousin had produced one valuable piece of ammunition which he was holding back to make use of at what seemed the proper time. This was a letter, dated 1 June 1665, which gave him 'latitude to grant or not commissions against the Spaniard, as he found it for the advantage of his Majesty's service and the good of this island'.[22] It was this letter which gave him the confidence to reverse royal policy and declare war on the Spaniards on 4 March 1666, just in time to make Mansfield's capture of Santa Catalina look almost legal.

Modyford's declaration was made after consultation with the Council of Jamaica, and it is interesting to look at the reasons they gave to justify their action.[23] Letters of marque against the Spaniards were seen to be a good thing because they enabled the island to acquire prize-goods at cheap rates which encouraged merchants to settle in Port Royal and provided the returns for ships bringing down foodstuffs for the island from New England. Small planters benefited from selling provisions to the privateers. Men were attracted from the Lesser Antilles and 'many of them after a voyage or two, having gott something turne planter'. The buccaneers would now fight for them and not against them, and the privateers would have early news of any Spanish attempt against the island and their ships would, of course, provide the defence against any such attempt. Only in the very last of the twelve reasons offered was any mention made of hostility by Spain which might justify such a revival of privateering activity. 'It seemes to be the only meanes to force them in time to a free trade . . . for although all old commissions have bin called in and no new ones graunted . . . yet they do continue all acts of hostility against us, by takeing our shipps when they cann, sometimes murdering our people or at least make them work at their fortifications'. The poor Jamaicans! It was at least some consolation that the solution would give such a boost to the island's economy.

The decision to issue commissions against the Spaniards very quickly had the effects that Modyford had anticipated. The privateers returned, economic activity increased and Port Royal became once again the bustling place that it had been in the early 1660s. Modyford waxed lyrical in a letter to Lord Arlington describing the new situation.[24] 'My Lord, you cannot imagine whatt an universal change there was presently after this declaration in ye faces of men and things; the shipping that was laid up presently a-repairing; great resort of workmen and labourers to Port Royall; many returning that were gone . . . many released out of prisons or engageing ye shares they should gett for ye payment of their present debts.'

Such activity boded ill for the Spaniards; but they were not to feel the full weight of this new generation of privateers for some time and, indeed, as we have seen, it was the Spaniards who had the first triumph. There was no immediate revenge for the recapture of Santa Catalina. Some Spanish shipping was taken, and there were a few raids ashore, but the English were too busy elsewhere to take full advantage of Modyford's new policy. They were still at war with the Dutch, and 1666 was to bring the first of the many Anglo-French wars in the West Indies. Many small islands in the Lesser Antilles were devastated, and most privateers were busy in what was seen by everybody as their legitimate occupation. Jamaica remained untouched but watchful.

The Treaty of Breda in July 1667 brought peace with both the French and the Dutch and left the English in the West Indies a free hand to attack the Spaniards. Ironically, the same year saw a formal treaty of peace, alliance and commerce between Spain and Great Britain which was ratified in London on 21 September 1667. The first clause stated that the subjects of the two kings should 'serve each other well by mutual help, aid, kindness, and all manner of friendship'.[25] This was to be interpreted rather oddly by the English in the Indies. Later in the same year, all the English privateers were drawing together to inaugurate the most intense campaign against the Spaniards that the Indies had seen for a very long time. There was to be no peace beyond the line.

CHAPTER FOUR

One Ship at Orange Island

THE HOT, sticky afternoon of Tuesday, 10 July 1668, was drawing to a close when the gang of negroes returned to Portobello.[1] They had spent the day cutting wood high up in the mountains to the west of the city and, from their vantage point, had spied a strange ship anchored in the shallow stretch of water between Isla de Naranjas ('Orange Island') and the coast. The news gave rise to a buzz of conjecture among the two or three dozen Spaniards, mainly old soldiers and royal officials, who made their home in the half-empty town. Ships were always news. Could it be a slave-ship which had overrun the harbour mouth on its way from the slave-depot at Curaçao? Or the long-expected advice-boat with news and mail from Spain? Or, only too likely, one of the accursed English corsair ships from Jamaica? There had been plenty of news of them that summer. Only ten days before, letters had arrived from Panamá reporting a fleet of twelve corsairs off the coast of Nicaragua. A small ship had been sent out on a reconnaissance voyage, but had not yet returned. Still, corsair or not, a single ship posed little threat to the well-defended city, and the Mayor, Andres Fernandez Davila, grumbled as he agreed to send a canoe to check on its identity. He would have to pay the canoe crew out of his own pocket, and the chances of recovering his expenses were negligible. Money was always hard to recover from Spain.

The swift tropical night had fallen before the canoe set out, and the initial interest in the strange ship soon died down as the people of Portobello prepared for bed at the end of another miserable day in what was generally considered the very worst posting in the Spanish Empire.[2] It really was a terrible place, especially now at the beginning of the worst of the wet season, humid, smelly and suffocatingly hot, cut off from the cool breeze of evening by the mountains and hills which surrounded it. Strangers to the town invariably complained of the heat, the constant rain, the hordes of flies and mosquitoes, and the stench of the filthy black mud that was laid bare at every low water. That is to say, they complained if they managed to survive the fevers that tended to sweep through the crews of every ship that spent any time in the port. Locals might become inured to the conditions, but many suffered from recurrent malaria and other tropical diseases and nearly everyone sooner or later became sunk in a terrible lassitude, due as much to the fact that there was rarely anything to do in the town as to its appalling climate.

Portobello had only one economic function: to provide a safe harbour for the Spanish treasure fleet. When that fleet was in, the place was a hive of activity for four or five weeks as the galleons were unladen and their cargoes of European luxuries were sold to the merchants of Panamá and Peru, who arranged for their carriage by mule-train and river-boat across the isthmus. In return came the produce and treasure of the New World: hides, drugs and dyes but,

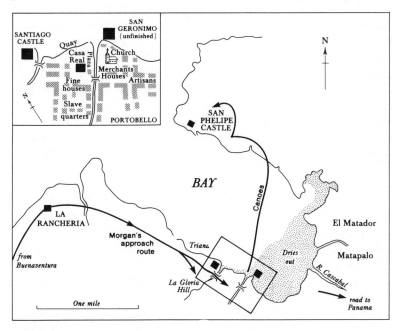

Portobello

above all, silver – silver in coin, silver in bars, millions and millions of pesos of silver stacked up in warehouses, in counting-houses, even in the public squares of the city, ready to be laden on the galleons for the long and dangerous return voyage to Spain. When the fleet was in there might be twenty or twenty-five million pesos of treasure in the town, twice the total revenue of the King of England, and a transient population of some ten thousand sailors, soldiers, merchants, shopkeepers and slaves to guard it. Every house and shack would be bursting at the seams, rents were astronomical and a great tented camp surrounded the city for those who could not afford a roof over their head. The fairs of Portobello were a very jolly, busy, moneymaking time for those who managed to stay alive.

But there was only a fair when there was a fleet, and the fleet did not come very often in these days of Spanish economic decline. It was nearly a year since the last one had arrived, under the command of the Prince of Montesarcho, and over a year before the next one was due. In the meantime, Portobello was a ghost town. The city might look quite impressive with its hundred and fifty handsome houses, two fine squares, two churches, royal treasury, hospital, Mercedarian convent, warehouses, acres of shacks and shanties for slaves and artisans, and huge stables for the mules that carried the treasure over the isthmus from Panamá. But, except for a few weeks every two or three years, most of this property was empty. Merchants and artisans preferred to live in the much bigger and slightly more healthy city of Panamá, only visiting Portobello occasionally to check that their property was in good order. The permanent population of Portobello was very small – a few score Spaniards, a few friars and nuns in the hospital and convent, and perhaps a couple of hundred mulattoes, free negroes and slaves. There were few women or children. Portobello was hardly the place that one would choose in which to bring up a family.

The city might be half empty, but it was still well defended, and in fact there were probably as many soldiers in the garrison as there were citizens in the town. Indeed, it was said to be the third strongest city in the Spanish Indies after Havana and Cartagena. The private citizens, whether they actually lived in Panamá or Portobello, had property to protect, and the Spanish Crown was vitally interested in the maintenance of this terminus of the long route to the Indies. The main defences of the port were two big fortresses or castles, one each side of the harbour. On the west, separated from the town by a small river, stood the castle of Santiago with a garrison on paper of 200 men and 32 guns placed to cover the port itself and the approach to the city. On the other side of the bay was the smaller castle of San Phelipe with 12 guns and a theoretical garrison of 100 men. No ship could reasonably hope to run the gauntlet between the cross-fire of these two castles. Beyond the castles were blockhouses and sentry posts, and to east and west along the coast there were armed lookout stations. These castles and outworks were manned by what the Spanish authorities euphemistically called 'paid' soldiers.

There is no doubt that, in July 1668, morale in the castles was low. None of the men had in fact been paid for over eighteen months – a common enough condition for the soldiers of any country in the seventeenth century, but a condition that was likely to lead to neglect of duty. Many soldiers had deserted. Others had permission to make a little money for themselves by setting up as tailors, shoemakers, grocers or tavern-keepers in the town and were allowed to sleep out – a privilege which cost them a percentage of their takings as a bribe to their castellans. The absence of such soldiers from their posts was potentially dangerous since both castles were already seriously undermanned. Many men were on detachment in the garrison of Santa Catalina, many others were sick or had deserted, with the result that, on the night of 10 July 1668, neither castle had as many as a half of its proper garrison.* These somewhat thin garrisons were reasonably well equipped with personal weapons. There had been a fresh supply in the last fleet, and each man had sword, musket or arquebus, cord, powder and ball, and was certainly supposed to be trained in their use. There was, however, a shortage of bombs and grenades and, more seriously, a shortage of gunners – not nearly enough to man every gun. The guns themselves, though they had passed muster six months previously, were not in very good shape. It was in fact very difficult to keep any military equipment in good order in the humidity of Portobello. Barrels rusted, cord rotted,

---

* Witnesses vary a little on numbers, but the consensus seems to have been that there were between 75 and 80 men out of a proper complement of 200 in Santiago and just under 50 out of 100 in San Phelipe. There were eight men in San Geronimo and another six in the Royal Treasury.

powder got damp, with inevitable results. For all that, there was no reason to believe that the castles of Santiago and San Phelipe would not provide adequate defence for the city, if defence were needed.

The city itself had no walls and was open to the country, although a fort called San Geronimo was currently being built, just off the quay in the sea itself. Most of the work was being done by a gang of English prisoners, the survivors of those captured in Santa Catalina in 1666. All night they were chained up in a prison attached to the offices of the Royal Treasury where there was an armed guard. These were the only regular troops in the town. The citizens were, however, mustered into four militia companies according to race – Spaniards, mulattoes, free blacks and slaves. At a muster late in 1667 there had only been 129 men in all four companies, a reflection of the small permanent population of the city. On the night of 10 June 1668, there were fewer even than this. There were less than twenty Spaniards fit to bear arms, most of the free blacks were out in the mountains hunting runaway slaves, while the slaves who had not run away were mostly at the farms and plantations in the countryside. Even including those men who were not mustered into the companies, such as the royal officers and the elderly, it seems unlikely that there were as many as a hundred people in the town who could have played any part in its defence. These hundred behaved this night the same as they would have done any other night. They went to bed in their own houses, many sleeping on their balconies to catch what air there was in the suffocating town. No provision was made for a special alert in the town or in the castles. Why should there have been? What danger could there possibly be to the city of Portobello from a single ship anchored off Orange Island?

Well, there was just one small problem. That ship was commanded by a man called Henry Morgan, a Welsh gentleman in his early thirties who was just beginning to be known as a man who could cause serious problems to sleeping cities.[3] Morgan's early career is little known, but he almost certainly came out to the West Indies as a soldier with the expeditionary force which captured Jamaica in 1655. We can presume that he served as a soldier and with the privateers for the next ten years, but we know few details until the day in 1665 when he returned to Port Royal, tanned, bearded and wealthy after nearly two years spent in a series of daring and success-ful raids in Central America.[4] Sir Thomas Modyford was immensely impressed by the achievements of Morgan and his colleagues and found no difficulty in believing that they had no knowledge of his proclamation calling in the privateers over fifteen months before their arrival back in Jamaica. Morgan was to have no problem in realizing the value of his prizes, and from now on he was to rise fast in the hierarchy of Jamaica. His success, his good birth and his influential friends and relations recommended him to Sir Thomas Modyford, whose first lieutenant-governor had been Morgan's uncle. His skill, his daring and his good fortune recommended him to the privateers. He may have sailed to Santa Catalina with Mansfield, as some accounts suggest,[5] although his name appears in no docu-ment connected with the expedition. What is more likely is that he spent the two years after his return from Central America quietly in Jamaica, getting married and investing his prize-money in the first of the plantations that were to make him one of the island's richest planters after his retirement from the sea. But this was just the calm before the storm that was to make his name renowned throughout the Spanish Indies. In 1667, Edward Mansfield, who had gone to Tortuga after Modyford ceased issuing commissions in Jamaica, was captured by the Spaniards and taken to Havana where he was 're-ported to be suddenly after put to death'.[6] Morgan, despite his youth, seemed to be the old privateer's natural successor. And so, now, in 1668, he was an admiral commissioned by Modyford 'to draw together the English privateers and take prisoners of the Spanish nation, whereby he might inform of the intention of that enemy to invade Jamaica'.[7]

Such a commission, issued late in 1667, hardly reflected the peace treaty which had been signed between England and Spain just a few months previously, but it does reflect the very real fear of the Spaniards which the more pacific planters and merchants of Jamaica continued to feel. There was no very strong reason to believe that the Spaniards in the Indies would necessarily take all that much notice of a document signed by Spaniards in Madrid, especially when that document neither confirmed the English presence in Jamaica nor indeed made any mention of the Indies at all. Did peace in Europe mean peace in the Indies? It never had before, and so the settlers of Jamaica, isolated by three thousand miles of sea from the nearest ship of the Royal Navy, continued to feel extremely vulnerable and ready to listen to and shiver at the merest rumour of Spanish preparations to attack the island. As the Council of Jamaica had reported early in 1666, when it resolved to commission the privateers once again, 'it is a matter of great security to the island that the men of war, cruising in all parts of the Spanish dominions, do often intercept their advices and thereby give seasonable intelligence to the Governor'.[8]

The fears of Jamaicans provided a superb loophole for the privateers, whose vaguely worded commission gave them in practice the right to do exactly what they liked with very little fear of future punishment. Morgan's commission gave him powers to capture Spanish ships at sea to collect information but, unlike the blank commissions captured on Santa Catalina, it did not give him permission to take action against the Spaniards on land. But if the information he collected at sea should establish that the Spaniards were arming against Jamaica, then he knew that a landing to confirm such information and perhaps to nip an invasion in the bud would never be punished by the authorities. For all they knew, the information could be true. What made such expeditions ashore particularly attractive was the fact that, since Morgan had no commission to make them, the normal conditions of privateering did not apply and no deduction had to be made from the loot for the King, the Lord High Admiral nor even for the owners of the privateers' ships. Since these deductions normally amounted to nearly a half of all prizes, it is easy to see why the privateers preferred the much more dangerous but much more profitable activity of seizing cities and towns rather than ships at sea. Modyford was to emphasize this point when clearing himself of accusations that the royal takings from privateering were rather low, considering the great wealth that the privateers were said to get. 'Of that from shoare they pay nothing because not commissionated to it.'[9] The point is also made absolutely clear by the first two articles of association drawn up by Morgan with his captains and his men for the expedition of 1668.[10]

1. It's agreed and concluded upon by and between the abovesaid parties that whatsoever gold, silver, pearls, jewells, rings, precious stones, ambergreece

and beazee* or other goods and merchandizes which are or shall be within
the terme of this voyage *taken on shore* shall be divided man for man as free
plunder.
2. It's agreed and concluded that what shipp or shipps shall be *taken att sea*
within the terme of this voyage, the tenths and fifteenths being deducted, the
fourth part of what goods are in the hould of such shipp or shipps shall be for
the respective shipps of this fleet and their owners, and the other three
fourths to be equally shared among such shipps company generally. . . .
[My italics]

This huge difference in their potential gains makes it abundantly
clear why the privateers should choose to spend so much more time
taking goods ashore than they spent capturing ships at sea.

Morgan had already conducted a successful, but not particularly
profitable, raid far into the interior of Cuba in alliance with a large
party of Frenchmen from Tortuga and northern Hispaniola. The
city of Puerto de Principe had been sacked and held to ransom.[11] The
privateers had had no trouble in collecting information which would
satisfy any qualms which might be felt in Jamaica at this breach of
their commission. 'They found that 70 men had been pressed to go
against Jamaica; that the like levy had been made in all the island, and
considerable forces were expected from Vera Cruz and Campeachy,
with materials of war to rendezvous at the Havannah, and from
Porto Bello and Cartagena to rendezvous at St Jago [Santiago] de
Cuba, of which he immediately gave notice to Gov. Modyford.'[12]
The quality of this information may be judged by what we have
already seen of the 'considerable forces' and 'materials of war' which
at this time could have been found in Portobello.

After leaving Cuba and dividing their plunder, the joint fleet had
then sailed to Cabo Gracias a Dios on the north-east coast of Nicaragua, where a council of war was held between the English and the
French to determine where they should sail next.[13] Since they had
'information' that practically everywhere in the Spanish Indies was
arming against Jamaica, they had plenty of choice. Morgan, no
doubt after consultation with his captains, had suggested Portobello.
This was certainly sticking his neck out. Portobello was known to be

* Ambergris: a secretion of the sperm-whale used in perfumery and cookery.
Beazee: bezoar-stone.

extremely well fortified, and there were scores of unfortified towns along the coast and in the interior which could have provided the same promise of plunder.

But Portobello had the right ring to it. The very name sounded glamorous even if, as we have seen, the reality was a stinking, half-empty fever-hole. Few Englishmen knew this and, even if they did, tended to forget it and to substitute in their minds an almost legendary place which brought memories of a golden past and promises of a golden future. Portobello, where Drake had died in 1596; Portobello, which William Parker had captured in 1601; Portobello, the terminus of the treasure fleet, the home of the richest merchants of the Indies, whose wealth could be squeezed out in plunder; Portobello, the key to the even greater riches of Panamá and Peru, one of the King of Spain's most precious jewels in the Indies. It was true that the city was well fortified, but surely a thousand well-led men. . . .

The French would have none of it. 'They wholly refused to joine with us in that action as being too full of danger and difficulty', as Morgan later reported.[14] Very well, said Morgan, we will take it ourselves. And when some of his men demurred at the thought of taking such a powerfully defended city with a force which was now reduced to less than five hundred men, Morgan is said to have replied in a paraphrase of Shakespeare: 'If our numbers are small our hearts are great, and the fewer we are the better shares we shall have in the spoils.'[15] Bravado! Or was it? Morgan's victories sometimes appear astonishing, but that is usually because we rely for our information on his own descriptions of them or those of his contemporary, the Dutchman Alexander Exquemelin. Things look rather different when we view them from the Spanish point of view and use Spanish rather than English sources for our information.

We have already seen that the city of Portobello, though potentially very powerful, was in fact rather vulnerable – short of men, low on morale and not particularly well equipped. The point to remember is that Morgan knew all this before he decided to attack the city. His informant was an Indian from Portobello itself who told him the strength of the garrisons and promised that he could put him in the city with only three hundred men.[16] As Morgan parted with the French and sailed south along the coast of Nicaragua, the Indian's information was to be confirmed from other, perhaps more reliable, sources. First, he met and captured the small ship that had been sent out from Portobello to confirm his presence on the coast. A little gentle persuasion quickly enabled him to discover that the rather vague news of corsairs had not led to a massive increase in the city's defences. Farther down the coast, the leading corsair ship spied a canoe paddled by six emaciated and half-naked men whose skin had been burned almost black by the sun. To their surprise, the corsairs were hailed in English and discovered that the men belonged to the gang of English prisoners working on the fortifications of Portobello. They had managed to escape from their guards and had seized the canoe from some fishermen. So Morgan now had absolutely up-to-date information on the defences of the town as he continued to sail south along the Mosquito Coast and made his plan.

What the former prisoners told of the conditions of their imprisonment produced a growl of anger from the privateers.[17]

They were chained to the ground in a dungeon 12 foot by 10, in which were 33 prisoners. They were forced to work in the water from five in the morning till seven at night, and at such a rate that the Spaniards confessed they made one of them do more work than any three negroes, yet when weak with want of victuals and sleep they were knocked down and beaten with cudgells, and four or five died. Having no clothes, their backs were blistered with the sun, their heads scorched, their necks, shoulders, and hands raw with carrying stones and mortar, their feet chopped, and their legs bruised and battered with the irons, and their corpses were noisome one to another.

That innocent Englishmen should be kept in irons and worked as slaves! A thirst for revenge was added to the ever-present lust for plunder that motivated the privateers. Morgan simply noted that 'the enlargement of our countrymen' provided a second reason for his invasion in addition to gaining 'what further intelligence we could of ye enemies intention against Jamaica, and if possible to scatter those forces which might there have been brought together'.[18]

Success, as always, would depend on surprise. The garrison might be undermanned but, if alerted, the guns of Santiago would blow his tiny army to bits and the survivors would find themselves chained in a dungeon in Portobello in their turn. Surprise depended on concealing his strength and his intentions from the lookout posts at Chagres and Buenaventura, but Morgan had thought up a scheme for doing that. He called his fleet of twelve small ships to anchor in the huge deserted bay of Boca del Toro, the same base as Mansfield had used in 1666, and put his plan into action. Leaving skeleton crews in all but one ship, he transferred his men to a fleet of twenty-three canoes which he had captured in Cuba and carried south on the decks of his ships for just such an eventuality. These canoes, about forty feet long and equipped with a small sail as well as paddles, were a common sight in the coastal waters of the West Indies. Morgan knew them well. It was in canoes, paddling down this same Mosquito Coast that they had just left behind them, that he had first made his reputation in his series of raids into Central America.

Morgan's twenty-three canoes, each carrying a score of well-armed privateersmen, must have made a stirring sight as they paddled out of Boca del Toro, rushed along on their way by the fast east-going current. But there was nobody there to see them, except their friends in the ships they left behind, as they set off on this last stage of their voyage along the isthmus, protected by just one large ship. They paddled by night, hugging the coast 'to be ye more undiscryed', and lay up in hidden places by day. It took them four nights to paddle the hundred and fifty miles down to Orange Island with the coast, now rocky, now sandy, just a blur to starboard and so close that the smell of rotting vegetation in the steamy July nights was always in their nostrils. No one saw the splashes of their paddles as they dipped them in the phosphorescent sea. No one heard their curses and grumbles. No one knew anything about them at all until the negro woodcutters spotted their escort-ship at Orange Island on the afternoon of 10 July – and they were too far away to see the canoes and so did not realize the danger.

So far so good! There had been a certain amount of risk in leaving the ships, but the chance of surprise clearly outweighed it. This coast was largely deserted, except for the great fortress of San Lorenzo at the mouth of the River Chagres, and they managed to creep past that at night without giving the alert. The danger from ships was minimal. Few sailed at night so near the coast and, indeed, there were few Spanish ships likely to be sailing at all. The corsairs themselves had brought the commercial traffic of the Spanish Main virtually to a standstill; at the time of Morgan's invasion there was just one ship, a frigate from Cuba, in the harbour of Portobello. Nor was there any danger from the ships of the Spanish Crown, for the only guard-ship on the entire coast was based at Cartagena. There was no ship to defend Portobello – a point which was to be sadly made a few days later by an officer from Panamá: 'We have no ships in the Kingdom.'[19] So the only real danger to Morgan was that he might be detected by a fishing boat alert enough to get away and give the alarm. However, the one boat which they met they captured. This provided them with a useful additional guide, a zambo* who knew the coast better than the Indian who had suggested the enterprise in the first place and who promised to put them ashore at a safe place near the town. Such men, the enemy within, were often prepared to betray the Spaniards for revenge or money. But in his case the motive was certainly fear. The zambo had just seen the corpses of his two negro companions thrown into the sea for refusing to guide the privateers.

Night fell, and the canoe commissioned by the Mayor of Portobello set out to investigate the strange ship at Orange Island, guided by the negroes who had reported it. Meanwhile, in the shelter of the wooded reef-girt island, Morgan went over his plans for the last time, and we can take a somewhat closer look at the men who were about to set out on this audacious raid. Who were these five hundred men who dared to think that they could capture the city of Portobello? We know the names of twelve captains and twenty-six representatives of the men who signed articles of association with Morgan for the expedition of 1668.[20] These are fairly obscure men, whose biographies are difficult to trace, though some of the captains, such as John Morris, Edward Dempster and Robert Delander, were already famous as corsairs and were to remain with Morgan for the rest of his career. All but two† of the men who signed the articles had good English names, and they were clearly drawn from the soldiers and settlers who had been attracted by the promise of Jamaica as a place where you could possibly make a fortune and almost certainly

* Half-breed, half Indian, half negro.

† Their names sound as if they might be Indians or negroes – Ipseiodawas and John Mapoo.

have quite a good time trying to make one if you were not averse to a little violence. But not all the men were English by any means, even if they might describe Port Royal as their home port. There were forty Dutchmen, several Frenchmen, Italians, Portuguese, mulattoes and negroes, and, according to Spanish sources, at least one Spaniard, a citizen of Cordoba.[21] The invasion force was a mixed bunch socially as well as racially, ranging from gentlemen and impoverished planters and merchants to men whom even their best friends would have described as the scum of the earth. They were 'men of the sea, *canaille* of little social pretension', as a Mexican who had been a prisoner in Jamaica for five years put it. But their morale was good. 'They are very happy, well paid and they live in amity with each other. The prizes that they make are shared with much brotherhood and friendship.'[22] One could hardly imagine a greater contrast to the wretched, unpaid soldiers of the garrison of Portobello.

The crew of a privateer in the West Indies was just about the most democratic institution in the world of the seventeenth century. The very fact that articles of association should be drawn up between the captains and the representatives of the men they led is a good indication of this. Discipline and obedience were necessary for a military operation, and a man who 'shall, by meanes of drunckeness or any other manner or way, neglect, slight or deny the reasonable commands of his officer' would lose his share or receive such other punishment as 'shall by the Councell of Warr be thought most convenient'. But this was not one-sided. Any captain who neglected *his* duty was to incur the same punishment. Very careful attention was, of course, paid to the division of loot, 'man for man', though the custom of the corsairs decreed that not every man got exactly the same.[23] Boys only got a half-share; specialists, such as carpenters and surgeons, got rather more than one man's share; captains got two men's shares and the Admiral, Henry Morgan himself, got five men's shares 'for his care and expence over us'. By the terms of Morgan's commission, prizes taken at sea could not be shared until they had been declared good prize by the Admiralty Court of Jamaica but, as we have seen, booty taken on land was not covered by the commission and this would be shared out before returning to Jamaica to prevent any argument with the authorities. Very great care was taken that all such booty went into the common pool and everybody was made 'to swear an oath on the Bible that he has not kept for himself so much as the value of a sixpence'. Then the division was made, but not before various special deductions had been made. Any man, for instance, who 'shall loose a legg or an arme or other limbes in the terme of this voyage' and could prove the loss on the oaths of two surgeons was to be paid £120 or 'six able slaves'. There were also bonuses to be paid as an incentive to the brave. 'In case wee should meete with any strong opposition in any place . . . that wee are intended and bound for, as castles, fortes or other strongholds, the first man entering such place or places shall have £20, alsoe he that first displayes his colours in such place . . . £20; as alsoe to all those that carry ladders, for every ladder soe carried and pitched upp against the walls . . . £10.'

There were plenty of castles, forts and strongholds in the place that Morgan's men were bound for that night, and even greed was unable to overcome a certain nervousness as the privateers got back into their canoes and checked their weapons. They carried no artillery at all, just cutlass, two pistols, musket and what a contemporary described as 'an insatiable desire of riches, courage and disdain of risk'.[24] But their weapons, though simple, were of very fine quality, and the privateersmen looked after them lovingly. Their cutlasses were razor sharp; pistols were oiled and clean; powder was dry; and their muskets, four and a half feet long and manufactured in France, were the very best in the world. There was no one who could fire a musket so accurately as these mercenary ruffians whose 'main exercises were target-shooting and keeping their guns clean'.[25] These guns were gleaming as the privateers paddled away from Orange Island just after midnight for the last few miles of their voyage to the sleeping city of Portobello.

CHAPTER FIVE

The Capture of Portobello

THE FLEET of canoes paddled quietly and gently along the coast in the darkness, the men conserving their energy for the burst of activity that lay ahead.[1] Just before two o'clock in the morning, the lookout in the lead canoe saw the splash of paddles ahead of him. It was the canoe that had been sent out from Portobello to inspect the ship at Orange Island. The privateers put on speed but were unable to close with the lighter and faster vessel, which turned and headed quickly back to the city to give the alarm. Now there was no time to lose, and the whole fleet raced along at full speed, lest surprise should be lost. At three, guided by the zambo, they landed near the lookout post at Buenaventura, about three miles from the city, and a small party crept ahead and captured the sentry 'without firing a shot or making any noise'. The man was quickly questioned and was able to reassure them that no special preparations had been made against their coming. His hands were tied behind his back and he was forced to march with the vanguard, a silent, frightened man, reminded by frequent prods from the muskets of the privateers that his life was forfeit if he should prove to have lied.

Morgan's men marched fast, but still silently, across country to the first real outpost of the city, a blockhouse at the old pearling station of La Rancheria where a guard of five men kept a watch for ships moving along the coast. The blockhouse was surrounded, and Morgan called on the defenders to surrender. But, hopeless though their own position was, the men of La Rancheria knew their duty and opened fire on the invaders, wounding two of Morgan's men. This was enough. The defenders were quickly overwhelmed, but their musket-shots were heard by the sentries in the castles of Santiago and San Phelipe and even by the citizens sleeping on their balconies in the city of Portobello.

The scene in the city was one of total confusion in this half-hour before dawn on 11 July 1668. One of the first to get up was the *Alferez Real*, Cristoval Garcia Niño, who got dressed quickly when he heard the shots and rushed out to the plaza in front of the Royal Treasury. Here he was hailed by the Mayor, who was getting dressed on his balcony. What was happening? Garcia did not know, nor did any of the other citizens who appeared tousle-haired and sleepy-eyed in the streets and squares or at the windows and balconies of their houses. The first real news came from the reconnaissance canoe which came racing up the bay, the exhausted crew firing their guns in the air and crying in a babble of voices, 'To arms, to arms'. Now things began to happen, though many could still not believe it was a real invasion. The drums beat the call to arms; men rushed back into their houses to buckle on their swords and get their muskets, only to find that they were useless, since the powder and ball had been removed to Santiago Castle to protect them from the humidity of the city. Some did not bother with defence, but used the few minutes of grace to try to hide their valuables or grabbed what they could and fled the city in their nightshirts. Silver and jewels were flung down wells or cast into secret holes in the walls of houses, and frightened men and women could be seen hurrying towards the east end of the city on their way to hideouts in the mountains. Others paid no heed to the alarm at all, but just turned over to shut out the noise and were still asleep in bed when the English captured them half an hour later.

One might expect a certain amount of confusion in a city woken before dawn by a call to arms, but the situation was little better in Santiago Castle. The sentries heard the shots, and minutes later the danger was confirmed by the crew of the canoe, who shouted as they paddled past the castle: 'To arms, to arms, the enemy are marching over land.' Sergeant Nicolas Trejo was one of the few who kept his head. He ordered the gate to be opened until the enemy actually appeared so that those of the garrison who slept in the city could get back to help in the castle's defence. A few made it, including the Genoese Constable of Artillery, Manuel de Olivera – though, as we shall shortly see, this was to be no great benefit to the garrison. Trejo told him to check that the guns facing the enemy's likely line of advance were loaded with grapeshot and then went to rouse the Castellan, Juan de Somovilla Tejada, who had not yet stirred from his bed. When he heard that the English were coming, Tejada drowsily told his sergeant not to bother himself; they were probably only the six English prisoners who had recently escaped. When told that there were far more than six, he said that they were probably the crew of a wrecked ship. It was only when he was informed that several hundred well-armed men were coming along the beach at Triana, only a musket-shot from the castle, that he actually got up to take charge of the defence. Tejada was a military engineer who had spent the last twelve years supervising the fortifications of Tierra Firme,[2] so it was the castle's own Castellan who was mainly responsible for the layout of Santiago. He was shortly to see just how good a job he had made of it.

Morgan had forced the pace once the alarm had been given, and it took him well under half an hour to cover the couple of miles between La Rancheria and the beach at Triana. But, as he climbed up from the beach and rounded the great crag called the Peña del Angel, he checked in a rare moment of panic. There, outlined against the dawn sky, was the towering castle of Santiago, its walls crowned with guns and manned with musketeers, all apparently ready to blow his army to pieces as they came, man by man, through the narrow defile into the open space before the castle. Morgan turned and grabbed his Indian guide by the throat. 'We cannot go that way,' he shouted. 'This is a trick to slaughter us all.'[3] But Morgan's friends laughed and patted him on the back, and Daniel, one of the men who had escaped from prison, told him that the guns of Santiago were in total disarray and he had nothing to fear.

Morgan was persuaded. He gave the order to charge and, with a bloodcurdling scream that was heard right across the bay, the privateers poured out through the defile and, splitting up into two parties, raced across the open ground. The smaller group of some seventy men sped towards a ravine that led up to a small hill called La Gloria which dominated the castle on the landward side. The rest of the men ran straight towards the castle itself and then, moving round the castle under cover of the walls, crossed over the bridge and charged into the city, 'firing off their guns at everything alive, whites, blacks, even dogs, in order to spread terror'.[4] In all this time not a single privateer was killed. Daniel's estimate of the gunners of Santiago proved only too correct. A few musketeers fired from the walls and missed. But what about the guns, those great guns supposedly loaded with grapeshot which had so frightened Morgan when he first saw them from the Peña del Angel? The Constable of Artillery had rushed up to supervise their loading, but he had been in such a panic that he had only managed to load two of them and these with comparatively harmless ball instead of lethal grapeshot. Nor was this the end of his incompetence. In the first gun he loaded the ball before the charge, so that it did not fire; while the second gun, though correctly loaded, was wrongly elevated and the ball sailed over the heads of Morgan's men and landed with a mighty splash in the sea. By the time he had reloaded, all Morgan's men had passed the danger zone and his marksmen were picking off the defenders of the castle from the safety of the hill on the landward side. The very first shot took off a gunner's head and soon the long French muskets were causing havoc in the depleted garrison.

The main body of Morgan's army had little trouble in capturing the city. Splitting up into their component companies, they raced through the streets, shrieking, firing their muskets and slashing with their cutlasses at anyone who dared to face them. There were few who did, although some bold spirits put up a token resistance before being killed, wounded or taken prisoner. Five men were told off to search each important-looking house and to drag the inhabitants from their beds, while parties were sent to take possession of the convent, the hospital and the Royal Treasury, where a great cheer was heard as the irons were hacked off the legs of the remaining English prisoners.

Only in the half-built fort of San Geronimo was there any serious attempt to halt the English fury, and even there the situation was really as hopeless as anywhere else. The fort looked quite strong with its walls rising out of the sea, but there were only a handful of men inside to defend it. Only one gun could be brought to bear and that proved to have damp powder. For a while there was stalemate as the privateers, not sure how deep the water was between the fort and the quay, took cover behind some canoes drawn up on land and engaged in a musketry duel with the defenders. The English offered quarter, but the Castellan refused, replying in the best Castilian manner that 'they would fight unto death like good soldiers'. But, just then, some of the former English prisoners came up and, laughing at their colleagues' hesitation, led them through the knee-deep water to the fort. The Castellan rapidly changed his mind, accepted quarter and was led off with the other survivors of his tiny garrison to the great church where the rest of the population of Portobello who had not fled to the mountains or been killed in the fighting were already assembled under guard. From start to finish, from Morgan's first sight of Santiago Castle to the surrender of San Geronimo, the capture of the city of Portobello had taken just half an hour. The sun was just rising as Morgan's men helped themselves to breakfast and considered how to achieve their next objective, the capture of the castle of Santiago.

The castle had been successfully by-passed as the privateers rushed in to capture the city, but unless both Santiago and San Phelipe were taken there was no way that Morgan's ships could get into the port and take his men and their loot away to safety. So there was only a brief pause after the capture of the city before Morgan recalled his men to their duty. Forty men were left to guard the prisoners in the church and another company was sent to reinforce the musketeers on the hill who were still keeping the garrison well pinned down. The rest of the army went back to the west end of the town and began to engage the garrison from the windows of the houses nearest to the castle. Covered by their friends, a party dashed out to try to set fire to the gate of the sally-port, but the defenders dropped powder-barrels fitted with short fuses on top of them and forced them to run back to the shelter of the houses. There was little other offensive action by the garrison. The shortage of gunners was keenly felt and was becoming worse as the marksmen picked off more and more men from their vantage-point in the hills overlooking the castle. The guns that were fired continued to show various defects. Several misfired because of damp gunpowder, another came off its carriage, and virtually no casualties were suffered by Morgan's men. He could have taken his time and trenched his way up to the main gate according to the textbook rules of seventeenth-century siege warfare, but that was hardly the dashing way of the privateers and there was always the danger that a relief army might come to disturb him. Many people had escaped from the town and Panamá was only seventy miles away, a short enough journey for a man on a good mount. He decided to speed things up a little by using a somewhat unconventional method to get his men up to the main gate under cover.

Morgan took a squad of men back to the great church where generations of soldiers and sailors from the galleons had worshipped. But now it was occupied by just a few score wretched prisoners, many still clad in their nightclothes. The usual racial divisions were forgotten in their common plight, and black, white and mulatto huddled frightened before the muskets of their guards. What was going to happen now? At a word from Morgan, the privateers went up to this terrified crowd of men, women and children and selected those who looked important enough or weak enough to suit his plan. They included the Mayor of the city, two friars, several women and nuns, and a number of old men. They were marched at gunpoint through the city and then, wailing and screaming, forced to walk forward over the bridge and across the open ground between the last houses of the city and the main gate of the castle. Bent low behind them and using them as a human shield were several privateers with axes and flaming torches ready to assault the gate. The defenders watched helpless. What were they to do? Could they fire on their own people who stood or knelt before them, pleading for their lives and begging them to surrender the castle? But they knew their duty and, at last, someone summoned up the courage to put a match to the touch-hole of a cannon loaded with chainshot. Two friars fell wounded and one of the English soldiers behind them was killed, but the gun, like so many others in the castle, was faulty and the explosion threw it off its carriage. The English were able to force their prisoners the rest of the way and get to work with their axes and torches on the main gate.[5]

While nearly the whole garrison was watching the drama at the gate, another party of privateers had slipped round to the seaward side of the castle with ladders which they had found in the city. Their first attempt to climb over the battlements was repulsed by the few defenders left in that part of the castle, but on the second attempt they were up and over and planted their red flag on the castle walls. Seeing the flag, the men on the hill rushed down to assist them and, after some last desperate fighting by those defenders who refused quarter, the whole castle was seized. It was still only ten in the morning. Forty-five of the eighty men in the garrison had been killed outright, among them the lethargic Castellan, who had been picked off by the marksmen. Many others were wounded, including a sergeant who was left for dead for four days in a pile of corpses before it was realized that he was still alive. The Constable of Artillery was just about the only man of rank who survived the assault unhurt, but he was too ashamed of his own incompetence to be able to face his future ignominy. Getting down on his knees, he begged one of the English captains to kill him. The obliging captain remarked that it would give him great pleasure to kill such a traitor to his King, drew his pistol and shot him in the heart.

We have little evidence about what happened during the next twenty-four hours, except that there was a rather desultory artillery duel between the English in Santiago and the Spanish garrison in San Phelipe across the bay. But it is fairly easy to imagine what the privateers got up to after seizing a city and a powerful castle between dawn and ten o'clock in the morning, and this is one occasion when there seems no good reason to doubt the words of Alexander Exquemelin. 'After the surrender of the fort . . . all the prisoners were brought inside the town, the men and women being housed separately, and a guard set to look after them. The rovers brought their own wounded into a house near by. Having put everything in order, they began making merry, lording it with wine and women. If fifty stout-hearted men had been at hand that night they could have wiped out all the buccaneers.'[6]

There was also the small matter of collecting the loot. The castles, public buildings and private houses were searched and a start was made to the unpleasant business of persuading prisoners to indicate where treasure was hidden. The Spanish evidence is silent on the details of torture and betrayal, except in relation to two women who were later accused of being very friendly to the enemy, spending much time in their quarters and pointing out other women prisoners who might have silver and jewels hidden away. These prisoners were 'maltreated and oppressed', or more precisely, in the words of Don Pedro Ladron de Guevara, were 'burned in parts that for decency he will not refer to'.[7] A disgruntled Jamaican, who had a grudge against the privateers, later declaimed at some length on the barbarities inflicted on the citizens of Portobello 'because they would not discover wealth they knew not of. A woman there was by some set bare upon a baking stove and roasted, because she did not confess of money which she had only in their conceit. This he heard some declare boasting, and one that was sick confess with sorrow.'[8] What is certain is that the privateersmen were past masters in the art of torture and there would not have been much hidden in the city which escaped their search. There are few people who can resist for long the pain of the bastinado, of flesh seared with a hot iron, or the terrible torture of 'woolding', which involved tying a band round the victim's forehead and tightening it with a stick till his eyes popped out. There is no reason to believe that the people of Portobello were tougher than any other men and so we can imagine that there were steady accretions to the pile of treasure under guard in Santiago Castle, ready to be divided when the expedition was successfully completed.

Next morning, the privateers may well have had bad hangovers, but there was still much work to be done. Most important, there was still the castle of San Phelipe to be captured before their ships, which had come up from Boca del Toro, could sail into port. They had orders to enter the harbour only when they saw the English flag flying from both castles. Morgan hoped to take San Phelipe without risk or bloodshed and, at about nine in the morning, he sent two men in a canoe to demand the castle's surrender. The young Castellan, Alexandro Manuel Pau y Rocaberti, ordered the guns to fire at the canoe and so forced it to return to the city. He would defend his castle to the death. Brave words, but how brave did young Alexandro feel as he looked out across the bay at the captured city? He had only forty-nine men to man the guns of his castle, half the proper complement. Their weapons were in good order but, alas, they had no food. It was typical of the lackadaisical way in which the defences of Portobello were organized that this isolated castle should have no stock of food to stand a siege. Each day, a supply of bread and meat was sent over from the city and the garrison had finished yesterday's ration at the evening meal. Now they had nothing left to sustain them through the trials and tribulations of a siege. To be precise, they had exactly four pounds of bread between all forty-nine men and a stock of tobacco and wine to calm their nerves and give them courage. How long could they possibly hold out? The Castellan was not to know that the citizens who had fled the city had already arranged for a canoe full of maize and plantains to be sent to the castle that very night. Nor did he know that the news of the fall of Santiago had already reached Panamá and that the advance guard of a relief army was on its way across the isthmus. All he knew was that he felt very frightened.

At eleven in the morning, the men on the walls of San Phelipe saw a dozen canoes and some two hundred men set out from the quay near the fort of San Geronimo. Even now, the privateers carried no artillery, just their muskets, pistols and cutlasses. They paddled across the head of the bay and landed a long way east of the castle of San Phelipe. The Castellan ordered the gates to be reinforced with earth and rocks and then sent his men to their posts on the walls and turrets.

At first, the men at their guns could not believe their eyes. The privateers, guided by two prisoners from the city, were marching near the seashore, straight along the main road towards the castle. If they came much closer they would be in range of the guns and, this time, the guns really were loaded with grapeshot. The heroic prisoner leading them to their fate deserves to be remembered. His name was Sergeant Juan de Mallvegui, and when his companion, *alferez* Alonzo Prieto, said that if they went much farther they themselves would be killed as well as the English he boldly replied that 'it was very possible that God would save them for their good intentions and, if he didn't, it was better that they should both die and kill all the English than that the castle should be lost'. 'Oh, no, *amigo*,' said the *alferez*. 'I have a wife and children and I do not want to die.'[9] Well, at least, that is the conversation that Spanish witnesses reported after the event. Whatever the two guides really said to each other, the sergeant's bold ruse was not to work. There were too many Englishmen familiar with the geography of Portobello for Sergeant Mallvegui to get away with it. One of them saw what he was trying to do and smashed him over the head with the butt of his musket. He then directed the marching privateers to a path which led up some low hills towards a watchtower well out of range of the castle. It was not until about two o'clock in the afternoon that the defenders again saw the English as they emerged from a ravine within musket-shot of the castle.

A barrage of well-directed artillery and musket-fire soon drove them back, killing several men. Two further sorties from the ravine were similarly repulsed. But then another party of Englishmen managed to move in the shelter of some rocks to the wall of the castle that faced across the bay. Here, there were no buttresses and it was impossible for the defenders to get their guns to bear on the English, who remained tight up against the wall and tried to set fire to the gate on that side. Rocks rained down on them from the walls, but little damage was done on either side.

The garrison might feel safe enough, if rather hungry, but the Castellan was beginning to lose his nerve as he looked down on the English beneath the walls and across to their colleagues at the end of the ravine. He walked down to the *place d'armes*. How much longer could he hold out? He called up to Lieutenant Juan Saborino, who was in command of the battlements, and told him to come down for a conference. 'What shall we do, Señor Theniente?' he is said to have asked. 'We shall have to surrender.' Saborino looked at him in amazement. There seemed no reason to surrender. Up till then, the enemy had only killed five men and they had only been fighting for two hours. 'We must fight until the last man,' he replied, and the Castellan ordered him back to his post.[10]

Scarcely had he returned when he heard the drums beating the ceasefire. He raced down the turret stairs to find that the Castellan had agreed to parley with the English and had let a ladder down from the *place d'armes* to allow two captains to come up for that purpose. Within minutes the conditions for surrender had been agreed. The garrison would be allowed to march out on the road to Panamá with the full honours of war, 'banners flying, drums beating, matches lighted and bullet in cheek'.[11] Officers crowded in from all over the castle to expostulate with the Castellan. How dare he surrender without consulting them? What possible reason was there to surrender anyhow? Had he no honour? But it was too late. While they were still arguing, the English swarmed up the ladder and opened the main gate and now the castle was full of them. Their cheers as they occupied San Phelipe could be heard right across the bay by the prisoners in the city. And now that they had taken possession of the castle it seemed that they were not prepared to let the garrison have the full honours of war, after all. As the men filed out of the castle on the road to Panamá, the English disarmed them of all but their swords. Lieutenant Saborino had his banner and lance taken from him and turned to the Castellan to complain of this breach of the surrender terms. But the Castellan said nothing in reply. He just stood there, staring at him like a madman, appalled at what he had just done. His world had collapsed. He was dishonoured and branded as a coward for ever. He could no more face the future than could the Constable of Artillery of Santiago. That night he begged his captors to give him a flask of vitriol, which he drank, and died in agony two days later.

Now Henry Morgan really was the master of Portobello. The English flag was raised on the castle of San Phelipe and the ships which had been waiting outside the port sailed in. Apart from the flagship, Morgan had three other frigates and eight small ships of the type described by the Spaniards as *balandras*, undecked ships little bigger than fishing boats, and they had no trouble navigating to their berths.[12] Indeed, there were many men who had sailed in here before, sailors from the Spanish slave-ships and galleons, men who had willingly exchanged the harsh conditions of service under the Spanish Crown for the adventure, freedom and potential gain of a cruise with the privateers. The ships were anchored in an arc at the head of the bay, 'so many moving castles' as they were later described by a Spaniard, whose guns were able to cover every possible approach to the city from the hills and mountains around the bay.[13]

Morgan had twice as many men to defend the city as had the Spaniards and, as we have seen, the average privateer was very much more effective as a soldier than his Spanish counterpart. Garrisons were placed in the captured castles, the lookout posts along the coast were manned, and sentries were posted on the brows of the hills around the city to give advance warning of any attempt at a relief from Panamá, the only place for hundreds of miles where there were sufficient Spaniards to attempt it. Interrogation of the prisoners had made it clear that there was no immediate danger of the city being relieved from the sea.

The privateers could take their time, could eat and drink their way through the supplies that they could find in the town, scatter through the surrounding countryside to round up any slaves left on the farms, torture and search at their leisure, and pile up treasure in the castles ready to be laden in the ships and taken back to Jamaica when they had exhausted the possibilities of the town. No doubt such possibilities included the entertainment of their female prisoners, although the historian must be careful not to allow his lurid imagination and the modern reputation of the buccaneers to overcome the facts. No Spaniard actually mentioned rape in the evidence given later to the official court of enquiry, and Morgan himself was pleased to report that ladies – at least, those of quality – were safer with his men than they were with the Spanish soldiers who later came to attempt to recapture the city. 'We do averre', he was to write in reply to some unknown criticism, 'that having severall ladies of great quality amongst other of our prisoners, which after six dayes possession we proffered theyre libertyes, and to goe to ye President's camp . . . they refused, sayeing they were sure now to be prisoners to a person of quality, who was more tender of theyr honors and reputation than they doubted to find in ye President's camp amongst his rude Panamá soldiers.'[14] This section of Morgan's report was bitterly attacked two years later by a mulatto ship-owner from Cartagena who had gone to Jamaica to attempt to recover what he felt quite rightly was an illegal prize. He said that the English killed the daughter of Castellan Tejada as she was weeping beside her father's corpse and that they tortured the leading lady of Portobello, Doña Agustina de Rojas, in the most terrible way. She was stripped and placed in an empty wine-barrel which was then filled with gunpowder. The grinning privateers then held a lighted slow match to her face and asked her if she could still not remember where she had hidden her treasure.[15] So perhaps Morgan was not quite telling the truth, or only what a Welsh gentleman might like to think was the truth. In any case, there seemed nothing to stop the masters of Portobello from enjoying themselves in any way they chose, if enjoyment was possible in the stinking heat of that miserable town.

CHAPTER SIX

Ransom

THE ONE MAN who could bring a halt to Morgan's leisurely enjoyment of his captured city was Don Agustin de Bracamonte, the young nobleman who had been appointed interim President of Panamá when Don Juan Perez de Guzmán was suspended by the Viceroy of Peru. No doubt, Don Agustin was eager for glory since his acting appointment would last only as long as Don Juan remained a prisoner in Lima. So we can imagine that it was with a certain excitement that he received the news of Morgan's capture of Portobello in the early hours of Thursday, 12 July, only twenty-four hours after Morgan's first appearance outside the city. Bracamonte was appalled by the news. What combination of incompetence and cowardice could have allowed the castle of Santiago to have fallen in so short a time? But he could draw some consolation from the fact that San Phelipe was still in Spanish hands. If he moved fast, he could avert total disaster and, perhaps, gain a glorious victory over the heretical invaders.[1]

One's first impression of Bracamonte is one of admiration. Rarely did Spanish colonial governors move with such speed. He did not hesitate. He did not call a *junta* to discuss the problem. He acted. Directly he heard the news, he gave the order for the city's drummers to beat the call to arms and went out into the plaza to make the necessary arrangements for a relief army to march to Portobello. At nine o'clock on that same Thursday morning, he had given his orders and was riding off ahead with a couple of aides across the savannah and into the narrow winding jungle paths of the mule-trail across the isthmus. By afternoon he was at Venta de Cruces, a third of the way to Portobello, where the trail met the River Chagres. He sent a messenger ahead on a fast mount to tell the Castellan of San Phelipe to stand firm. Relief was on its way. Later that evening, the first contingent of the relief army, the two hundred regular soldiers of the garrison of Panamá, marched into Venta de Cruces. More men were to come during the night. 'I swore to God', wrote Bracamonte later, 'that I would leave on Friday morning and be at Portobello on Saturday . . . to join up with the citizens who had fled to the mountains.'[2]

But, sadly, Bracamonte's enthusiasm was unable to overcome completely the normal lethargy of the Spanish Main and, indeed, despite his promise to God, he soon succumbed to it himself. Another five hundred men from the militia companies of Panamá and the surrounding villages came in the next day to bring up his numbers to their full complement of eight hundred men.* But when Bracamonte mustered his small army he discovered that everybody had left Panamá so quickly that much of their equipment had been left behind. The mulattoes of the militia had come out without any weapons, and the army as a whole had very little food. He sent some men back to supply these deficiencies and also to bring all the handguns they could find as well as a consignment of rope-soled sandals (*alpargatas*) to enable his barefoot militia to march with some comfort over the mountains. The mules arrived with this extra equipment three days later, and so it was not Friday but Sunday before the relief army set out from Venta de Cruces along the narrow track through the jungle and over the mountains on the second stage of their march to Portobello.

On that same Sunday, at the little village of Pequen, they met the dejected refugees from the castle of San Phelipe, who told the President of their Castellan's cowardice and surrender. This put rather a different complexion on matters and a *junta* was held here in the jungle to decide whether to retreat or to continue with their march. The majority decided it was too soon to retreat and so the army marched on.

Bracamonte rode ahead to the ford across the River Cascabal, seven miles from Portobello, where he waited for his army to catch him up. Here he was able to make contact with several of the men who had managed to flee from the city, and what he learned from

* Both Morgan and the prisoners in Portobello were to state that Bracamonte's army was much bigger than this – as, indeed, did some of the men who marched with him. However, both Bracamonte and his *maestre de campo* stated that the army was only 800 strong and, as they submitted the musters with the lists of all the men as evidence of this fact, we have to believe them.

them of the strength of the English made him think that the job of recapturing the city would be 'muy difficulto'. He sat down to write a letter to Don Benito de Figueroa, the Governor of Cartagena, some three hundred miles away by the direct sea route, asking him to organize some assistance.[3] Bracamonte had already written to the Viceroys of both New Spain (Mexico) and Peru, but it would be a long time before he could expect any help from those faraway centres of the Spanish Empire.*[4] Cartagena was much nearer, had a large garrison and some ships which could transport them. Bracamonte also hoped that Figueroa might be able to arrange for relief from an even stronger source. This was the fleet of six ships, known as the Armada de Barlovento ('Windward Squadron'), which after an absence of over twenty years had just returned to fulfil its function to 'clean the coasts of the Indies of the pirates which infest them'. The fleet was at present stationed in Havana and, combined with the *capitana* of the Cartagena coastguard and what other ships Figueroa could rustle up, would have been more than a match for Morgan's motley armada.[5] Bracamonte sent a messenger with his plea for help who went over the mountains to the east of Portobello and then made his way by canoe along the coast to Cartagena. The messenger did his best, but he was molested by corsair ships on the way and it took him nineteen days to deliver the letter. Figueroa called a *junta*, which decided to send a relief force without waiting for the Armada de Barlovento. Eventually a fleet of seven assorted ships was assembled, but they only sailed on 31 August, fifteen days after Morgan had left Portobello of his own free will. Needless to say, the Armada de Barlovento got the news much later and never sailed against Morgan. The long distance between the main centres of population, the usually unprepared state of Spanish ships and men, and the fact that the corsairs were nearly always the masters of the sea meant that such disappointments and frustrations were virtually inevitable in the defence of the Spanish colonial empire. Bracamonte would just have to do the best he could with his eight hundred men.

---

* The Viceroy of New Spain first heard of the fall of Portobello on 23 October, over three months after the event. The Viceroy of Peru received the news on 31 August and, within six days, a relief force had been sent. 'The brevity [of preparing and sending the relief] had neither been done nor heard of in our times.'

What was not inevitable, and was indeed a frightening sign that the English privateers had a new leader never equalled before for wit, intelligence and sheer effrontery, was the letter which was brought to Bracamonte by Sergeant-Major Antonio de Lara, one of the prisoners from Portobello.[6] 'Señor,' the letter began and continued in good Spanish, 'tomorrow we plan to burn this city to the ground and then set sail with all the guns and munitions from the castles. With us we will take all our prisoners . . . and we will show them the same kindness that the English prisoners have received in this place.' However, the letter continued, departure could be delayed and the city saved on payment of 350,000 pesos. The letter was signed: 'Portobello. 14 July 1668. Henrrique Morgan.'

Enclosed was a set of capitulations signed by Morgan and six of his captains and by eleven citizens of Portobello, including the Mayor and the only one of the three castellans who had survived. Lara explained that he had been forced to conduct the negotiations with John Douglas, Morgan's commissary, and that he and the prisoners had only signed the capitulations after being threatened with death if they refused.

Don Agustin was appalled at the insolence of Morgan. That a mere pirate should dare to treat him on equal terms with the President of Panamá! If their two countries had been at war and Morgan had been the commissioned servant of his King, then things might have been different. As it was, Bracamonte felt bound to reject even the possibility of discussion. 'I take you to be a corsair and I reply that the vassals of the King of Spain do not make treaties with inferior persons.' He would not treat. He would fight.

Morgan was unabashed. He replied on the same day in a second letter which was far more insolent than the first. It is worth quoting at some length.

Although your letter does not deserve a reply, since you call me a corsair, nevertheless I write you these few lines to ask you to come quickly. We are waiting for you with great pleasure and we have powder and ball with which to receive you. If you do not come very soon, we will, with the favour of God and our arms, come and visit you in Panamá. Now, it is our intention to garrison the castles and keep them for the King of England, my master, who, since he had a mind to seize them, has also a mind to keep them. And since I do not believe that you have sufficient men to fight with me tomorrow, I will order all the poor prisoners to be freed so that they may go to help you.

All this, it will be remembered, was written by a man who had no commission to invade Spanish territory and at a time when a treaty of peace and friendship had recently been signed between the two nations. Morgan ended the letter with a typically insolent flourish: 'Portobello, City of the King of England.'

As Bracamonte's men filed over the ford across the River Cascabal, he could see that, corsair or not, Morgan's words were true. He had not enough men to fight him, tomorrow or any other day. Nor was there much sign of the initial spirit which had been felt in Panamá, as the footsore, weary and already hungry men climbed up the track to a place called Matapalo where they made camp in the mountains, just a mile or two from the outskirts of Portobello.

Here they quite literally became bogged down. Matapalo was not a good site for a camp, a deep valley surrounded by hills which blocked out any possibility of a breeze. The heat and humidity would have been enough by themselves to depress the army. But then there was the rain. It had started on the march and was to continue the whole time they were in camp – a few hours of torrential rain followed by a few hours of sickly heat from the sun which brought out every possible variety of insect to plague the miserable men. Soon the place was a quagmire and the soldiers began to fall sick, 'suffering in their feet and chests from spending day and night in mud up to their knees, continually soaked from head to foot by the rain'.[7] Feet swelled up from a disease, 'vulgarly called *mazamorra*', and many men could no longer walk. The rain spoiled food and gunpowder as well as feet and, after a few days, it was a hungry, sick and nearly defenceless army which rotted in the mud of Matapalo.

Bracamonte's army was not only bogged down in its own camp; it was also unable to make any impression on the English enemy. So soon as a company climbed the hills that surrounded the camp and started to descend to the city, they were driven back by the English sharpshooters and by the guns of the ships in the harbour. Movement was a little easier at night, and one daring patrol, led by a man whose mother was a prisoner of the English, managed to creep into the city one night and release some prisoners, though not, alas, the captain's mother. They were also able to take back with them to the mountains some images of the Virgin Mary which they knew 'were being treated with indecency'.[8] But other similar patrols came to grief, trapped in well-placed ambushes to which the privateers had been led by former slaves and other malcontents from the city. There were not many such actions. Most of the time nothing happened at all. The English amused themselves in the city, and the Spaniards rotted away in the mud and rain of the mountains. After five days of stalemate, the English became bored and Morgan sent out a powerful sortie of some two hundred men to engage the Spaniards on the slopes of a mountain called El Matador. The skirmish that followed was not very exciting. Eight Spaniards and one Englishman were killed and then the privateers returned to the safety of the city, leaving one prisoner, a Yorkshireman called Robert Burney, in Spanish hands.

It so happened that, on the same day, two Spanish seamen escaped from the English and fled to the camp. They claimed to have been taken prisoner at sea by John Morris, one of Morgan's captains. Bracamonte arranged for their interrogation and that of the English prisoner, using an Irish soldier in the Spanish service as an interpreter.[9] He was able to discover fairly accurately the disposition of the English in the castles and the ships. He also learned what must have been only too obvious, that it was the intention of the English to take all the silver and slaves that they could find and then burn the city to the ground and throw all the guns from the castles into the sea. Burney, however, added that he was sure that Morgan would be prepared to leave the city intact if he should receive a sufficient ransom in silver. Bracamonte knew this already, but the Spanish seamen supplied some further information which made the President, already sickening from the same fever as his men, quite ill with apprehension. They told him all about the council of war between the English and the French off the coast of Nicaragua and the French decision not to sail with the English to Portobello. But then they added that the reason for this was that the admirals of the two corsair fleets had made a pact. The English would occupy Portobello and draw the people of Panamá to its relief. The French would then march across the isthmus to the deserted city and sack it.

Bracamonte's instinct was to march straight back to defend his threatened city. But he could hardly desert Portobello on the unsubstantiated word of two seamen whom he had already arrested as suspected spies. So, the next morning, 23 July, he called a *junta de guerra*. The declarations of the two seamen and the English prisoner were read out, and then Maestre de Campo Juan de Salina, commander of the advance guard of the Panamá army, stepped forward to speak his mind. 'We find ourselves today,' he said, 'with just eight hundred men, inexperienced and poorly armed people who, man for man, are not the equal of their enemies. These men are the only defence of this Kingdom and so of all Peru. . . . I consider it impossible for us to recover Portobello and its castles. . . . What we must do is to leave sufficient men here to hold the enemy back if he advances and retreat with the rest to Panamá.'[10] He then went on to give his reasons – the sickness amongst the men, the shortage of food and powder, the danger from the French, the strength and dedication of the English. 'With such a prize one can expect the enemy to fight well. We would get smashed to pieces if we attacked, whichever way we went.' Thirty-three captains and other officers were of the same opinion – much to the relief of Bracamonte, who ordered that the retreat should begin the following day. Just in case the evidence presented by the *junta de guerra* was not sufficient to justify his decision, he took the precaution of getting medical evidence of the state of the men from two surgeons who had come with the army, one of them a former Professor of Anatomy in the University of Seville. These two declarations were added to the thick bundle of paper, sealed and attested by royal notaries, which he had already prepared.[11] Such precautions were always necessary in the Spanish service. No one but a fool would do anything, let alone order a retreat, unless he could fully document the reasons for it.

As the dispirited army marched back along the trail to Panamá and the rearguard took up its position, Captain Francisco de Aricaga set off down the hill towards Portobello, making sure that the white flag carried by his men was clearly visible.[12] Bracamonte had decided to do business with the pirate after all, and Aricaga had orders to seek an interview with Morgan on the pretext of exchanging the English prisoner and, while there, to try to negotiate a ransom for the city. Morgan saw him and said he would be quite happy to do business, but the terms had not changed from those set out in his letter ten days previously. If he was paid 350,000 pesos in silver, he would leave the city intact and hand over the three hundred slaves he had captured. If not, he would burn the city to the ground, demolish the castles and blow up the guns. Aricaga was staggered. There was not so much money in the whole of Panamá. The most he could possibly offer was 100,000 pesos – 50,000 in cash and the balance to be paid by a bill of exchange drawn on the Grillos, the Genoese firm which had the contract for the delivery of slaves to the Spanish colonies. Morgan laughed. Whoever heard of a corsair being paid by bill of exchange? His men wanted 350,000 pesos in cash and they wanted it now. The negotiations broke down.

But Morgan was not quite as confident as he sounded during his interview with Aricaga. The truth was that he was no longer as strong as he seemed. He had lost only eighteen men killed in the capture of the city and castles, but he was now losing more than that each day to the fevers that so regularly took their toll of strangers to the city. This fact was clear to some of the prisoners who were later to attack Bracamonte bitterly for his desertion of their city. According to Juan de Pineda, a prisoner in San Phelipe, the garrison of the castle had been reduced to only thirty or forty men and had to be changed every twenty-four hours because of the continuing sickness among Morgan's men. In such circumstances, Morgan had already had to abandon a plan to advance on Bracamonte's army, destroy it and march to Panamá. There was no guarantee that he would win. Now he began to feel that it would be dangerous to hang around in Portobello until the Spaniards agreed to his terms. He might have to wait for months, by which time he would be so reduced in men that even the army of Panamá might be able to recapture the city. So, two days after the negotiations with Aricaga, he sent one of the prisoners to arrange for a further parley with the commander of the rearguard, Cristoval Garcia Niño.[13] Morgan huffed and puffed and threatened, but the most that Garcia would do was to drop the idea of paying by bill of exchange. It was impossible, he said, for the Spaniards to offer more than 100,000 pesos. Both men knew that this sum, worth about £25,000, was a small ransom to pay for a city of such great importance to the Spanish Crown as Portobello. Morgan said later that it was barely sufficient to cover the value of the three hundred slaves which he left behind – a slight exaggeration perhaps since he could have bought a thousand slaves for £25,000, but nevertheless a sign of his disappointment. It looked as though this was going to be another of those peaces which the English have a habit of losing after winning the war.

In the end, Morgan agreed to the sum, stipulating that the money should be paid within the very short term of ten days. Garcia used up a little of this term by attempting to get Morgan to agree to a procedure for the actual payment of the ransom which would have been very favourable to the Spaniards. He proposed that the English as well as the Spaniards should deliver hostages in earnest of their good faith and that the exchange of hostages and the actual delivery of the money should be carried out after the English had sailed from Portobello. Each side would then sail to the mouth of the port, 'in two equal ships, one to deliver and one to receive the money, one to land with the Spanish hostages, the other to proceed to sea with the English hostages'. But Morgan would have none of this. He agreed that the privateers would produce hostages. Garcia himself could select six of his captains. He agreed that the Spanish hostages could inspect the castles, to make sure that the guns were intact, before the English left the city. But there was no way that the English would put to sea before the money was in their hands.

Garcia, now convinced that he had got the very best terms possible, galloped over the mountains to Panamá, where he arrived on Sunday, 29 July, only a day after Bracamonte had returned to the city with his army. The President had quickly discovered that the French were nowhere near the isthmus. It was, then, with some relief that he heard that Garcia had managed to get such good terms. It might take some of the sting out of the rebukes that he could expect for abandoning Portobello.

A *junta* was called to discuss the ransom terms.[14] Bracamonte made a moving address in which he expressed his grief and sadness 'that, in the time that he was Governor, the Kingdom of Tierra Firme had been afflicted by so great and just a punishment for his sins'. In the deplorable circumstances, he could see no alternative to accepting the terms. Nor could any other member of the *junta*, although the *contador*, Don Sebastian Gomez Carrillo, spelled out in detail the appalling precedent that they would be setting in paying ransom to a pirate. Now the pirates would be encouraged to spend every day attempting to seize the cities of the Kingdom – a true enough prophecy. But the alternative was unthinkable. Commerce would come to an end if Portobello was burned and indefensible. Nor would it be possible to find the money to rebuild the city and its castles, which had originally been built in the halcyon days of the early seventeenth century when Spanish American trade was at its peak and 'the coffers of the Kings of Spain were not so empty as they are today'.

The King might be poor, but individual merchants in Panamá were rich, and the whole ransom was raised in three days. Some came from the Royal Treasury, but most was borrowed, nearly half the total coming from one wealthy merchant in the Peruvian trade who had already provided much of the finance for Bracamonte's abortive attempt to relieve Portobello. The money was to be repaid by the city of Portobello from the profits that they made on the next fleet of galleons, on the grounds that the ransom was the responsibility of Portobello alone since eleven prominent citizens had signed capitulations agreeing to pay the much larger sum of 350,000 pesos. This clever move by the citizens and administrators of Panamá was to lead to endless lawsuits, as the men of Portobello argued that the capitulations had been signed under threat of death, that they had already suffered enough and that, in any case, they saw no reason why they should pay a ransom for castles and fortifications which belonged to the King and for property in the city which belonged to outsiders, prominent among whom were the citizens of Panamá.[15]

Such legal strife lay in the future. For the moment, everything went smoothly. On 3 August, two mule-train owners signed a receipt for the treasure and set off back along the track to Portobello. There was no hitch with the handover of the ransom and so the privateers became the proud possessors of twenty-seven bars of silver worth 43,000 pesos, several chests of silver plate worth 13,000 pesos, 4000 pesos in gold coins and 40,000 in silver coins – a grand total of 100,000 pesos.[16] Morgan received the treasure with great civility and begged the men who had delivered it to thank their master and to tell him that one day he hoped to have the pleasure of meeting him in the city of Panamá. He then loaded the ransom and the rest of his accumulated treasure in his ships and prepared to sail away, just one month after his first violent arrival in the city. 'Thence being under sayle', he reported, 'we sent the hostages on shoare, leaving both towne and castles entirely, and in as good a condition as we found them, though there wanted not temptation enough for souldiers through the gallant artillery and abundance of ammunition was left there.'[17]

And so ended perhaps the most successful and audacious amphibious operation of the seventeenth century. Morgan had just shown himself to be a privateer of genius. The secrecy of his approach, the timing and dash of his attack, and the discipline that he maintained among his men were impeccable, an example to any military commander. His men must have been quite satisfied, too, even if the ransom was a little low. The total value seized is difficult to ascertain, but it seems probable that it was in the region of a quarter of a million pesos, making a division of just over £150 a head for the four hundred or so men who survived the fighting and the fevers of Portobello – a huge sum for a seventeenth-century soldier or sailor and one that was subject to no deduction by the authorities in Jamaica, as we have seen. One should spare a tear for the poor people of Portobello, who were to take a long time to recover from Morgan's unwelcome attentions. It is difficult to feel much admiration for the soldiers who defended the city, but it would be unkind not to feel a certain sympathy for these men who, unpaid and neglected, served out their time in such an uncongenial station.

Morgan's success was to establish his reputation as the Admiral of the Jamaican privateers and to ensure that even today his name is well known when all his colleagues have been forgotten. But his daring, though much admired in Jamaica, was to cause heads to shake in London, while in Madrid there was horror at his outrage. It sometimes proved convenient for an impoverished government to forget or ignore a raid or two in Honduras or Campeche or Venezuela, but no one could be expected to take no notice of the capture of Portobello, the terminus of the King of Spain's lifeline to the Indies.

CHAPTER SEVEN

No Peace beyond the Line

THE NEWS of the capture of Portobello reached London, with its regular trading links with Jamaica and the rest of the West Indies, long before it arrived in Madrid. There was none of that sense of national shame which, in an ideal world, one might have expected at such a scandalous breach of a treaty on which the ink of the King of England's signature was hardly yet dry. The people of London were not interested in such diplomatic details. The last three years had seen one disaster after another – plague, fire and humiliating defeat at the hands of the Dutch. Now they could openly drink the health of those Englishmen who had restored English pride and struck such a blow against the hated papists. They might not know where Portobello was, but the name had a good ring to it and it reminded them of past glories, of Drake and Queen Elizabeth and everything which Protestant Englishmen found most glorious and exciting. A new name could be added to that band of heroes who had humbled Spain, the name of Henry Morgan.

Such a reaction might be expected from the ignorant populace, but the Conde de Molina, the Spanish Ambassador in London, was soon to discover that matters were not so very different at Court. Nor, indeed, was this to be much of a surprise to him. He had spent the autumn of 1668 complaining to ministers about the illegal seizure of Spanish shipping in the Indies and had received politeness, but no more. The truth of the matter, he had been told, was that 'beyond the line no other rule is recognized but that of force',[1] a fact which he had already discovered for himself. The treaty of 1667 had never been proclaimed in Jamaica, and no effort had been made on the part of English ministers to see that it was enforced in those faraway parts. Indeed, it was clear that the English saw the treaty as applying only to Europe and as a preliminary to a second treaty which would give them valuable trading privileges in the Indies and Spanish recognition of the *de facto* English possessions in America. The capture of Portobello would not be openly condoned by the English ministers – it had, after all, been done without commission in time of peace – but the fact that it could be done once with such ease and thus, by implication, could be done over and over again was a very valuable, if unspoken, factor in negotiations. Spanish weakness might be exploited again if Spain did not bend a little to English wishes, for England was not too noble to make use of 'that raffish instrument of foreign policy, the privateer'.[2]

Molina was diplomat enough to face the facts. Spain was weak and in need of friends. And, in a generally hostile Europe, there was probably no friend more valuable than England, a major trading partner and a potential counterweight to the ever present threat of France. No doubt some concessions in the Indies would sometime have to be made to retain England's friendship, but they did not have to be made just now. For, in December 1668, when Molina received his first news of Portobello, Spain was at peace with everyone, a fact which must have seemed something of a miracle for a native of a country which had been at war with someone or other for the past half-century. Now, in this interlude of peace, all the diplomats of Europe were engaged in a gigantic reshuffle, negotiating and re-negotiating, forming open alliances and secret alliances, making promises and breaking them, getting ready for the next series of matches in that favourite European game called war.[3] Even Spain had room to move in this period of peace, and there was no need for the Spanish Ambassador in London to pull any punches when, on 22 December 1668, he complained to the King of England of the unprovoked assault and capture by Englishmen of a Spanish colonial city in the West Indies.

Such a complaint could be dealt with in many ways. At the very simplest, it could be argued that, since the Spaniards denied the validity or even existence of English possessions in the West Indies, the King of England could hardly be held responsible for bad behaviour by people who in Spanish eyes did not exist. This, of course, was simply a rather unsubtle hint that if the Spaniards would recognize such English possessions there might be no more bad behaviour. Another way of denying all responsibility was to say, quite correctly in this case, that the privateers had no commission for what they did and to regret that it was quite impossible to bring such rascals to account for their action – a statement which was also quite correct in the absence of any naval forces in the West Indies. But, on this occasion, the King decided to take a rather more positive approach.

At a Privy Council meeting on 28 December, a clerk was ordered to produce and read from a much-thumbed file of depositions relating to Spanish hostilities to Englishmen in the West Indies.[4] The file might be rather slender compared to a similar file of English depredations kept by a clerk in Madrid, but there was a file and heads shook at these fresh reminders of Spanish treacheries and violent interruptions to peaceful English commerce. The King, now briefed, granted Molina an audience in the evening.[5] Yes, he had heard something about Portobello, although he had no official news as yet. Such behaviour, if the rather vague reports were confirmed, was regrettable but, alas, only too easy to understand when the Spaniards behaved as they did to Englishmen in the Indies. Since there were faults on both sides, he suggested that the best course would be for such past damages by the men of both nations to be buried in oblivion, as if they had never occurred, and that the peace which had been concluded between the two crowns should be solemnly published and proclaimed in the Indies as it had been here in Europe. It might also make for better relations in the future if the ships of each nation could call at each other's ports 'to make provision of food, water, wood and other things necessary for sustaining life'. At the moment English mariners in distress were treated in a most un-Christian way. Here was a deposition from a Robert Delander, who was dismasted on the coast of Cuba and sought permission to enter the port of Havana to repair the damage. Permission was granted by the Governor, who then proceeded to sell the ship at auction and to send Delander and his crew as prisoners to Seville.[6] The King did not mention that Delander was a notorious privateer who had been extremely lucky to get his release from Seville in time to serve as one of Morgan's captains in the capture of Portobello.

Molina heard all this unmoved. He had heard it all before. He knew how keen the English were to get permission to call at Spanish ports in time of distress. This was the thin end of the wedge, the way to crack open the Spanish monopoly of colonial trade. Once in a Spanish port, what was to stop the distressed English ship's captain from trading? There would be no shortage of Spanish colonists prepared to do business with him. And who was to know if a ship was really in distress? But there was no future in arguing with a king. Molina repeated his demand for punishment for those responsible for the scandal at Portobello and insisted that reparation be paid for Spanish losses. The audience ended.

In the early weeks of 1669, Molina received unwelcome confirmation of the reality of the Portobello expedition as ships from Jamaica began to arrive in the Thames with Spanish booty in their cargo. The Ambassador put a claim into the High Court of Admiralty for restitution of this Spanish property. But here again he was to be thwarted. The Portobello booty was declared good prize. When Molina remonstrated with the Duke of York, Lord High Admiral and a recent convert to the Catholic faith, there was no sign of brotherly feeling for his co-religionists. The Duke insisted 'that the Spaniards forced them to declare war beyond the line of the Tropic by their constant acts of hostility against English ships, even those which sought refuge in their ports from storms'.[7]

Further protests to the King and Lord Arlington brought no better response. On 5 March, after much prodding, the Secretary of State sat down to write a letter to the Queen of Spain.[8] The King, he said, was 'very sorry for the accidents which have happened in those remote parts, to the great prejudice of good relations between the two crowns and against his royal orders. However, he does not know how he could punish the Governor of Jamaica, since he has seen from the most recent despatches that there has never been any cessation of hostilities on the part of the subjects of Her Catholic Majesty.' He then brought in a new issue. News had been received in England 'of a design to invade and take Jamaica in the same way that Santa Catalina was captured two years ago, which he could prove by the sworn evidence of many Spaniards'. The wretched island of Santa Catalina, recovered and lost again in 1666, was now a grievance to be weighed in the balance against the city of Portobello, just as one captured English ship could be weighed against the sack and plunder of a string of Spanish towns and villages in Honduras or Nicaragua. The English were never short of grievances to be put on file and brought out as necessary to trump a Spanish complaint. Arlington knew this game as well as anybody and he ended his letter by referring to the King's previous conversation with Molina and suggesting that the only answer to such mutual hostilities was to reopen negotiations for a fresh treaty. This would clarify the rights and interests of both nations in the Indies and so lead to a real and permanent peace. He had in fact issued instructions to Sir William Godolphin to go to Spain to negotiate just such a treaty only a few days previously.[9]

Molina continued to complain. He saw Arlington and the King on successive days in early March. He threatened to leave the Court and return to Spain, a threat which he was to carry out after some delay in July.[10] But there was no crack in the cold politeness of the English response. There would be no restitution of the Portobello booty. Sir Thomas Modyford would not be recalled or punished. There was no peace in the Indies, as the King remarked in a letter of his own to the Queen of Spain.[11]

This diplomatic hard line was not simply a means of exploiting the unexpected news of the capture of Portobello for the benefit of future English merchants and ship-owners. It also reflected a general feeling in some distinguished English circles that more could be made of the weakness of the Spanish Empire than simply to turn a blind eye to the activities of Sir Thomas Modyford and the Jamaican privateers. If a well-garrisoned city could fall to five hundred men, what could not be achieved by a full-scale invasion? It was the dream of Cromwell all over again. Such thoughts were hardly spoken, and they were soon to give way to a more proper diplomatic approach, but they were clearly in the air in the winter of 1668 and the spring of 1669. This was one of those recurring periods when the enemies of Spain were in the ascendant, when Modyford and the privateers could do what they liked, and the apparent friends of Spain, such as Lord Arlington, kept their mouths shut or acquiesced in the greedy ambitions of their betters. These betters were only too easily impressed by flashy schemes which promised imperial expansion and mounds of cheaply won Spanish plunder. The King himself, who was currently engaged in secret diplomacy with France, whose object was to doublecross and eventually destroy his present Dutch allies, had been easily tempted by the merest hint from King Louis XIV that the French and English might also join together to conquer and divide the Spanish American empire.[12]

The Duke of York, whom we have seen defending a hard line in the High Court of Admiralty, was also interested in such aggressive imperialism. Both he and the King had been impressed by the information brought to England by two colourful South American adventurers, Don Diego de Peñalosa and Carlos Henrique Clerque.[13] These men had separately stressed the general weakness of the Kingdom of Peru, and Clerque had offered to lead an English expedition to Chile, a province which he said was ready at any time to throw off its hated Spanish overlords. The Duke was not prepared to go quite so far as yet, but he had agreed to send out a reconnaissance party to check the truth of Clerque's information. In the summer of 1669, two ships were fitted out in great secrecy, under the command of Admiral Narborough, to sail with Clerque to Patagonia and so through the Straits of Magellan to Valdivia in Chile. They had orders to chart the coasts, investigate the fauna and flora, make friends with the Indians and determine which ports might be best established as fortified trading-posts. They were expressly forbidden to do harm to Spaniards on land or sea except in their own defence, but there was no mistaking the aggressive intentions of this English expedition to rediscover the back door to the wealth of Peru. This was the way that Drake had sailed and raided in the course of his circumnavigation, an example which had later been followed by the Dutch. It was now twenty-five years since a foreigner had sailed in the waters of Chile, and there was little likelihood of the local Spanish governors accepting Narborough's plea that he had come in peace and friendship.

The Duke of York was also said to be directly involved in a plan to revive a scheme which had been actively canvassed in the late 1650s. This was to establish a West Indian or Jamaica Company, on the lines of the now defunct Dutch West India Company, whose only function would be to attack and plunder the Spanish colonies.[14] There is no English evidence that this scheme ever materialized, but Spanish sources stated that the Company was established in 1669 with a capital of more than £300,000 and that it had sent progressively greater resources in ships, arms and men to Jamaica. The Duke of York was thought to be the Company's patron and to have a large investment in it. Some substance had been given to this suspicion of the Duke's direct involvement in privateering by the fact that he had ordered a royal frigate, *Oxford*, to be sent to Jamaica late in 1668, ostensibly to help put down piracy. But, on arrival, the frigate had immediately been fitted out as a privateer by Governor Modyford – a fact which had led to no recriminations by the English Admiralty.[15]

We should not leave this brief discussion of the apparently hostile attitude of the English royal family towards their Spanish allies without mentioning the King's cousin, Prince Rupert, the Cavalier hero of the Civil War. There were very strong rumours around the Court in 1669 that he was about to be sent to the West Indies as a Viceroy with jurisdiction over all the governors of the separate islands.[16] Some said that this would be simply a sinecure to increase the Prince's income, but it seems probable that there was more to it than that, for the Prince had recently acquired a personal motive for wanting to strike a blow in the Indies. Henry Morgan had reported a rumour that the Prince's brother, Prince Maurice, whose ship had disappeared in a West Indian hurricane in 1662, was alive and had recently been a prisoner in Portobello.[17] Whatever his motives, Prince Rupert gave his ambitions away at a Council meeting in June 1669 when he blurted out that 'they ought not to wait any longer or to delay uniting themselves with France to divide between them the part of America held by the Spaniards'.[18] It was clear that he thought that he himself would make a good leader of the English part of such an expeditionary force.

Such facts, half-truths and rumours were fed back by Molina and by other Spanish agents to Spain, where they provided background information to a lengthy debate on West Indian affairs in 1669. Molina's first report of the loss of Portobello had reached Madrid in January, where it was received with all the distress that one might imagine. Spain had no need for any further humiliation and what could be more humiliating than to lose a city to a pirate? So much had been lost already, and no year had been worse than 1668: the year which had seen Spain forced to grant independence to her former province of Portugal after twenty-eight years of civil war; the year which had seen a string of Flemish cities lost to the greed of France at the close of the so-called War of Devolution. The country was at the very nadir of her fortunes, bankrupt, defeated and supposedly ruled by a Council of Regency in the name of King Carlos II, the last Spanish Hapsburg, a deformed, degenerate, miserably inbred boy of eight who was to upset the plans of the assembled vultures of European diplomacy by surviving for another thirty-two years. His mother, Queen Maria Anna of Austria, was said to be totally devoid of political capacity, but it was she, rather than the divided Council of Regency, who was actually ruling and, to the horror of Spain, was doing so under the attentive eye of Father Nithard, her Austrian Jesuit confessor. The King's father, Philip IV, who had died in 1665, had prayed that God would punish him alone for his numerous sins rather than his long-suffering people. But he had prayed in vain, and God had been unkind to Spain.

Spain might have to suffer humiliation in Europe with patience, but it seemed too much to have to do so in the Indies as well. Portobello was really the last straw, an insult which should not be swallowed even by so impoverished a nation as Spain. The body responsible for American affairs was the Council of the Indies, whose President was the Conde de Peñaranda, generally reckoned to be one of the few really able men in the country, a septuagenarian diplomat and former Viceroy of Naples who was also a Councillor of State and a leading member of the Council of Regency.[19] If anybody was going to do anything about English hostility in the Indies, it would have to be him, and it seemed at first that there would really be some speedy and effective action. At the first meeting that was held on the subject of Portobello by the Council's *junta de guerra*, on 17 February 1669, there was an aggressive as well as a defensive note to the discussion, and this note of aggression was to be echoed by the Queen.[20] It was not yet known whether Portobello was still in the hands of the English, and so the first priority was obviously to recover the city. It was agreed that the fleet of galleons due to sail to the Spanish Main under Captain-General Manuel de Banuelos should do the job, reinforced by the Armada de Barlovento and every other suitable ship that could be found in the harbours of the Indies. Extra men and weapons would be provided from Spain. And, if the galleons should find that the English had already left Portobello, they should go on to Jamaica to recover that island for the Spanish Crown.

But this was all talk. The galleons were not due to sail till June, and there was no way that the complicated timetable of preparations for their sailing could be accelerated. And it was not long before the news of the ransom and Morgan's departure was received in Spain. Now matters did not seem so urgent, and so, despite further meetings and further wishful thinking, nothing at all was done until 17 March. Then all that happened was that the Queen wrote letters to all colonial governors warning them to be on their guard and, if they were attacked, 'to resist as much as is humanly possible, always paying great attention (as is just and natural) to their security and conservation'.[21] The idea of using the galleons to attack Jamaica was quietly dropped. It was more important that they return quickly and safely with the treasure of Peru to Spain. They would, however, carry out arms and men to reinforce the garrisons of Portobello and Cartagena, and the General of the Galleons was to confer with local experts and military engineers to determine what was necessary to improve the castles and fortifications 'so that in a future invasion the enemy would not be successful'.[22]

All this was rather a feeble response to the wave of anger that had first greeted the news of Morgan's raid. It was felt that something more should be done to strike a blow against this aggressor in the Indies. But what could be done which would cost nothing? The answer was obvious in the seventeenth-century world; it had been demonstrated often enough by Jamaica. If the State had no resources, then the job must be sub-contracted to private citizens. If there was no peace in the Indies, as the King of England assured them, then Spanish governors must have permission to issue commissions to Spanish privateers to attack the English. It was a decision which was not made in haste. The Spanish Crown was nearly as suspicious of its own corsairs as it was of those of other countries. They had the disconcerting habit of using their commissions as a cover to break the official monopoly of trade, and it was suspected that most, if not all, of their prize-goods were acquired by clandestine trading with the enemy rather than by fighting. Still, there must be some bold spirits in the Indies, and it was a bold letter – a declaration of war, in fact – that the Queen of Spain wrote to colonial governors on 20 April.[23] 'I have resolved to give you notice that, on receipt of this letter, the vassals of the King my son can . . . proceed against the English in the Indies with every sort of hostility, keeping as good prize all ships belonging to subjects of the King of England which they can capture on those coasts and invading and occupying whatsoever island, town or place that the English have occupied or fortified in the Indies.' Governor Modyford would learn that two can play at the privateering game. The despatches were to go with the galleons when they sailed in June.

The session of the *junta de guerra* which had recommended that the Queen grant this long-awaited opportunity to those in the Spanish Indies desirous of revenge also discussed at length the *empresa de Jamaica*, the plan to send an expedition to recover Jamaica, 'since it is from there that all the damage comes'.[24] The *junta* emphasized the importance of early action for, if the English got much stronger, there was a real danger of losing all the Indies. They felt that a strong squadron from the Spanish home fleet would be successful in such an enterprise and pointed out that Spain had never had a better opportunity than was provided by the present interval of universal peace in Europe. Nor was there any diplomatic problem, since England herself accepted that the treaty of 1667 did not cover the Indies. It all sounded very sensible and convincing, but there were problems. Jamaica was said to be well fortified, and so they would need a considerable fleet. The fleet's absence would leave the coast of Spain unprotected against a surprise attack from any of the country's many potential enemies who took this opportunity to forget the peace. Finally, and predictably, there was the question of money. The enterprise would be expensive and the funds would have to come from the Royal Treasury, since the Council of the Indies had only sufficient resources to equip the silver fleets and 'we certainly do not want to impede them, since, if we did, the Royal Treasury would be starved of its returns in silver and the Kingdom would be starved of the commerce that the silver fertilizes'.

This perennial Spanish problem was to prove insoluble. The *empresa de Jamaica* was to be discussed at meeting after meeting through the remainder of 1669 and into 1670, but always the same difficulty remained.[25] Each new English outrage made it clear just how dangerous Jamaica was and how much the English occupation of the island was costing the Spanish nation. Bold men pleaded that, even if money was short, the recovery of the island would be a good investment since victory would bring a halt to losses to the English and lead to more tribute and more treasure being shipped home from the Indies. Great play was made of the glorious expedition led by Don Fabrique de Toledo in 1629 which had succeeded in rooting out the English and the Dutch from several of the islands, 'without letting shortage of means nor cost halt the resolution'. But it was no good. The Spanish Crown was even poorer in 1669 than it had been in 1629 and what money it had it needed to spend in Europe. At first it was decided to postpone action until the return of the Mexican fleet which was due in January. But, when the fleet did return, the silver on board was needed for something else. So it was decided to wait until the return of the Tierra Firme galleons in May. But their treasure, too, had by then been earmarked for another purpose which seemed to be even more urgent than the recovery of Jamaica. And so there never was to be an *empresa de Jamaica*.

By the spring of 1670 it is possible to detect a subtle change in the recommendations of the *junta*, reflecting a new situation in which the memory of Portobello did not rankle quite so much. Information had been received from many quarters that the English Government was not really very interested in Jamaica, an island which seemed to provide very little income for those in England. It was felt that it might be possible to persuade the English to sell the island. When the subject of the *empresa de Jamaica* came up once again in the *junta de guerra*, Peñaranda suggested a compromise.[26] He thought that a successful recovery of Jamaica would require sixteen or eighteen ships of good size. These should be fitted out in Spain but, while they were being fitted out, negotiations should be carried on with the English to buy the island. The *junta* found this scheme 'very convenient, since the cost of buying the island would be no more than the cost of an expedition and it is success we want'. Besides, there was no denying that an English alliance would be much more valuable than all-out war in the Indies.

Peñaranda was in fact already engaged in negotiations for a new English treaty. Sir William Godolphin had arrived in Madrid in June 1669 with instructions 'to cultivate and improve the present allyance to a further increase and strictness of friendship and love'.[27] In September, Peñaranda was appointed by the Queen to treat with him alone, a fact which gave Godolphin great satisfaction since 'he is of more generall credit than any other minister in this court'.[28] Progress was rather slow during the winter, and Godolphin was forced to endure 'many storms and loud outcries . . . not only from ye Minister but from ye common people, upon the assaults on the maineland and depredations at sea committed on them by our privateers in those parts since our last treaty'.[29] But, by May of 1670, he felt that he had talked his way out of this problem and thought that 'His Majesty will be noe further troubled with complaints of what hath past' and that he could look forward to a solid and lasting treaty which would lead to the 'increase of our plantations and navigation in the Indies'.[30] All of which might sound very encouraging but, in May 1670, there was still no peace in the Indies and little sign of any peace in the immediate future.

CHAPTER EIGHT

'Our Portobello Men'

DRUMS beat, flags waved, guns roared and the crowd cheered as the whole population of Port Royal, men, women and children, black and white, lined the sandy, sundrenched length of Thames Street to welcome home their very own Admiral Henry Morgan and his privateers. No doubts here about the ethics of privateering in peacetime. Privateering was good for business; indeed, in 1668 it was just about the only good business in Jamaica. There was certainly nothing else from which so much money could be made so quickly. At that heady moment when the privateers sailed in, one might agree with the rapturous boasting of a later historian of the island that there was so much money 'that Port-Royal was reckoned the richest spot of ground in the world'.[1] The town's inhabitants made haste to ensure that as much as possible would accrue to them.

Tavern-keepers set out their choicest brandy and madeira, skinny whores fresh out from London put on their finery, creditors reached for their account-books, and merchants beamed as they watched the bars of silver, the chests of gold and silver coins, the plate, the jewellery and the rest of the assorted finery of a Spanish colonial town unloaded on the quay. Oh, what bargains there would be! The privateers sold things so cheap. Of course, you had to have something to buy them with. 'Had I had monies by me when our Portobello men came in', wrote the Governor's brother, Sir James Modyford, 'I could with ease have doubled if not trebled that money in buying good substantial gold and silver.' Poor Sir James! He had come out to the West Indies to be Governor of Providence Island, a very poor choice of preferment. But 'his dearest brother' had looked after him quite well since his arrival, made him Lieutenant-Governor of Jamaica, Governor of the Town and Castle of Port Royal and sole judge of the Admiralty and Customs.[2] He would probably have money to hand next time the privateers came home.

For a few weeks Port Royal belonged to the crews of the privateer ships. It was no place for the squeamish. Respectable citizens counted up their profits and pretended not to notice as the town earned its reputation as the Sodom of the New World. Such a reputation was a small price to pay for the riches of the Spanish Main, riches which soon changed hands. Some of the privateers were really wild men, hunters of beasts and Spaniards, men who never saw a city except when they were sacking it or in the course of such a spree as this at the end of a cruise. Most were plain, unlettered, unvarnished soldiers and sailors with all the tastes that their kind have satisfied on leave throughout history. They drank, they whored, they fought, they gambled, they swore, they boasted and eventually they passed out into oblivion. But there was one difference here in tropical Port Royal in September of 1668. Each of these men had more money to spend than the common sailors of their day could earn in several years. And spend they did. By the time the stories trickled down to Charles Leslie, who wrote a history of Jamaica some eighty years later, the privateers' debauch had taken on an element of fable. 'Wine and women drained their wealth to such a degree that, in a little time, some of them became reduced to beggary. They have been known to spend 2 or 3,000 pieces of eight in one night; and one of them gave a strumpet 500 to see her naked. They used to buy a pipe of wine, place it in the street, and oblige every one that passed to drink. . . .'[3]

Drink! Governor Modyford smiled. The more they drank the better. The duties on drink paid the expenses of government, and their proceeds doubled and trebled when the privateers were in port – just one more benefit to the island from his decision to issue commissions. He could feel pleased with himself. The island had prospered in his term as Governor. The population had increased by leaps and bounds as poor or ambitious men and women from the other colonies, from England, Scotland and Ireland, even from Germany and Holland, had come to try their luck in this huge, fertile and nearly empty island. Even now, less than a quarter of the land had been granted away and the plantations that were to make Jamaica's fortune in the future were still in their infancy. They were nearly all along the seashore, and most of the rest of the island was still a wilderness of forest and mountain where English hunters and runaway slaves chased wild pigs and tried to avoid each other.

Port Royal itself was to grow three times as large in the next two decades before the city was destroyed and swallowed up by the sea in an earthquake in 1692.[4] But it was already quite large for a colonial town, with a population of some two or three thousand packed into its cramped sandy site at the end of a long, curving sandspit. Its buildings, constructed of brick and timber in Dutch and English provincial styles and set out in streets with homely and familiar names, such as Queen Street, Lime Street and Honey Lane, made a strange sight when seen from the sea against the luxuriant tropical vegetation of the mountainous island. The town was busy and prosperous, dealing in the goods brought in by the hundred or so small ships which visited the island each year, servicing the needs of the planters and, of course, satisfying the desires of the privateers whose booty provided the major returns to pay for the imported goods. The people of Port Royal were quite happy in their tropical, redbrick town, despite the sandflies, the heat and the very poor water-supply – quite happy, that is, as long as there was war against the Spaniard. It is true that 'death is more busy in this place than in many others', but that was in comparison with England, and Port Royal was certainly not such a death-trap as Portobello and the other cities of the Spanish Main. The city was hot and smelly, but the worst effects of the tropical climate were blown away each day by the trade wind – the 'Doctor' as the locals called it, and 'truly it deserves the title'.[5]

In 1667, Fort Charles on the seaward side of the spit was completed and its thirty-six guns made an impressive show of strength to any ship approaching the port. But, in fact, despite this menace, the centre of the town and especially the harbour were very vulnerable to attack and, indeed, the island as a whole was much weaker than was supposed in Madrid or Panamá. There were no regular soldiers and no royal ships, and when the thousand or so privateers were at sea the population depended for its defence on a militia which on paper numbered some 2500 men divided into five regiments. The number of actually effective men was probably much less, and the men were in any case scattered about the island and would have been slow to assemble to resist a determined invasion. Drill was taken fairly seriously and most men had at least got arms, unlike the militias of the Spanish Main, but they would have been hard-pressed to hold off an attack from the seasoned soldiers who travelled with the Spanish silver fleets. A Spanish invasion was therefore a real threat, not simply a figment of the privateering community's imagination, but from what we have seen of the men who served as regulars and militia in Panamá and Portobello it is clear that this threat was only imminent when the galleons were actually in the West Indies.

Sir Thomas Modyford was not, of course, prepared to agree with this analysis. The justification of his policy was that the threat was always imminent and never more so than when he found himself obliged to explain just why it was that the privateers had had the confidence to take two Spanish towns, when they only had a commission against Spanish ships. Henry Morgan helped him by providing a narrative of his expedition which demonstrated not only the boastful exaggeration of enemy numbers which was the characteristic of every privateer report, but also that command of effrontery, irony and understatement which he had demonstrated in his letters to the President of Panamá.[6] When he arrived in Portobello, he wrote, 'seeing that they could not refresh themselves in quiet, they were enforced to assault the castle which they took by storm' – not quite the way Castellan Tejada had viewed the course of events. The handful of citizens of Portobello who stood up to Morgan's men would have been amazed to learn that there were nine hundred men in the town who bore arms – almost as amazed as Bracamonte would have been to discover that he had marched to that city's relief with an army of three thousand men.* But such figures made the story sound better, and Modyford had no doubt that the Duke of Albemarle, to whom he penned his report more than a month after Morgan's return, would swell with pride at the thought of an English victory against such odds and would soon forget the illegality of the action.[7] Better still was the information about a threatened Spanish invasion that Morgan claimed to have collected in Cuba and Portobello. 'It is most certain', wrote Mody-

---

* Spanish sources indicate that there were well under 200 men in the town, including the soldiers in the garrison, and that Bracamonte's army was no more than 800. See above, pp. 57–58 and 81.

ford, 'that the Spaniards had full intention to attempt this island, but could not get men.' This was probably true. Given the men (and, of course, the money), the Spaniards would have conquered the world. 'They still hold the same minds', the letter continued, 'and therefore I cannot but presume to say, that it is very unequal that we should in any measure be restrained while they are at liberty to act as they please upon us.' Such sentiments sounded all right in Jamaica, but would they in England? God alone knew what changes in policy might have occurred by the time the letter arrived. Modyford was still a little alarmed at possible English reactions to Morgan's raid and threw himself on the mercy of his noble cousin. 'I beseech your Grace so to present my behaviour in this great affaire that no sinister construction may be put on the actions of your Grace's most faithfull and dutyful servant, Thomas Modyford.' He need not have worried. He seems to have got no answer, let alone a reprimand.

Even the best of sprees must one day come to an end and, although it must have seemed like an eternity, it was only a few weeks before the streets of Port Royal began to quieten down. The tavern-keepers closed their doors and refused to give any more credit, and Morgan's men 'came clamouring to their Captain to put to sea; for they were reduced to a starving condition'.[8] There was no reluctance on Morgan's part. The good times would not last for ever. Any day a letter might arrive from England commanding that hostilities cease and no more commissions be issued. Modyford might 'reprove' Morgan for exceeding his previous commission with a guffaw and a nudge in the ribs, but neither man was prepared to disobey a direct order from London unless he could think of a very good story to show he had never seen it. So, early in October 1668, Morgan rounded his men up, got his ships ready for sea and set sail. Isla Vaca ('Cow Island'), off the south coast of Hispaniola, was given as the rendezvous.

Shortly after the privateers had sailed, Port Royal greeted a welcome new arrival, the first royal ship to be assigned to Jamaica since 1660. This was the frigate *Oxford*, thirty-four guns, which had been sent out on the orders of the Duke of York to help defend the island and to put down piracy.[9] Her charges were to be paid by the Jamaicans and, since it had been so abundantly proved that the best and most profitable form of defence was attack, her crew was increased to 160 men and she was immediately fitted out for a six-month cruise as a privateer. An unfortunate incident, in which her captain killed the ship's master and then ran for his life, led to a change in command. Edward Collier, a privateer of great experience who had fought with Morgan at Portobello, took over as captain of what was now by far the most powerful English ship in the West Indies.

Collier's first action showed his willingness to put down piracy, so long as it was to be of benefit to his piratical colleagues. Just a few weeks after he had taken over his new command, he returned to Port Royal in company with a fourteen-gun ship from La Rochelle called *Le Cerf Volant*. Her captain and the forty-five members of his crew had been clapped in irons, accused of plundering an English merchant ship from Virginia. The master of the Virginian ship identified the French captain, and Sir James Modyford in the Court of Admiralty had no difficulty in finding him guilty of piracy and sentencing him to death, while his ship was condemned as a lawful prize. The captain was later reprieved, but the ship, renamed *Satisfaction*, sailed with *Oxford* to Morgan's rendezvous at Isla Vaca.

Here they found nearly the whole body of the Jamaican privateers and several Frenchmen from Tortuga – ten ships and some eight hundred men – eager and ready to sail for fresh action under the man who had so impressively proved his worth at Portobello. Morgan hoisted his flag in *Oxford* and, on 12 January, called a council of war of his captains to decide on their next objective. The names of many Spanish cities were bandied about by the confident captains, but it was Cartagena, the richest and best-defended city on the Spanish Main, that got the vote. This was a bold decision. Even a sleepy Cartagena would be a much harder nut to crack than Portobello. The city lay at the end of a lagoon whose entrances were narrow and guarded by powerful forts. But it was rich and it was Spanish and it was the only place which really had taken any action to oppose the privateers, as we have seen. The capture of Cartagena would make everyone rich and there would be sufficient evidence of Spanish hostility to satisfy any government enquiry. With a thousand men and the powerful *Oxford* to blast their way through the city's defences, the privateers could feel that the prize was already theirs.

Morgan's captains celebrated their decision with a rowdy dinner in the frigate's cabin, while his men echoed their leaders' conviviality in the forecastle. 'They drank the health of the King of England and toasted their good success and fired off salvoes.'[10] Night fell and the drinking continued until, in one terrible moment of destruction, the party ended with the most almighty bang, as some accidental spark or careless match ignited the powder in *Oxford*'s magazine. The blinding flash illuminated the demonic scene as spars and planks and bits of men were hurled into the air to crash down into the phosphorescent sea. Surgeon Browne, who survived to tell us the story, reported that only six men and four boys belonging to the crew were rescued. Some two hundred men were killed or drowned. But a strange fate was to save Morgan. For he, and every one of his captains who sat on the same side of the great table in the frigate's cabin, survived the explosion and were later recovered from the water. Their dining partners who sat opposite were all killed. No one ever knew what caused the disaster. Most men thought it was an accident. Some said it was a French revenge for Collier's treachery. But the citizens of Cartagena knew whom they had to thank. High up on a hill above the city stood a monastery, the home of Nuestra Señora de Popa, the patron of the city and well known to be the best defence against the privateers. Many men saw her come home wet and tired after her long journey on the night that *Oxford* blew up.[11]

The people of Cartagena were right to thank their patron, for she had saved the city. The loss of *Oxford* and a fifth of his men convinced Morgan to look for a lesser target, especially as Collier now decided to set off with *Satisfaction* on an independent cruise to the coast of Campeche. Morgan moved his flag to the largest remaining ship, the frigate *Lilly* of fourteen guns, very cramped after the spacious comfort of *Oxford*, and led his reduced and strangely sober squadron east along the south coast of Hispaniola. Progress was extremely slow as they beat straight into the strong east wind which shivered the timbers of Morgan's tiny ships. Many of these ships were completely undecked, and wind, weather and unremitting hard work reduced the men in their tattered rags to a state of complete exhaustion. Labour at sea was occasionally enlivened by raids ashore to replenish their dwindling stores with the wild pigs and cattle that roamed the island. But even these forays, usually such fun, were spoiled by the unaccustomed vigilance of the soldiers and militia of Santo Domingo who, on more than one occasion, chased the privateers back to their ships. The combination of contrary winds and contrary Spaniards was too much for some and, after a few weeks, 'three of our best ships, pretending inability through distresse of weather not to beat windward, left us', leaving Morgan with just eight ships and five hundred men, half his original numbers.[12] We know the names of six of Morgan's remaining captains,* and they were all men who had served with him at Portobello, men who were prepared to follow Morgan's star, however harsh the conditions.[13]

The original plan had been to sail to Trinidad and then to sail to leeward along the Spanish Main, raiding the poorly protected ports of eastern Venezuela and the pearl-rich island of Margarita, but it was clear from their present progress that they would take weeks, if not months, to get so far east. When they reached the island of Saona, a favourite corsair haunt at the east end of Hispaniola, one of the Frenchmen in Morgan's squadron suggested an alternative target. Two years earlier, he had sailed with the ferocious Tortuga corsair, Jean-David Nau, known as L'Ollonais, and they had raided the towns in the huge inland sea called the Laguna de Maracaibo. This lagoon, which is about five thousand square miles in area and is now a major centre of the Venezuelan oil industry, was even in the seventeenth century quite a wealthy area with a herding economy on the west side and plantations of cacao, cotton and particularly tobacco to the east and south.[14] The Frenchman reported that defences had been weak and pickings good and he felt that, after two years, the region should have recovered sufficient riches to be worth attacking again. Morgan had several men in his squadron who knew Maracaibo and since it lay just west of south from Saona, an easy sail, he decided to follow the Frenchman's advice.

The decision made, they 'stood away for the Main' and came to an anchor at the Dutch island of Aruba, where they stocked up with sheep and goats which they bought from the Indian herdsmen. Two days later they were on their way again, sailing out of harbour at

---

* John Morris the Elder, Jeffery Pennant, Edward Dempster, Richard Norman, Richard Dobson, Adam Brewster.

night to disguise their destination, and the next morning they entered the Gulf of Venezuela, a vast indentation in the Spanish Main which tunnelled down into the narrow channel leading to the Laguna de Maracaibo. The gulf is shallow and is notorious for its dangerous winds and currents, but Morgan's pilots seem to have had no trouble in traversing the gulf by night and bringing the fleet to anchor a short distance away from the breakers which crashed on to the Barra de Maracaibo, the three small islands surrounded by shoals and sandbanks which bar the entrance to the narrow neck of water which connects the gulf to the lagoon. It was 9 March 1669, over two months since they had left the wreckage of *Oxford* and the unpleasant sight of the bloated, dismembered corpses of their friends washed up on Isla Vaca.

Daybreak was to reveal an unexpected problem. The twisting and very shallow channel across the bar, which ran between the middle island of Zapara and the western island of San Carlos, was by itself a sufficient hazard for strangers. To his horror, Morgan saw that the Spaniards had increased the hazard since the raid of L'Ollonais by building a fort on the eastern extremity of San Carlos Island which completely dominated the channel. However, this hazard was to prove less terrible than it appeared. The Fuerte de la Barra was well stocked with food and ammunition and was armed with eleven cannon but, in the best tradition of the Spanish Main, it was somewhat undermanned, having a castellan and just eight soldiers in the garrison. These nine men were awake and did their best to disguise their numbers by firing on Morgan's ships and on his men as they landed from boats and canoes and advanced to assault the fort. They held out all day and did a fair bit of damage, later claiming to have sunk one of the privateers' ships, although Morgan does not mention this in his report and his privateers still had eight ships several weeks later. But, when night fell, the handful of defenders lost their nerve and, leaving a long slow fuse to the powder magazine, slipped out of the fort and took a boat to safety.[15]

The luck which had saved Morgan's life on board *Oxford* was to hold. He and his men inched their way up to the fort in the darkness, all prepared for a savage night assault, and they were 'amazed to find no defenders'. But amazement was tempered by caution, for the privateers were used to deserted forts and the habits of their defenders, and a rapid search was made for booby traps. The burning match was discovered, 'about an inch away from the powder', or so Exquemelin tells us with his customary sense of drama.[16]

Morgan now had to make an important decision. Should he man the fort and so hold the channel against any Spanish intruders who might venture to disturb his leisurely search for riches in the Laguna de Maracaibo? This would have seemed the wisest thing to do, but a proper garrison would have taken at least fifty of his already depleted force and garrison duty was not exactly what the privateers had signed on for. The only alternative was to dismantle the fort and render it harmless so that at least it could not quickly be put in order to bar his passage out of the lagoon. The guns were thrown down from the walls, spiked by driving a nail into the touch-hole and then buried in the sand, and all the powder, weapons and food in the fort was divided and transferred to the privateers' ships.

The fleet then sailed across the bar, preceded by canoes manned with leadsmen and keen-eyed lookouts to guide them through the winding channel. This was by no means the end of their navigation problems. Today, the entry to the Laguna de Maracaibo is simple enough, even for oil-tankers which can follow the well-marked dredged channel with no difficulty. But, in the days of sail without a single light or buoy, it was a really treacherous passage. Beyond the bar the water opened out invitingly into the very shallow Bay of Tablazo which was liberally sprinkled with shoals and quicksands to catch the unwary, including some of Morgan's fleet which went aground and had to transfer their crews to their more successful consorts. South of this bay was the long neck of the lagoon itself, and south sailed Morgan and his men, for it was on the western side of this narrow entrance to the lagoon that the city of Maracaibo stood, some twenty miles from the Fuerte de la Barra.

Maracaibo had already been warned of the enemy's approach by the men who fled from the fort. Juan Sanchez Vorrego, the captain of the city, was determined to resist and he ordered the city drummers to beat the call to arms. The result was disappointing. Just twelve men from the four hundred families who lived in the city answered the call. The rest could be seen moving rapidly westwards with their families, their slaves and as many of their worldly goods as they could carry to seek a refuge in the mountains. The drummers beat again and the good captain, after cursing his neighbours for their cowardice, issued a proclamation that all citizens should muster to their flags with their arms, 'on pain of their lives as traitors to the kingdom'.[17] But it made no difference. Morgan's reputation had preceded him, and the people of Maracaibo had no wish to suffer a repeat performance of what L'Ollonais had done two years before. The city had no fort and no regular troops, and few people doubted the outcome of resistance. 'The towne at our arrival wee found quitted,' reported Morgan. Even Captain Sanchez had taken to his heels.

Some of the citizens had not fled far enough. While most of Morgan's men searched the town, a raiding party of a hundred privateers set out into the country and returned the next evening with thirty prisoners and a train of mules laden with plunder. The prisoners were tortured with that brutal skill for which the privateers were notorious and soon revealed some of the hiding-places of their friends and neighbours. And so the process continued. Morgan's men took up their quarters in the houses round the market-place, and the church was turned into a guardhouse for their prisoners. Each evening saw drunken carousing in the town, and each day the raiding parties rode out into the country 'with complete liberty and no resistance'. At the end of a week, the raiders had taken a hundred prisoners and had cleared the country for thirty miles inland of cattle, slaves and all the valuables that they could find or could persuade people to find for them. It was time to move on. As Morgan succinctly put it in his report: 'After a few inroads in ye country wee tooke some of ye inhabitants who furnished us with fresh, but noe manner of dry provisions, neither did that side of the lake produce any; whereupon wee resolved to sayle farther to discover ye lake for ye service of our King and country.'

The huge lagoon, eighty-six miles long and up to sixty miles wide, was now completely open to them. Not that there would be all that much to find. The news of their approach had gone ahead, and the whole of the west side of the lagoon had been deserted and the herds which were the country's main riches had been driven far inland. Morgan thought that his best chance of still achieving a measure of surprise was to sail to the very far end of the lagoon where there was a settlement at a place called Gibraltar, 'a meane village but full of planting and coccao walkes and graine', just those 'dry provisions' which he had not been able to commandeer on the west side.

It was strange for privateers to sail across a fresh-water sea; by the time they reached Gibraltar they were nearly a hundred miles from the open salt water which was their usual habitat. But fresh water made no difference to their behaviour, and Gibraltar was to receive the same treatment as Maracaibo. Here, too, there was no resistance and the people had fled. Out went the raiders and back came those prisoners too old, too frail, too stupid or too careless to put sufficient distance between themselves and their booty-crazy pursuers. Out, too, came the same old instruments of torture which, according to Exquemelin, were worked overtime for the sake of the poor people of Gibraltar. But once again there is no evidence either to support or contradict the appalling details described by Exquemelin. The Spaniards, used as they were to torturing their own prisoners in very much the same way, make no mention of it, and Morgan's only comment was that 'having spent in Gibraltore some time and re-cruted ourselves with dry provisions, wee sayled for Marracaibo preparing ourselves for sea'. But, as his ships sailed north again from the bottom of the lagoon, they were carrying rather more than the grain of Gibraltar and the beef and pork of Maracaibo. They were carrying slaves and jewels and silks and the assorted luxuries which once had graced the planters' parlours in this backwater of the Spanish Empire. They were carrying prisoners eagerly awaiting a quick reply from friends and relations to whom they had written begging for a ransom to pay for their release. And, as usual, they were carrying pieces of eight, those misshapen discs of silver which drove the privateers to their exhausting exploits and which they had such a genius for finding wherever they might be hidden away.

The fleet which anchored in the still deserted port of Maracaibo on 17 April was rather larger than the one which had crossed the bar thirty-eight days earlier. The privateers had rounded up most of the shipping of the lagoon and their original eight ships had now been joined by five of the local trading craft, known as *plantaneros* or banana-boats, and one large merchant ship from Cuba which was bigger than any other vessel in the privateer fleet, but not big enough to save itself from capture. The privateers might well look pleased as they jumped ashore. There had been none of the glory of Portobello, but it had been quite a successful cruise. It was now just a question of getting home to enjoy the benefits of their success.

CHAPTER NINE

A Bad Day for the Admiral

NOTHING was more vital in the Spanish West Indies, and nothing more difficult to obtain, than accurate and up-to-date news. The normal problems of communication in the pre-industrial world, a world where speed was dictated by the horse and the wind that filled a sailing ship's sails, were here magnified by the scattered and amorphous nature of the empire in which the towns which housed the majority of the Spanish population were mere pinpricks of civilization in a vast and hostile world. Island was separated from island by great tracts of sea whose passage was made difficult or dangerous by reefs and shoals, by storms and contrary winds, and by the ever-present threat of the corsair. The mainland settlements, too, were little better than islands, separated from each other by jungle, swamp and mountains, often inhabited by wild Indians who had never bowed their heads to the Spanish yoke. The Spaniards tried hard to overcome these problems. A stream of advice-boats, canoes, horsemen and Indian runners passed from settlement to settlement with letters and duplicates of letters to pass on the latest piece of gossip, rumour or well-substantiated news. But, try as they might, it would often take weeks for such news to travel just a hundred miles, and Spanish colonial governors almost always acted on information that was out of date, if not totally incorrect.

Such problems had never seemed greater than in the aftermath of Portobello, where Morgan's coup had proved only too conclusively that not even the most powerful and well-defended towns could consider themselves immune from the privateers' attentions. Altruistic interest in the fate of Portobello itself soon disappeared in a more selfish concern with dangers closer to hand. Where would the privateers strike next was the question on every governor's lips; no one had any doubt that they would strike somewhere. Anxious eyes surveyed every scrap of information relating to the reported plans of the men who were drinking the nights away in Port Royal or Tortuga, and such information was so vague that all might be excused for fearing that it was their town, their riches, their person which would be next to feel the privateers' fury. The Viceroy of New Spain felt certain that Jamaican eyes were fixed on Vera Cruz, the only major port on the Caribbean coast of his huge dominions, and sent three hundred soldiers down to reinforce the garrison.[1] Other governors felt just as certain that their town would be the target and wished that they, too, had such reinforcements to hand as they surveyed the crumbling walls and depleted garrisons which were their only defence.

As 1668 passed into 1669, a wise man could discern a certain pattern in the information which was passed from island to island and from town to town. An escaped prisoner from Jamaica was just one of many people who reported that the privateers were drawing together to attack the Spanish Main – a big target, but a reprieve for Vera Cruz and Florida, for Cuba and Campeche. A Dutch skipper passed on the news that a fleet of privateers had been seen sailing east from Jamaica towards the island of Hispaniola. A herdsman noted the concentration of vessels at Isla Vaca and asked the privateers who came ashore where they were planning to go this time. 'Cartagena and the Spanish Main,' came the boasting answer, for it was hopeless trying to keep strict security amongst such a wild and undisciplined crowd of men. The herdsman told a turtle fisherman who told another turtle fisherman who reported to the authorities at Santo Domingo. The news hardly travelled fast but, with infinite patience, the royal scribes who wrote the Governor's correspondence did their duty and soon canoes and advice-boats were setting off to spread the word.

By early February the word had reached Havana, and here the Governor was able to pass it on directly to Don Alonzo de Campos y Espinosa, *almirante* of the Armada de Barlovento,[2] the one man in the West Indies who was really equipped to do something to stop the privateers before they had even reached their target. The Armada de Barlovento was supposed to be a permanent fleet of fast and power-ful ships whose function was to patrol the coasts and islands of the Indies and to clear them of the pirates who infested them.[3] To the twentieth-century observer it seems amazing that the Spanish West

Indian empire could exist without such a fleet, so hostile were the numerous intruders into the region, but in fact lack of money, lack of men, and the greater demands of Europe meant that this apparently essential institution was very rarely in existence and, even when it did exist, it was often used more to convoy the silver fleets than to put down piracy. The Armada had first been established in the late sixteenth century and had considerable success, but its very success had undermined its function and had led to the withdrawal of the ships to other stations. For many years there was once again no permanent squadron, and the corsairs soon returned in strength to dominate that supposedly Spanish sea, the Caribbean. Continuous pressure eventually led to the establishment of a new squadron in 1641, paid for by American taxation and based in Puerto Rico, but this squadron, too, was short-lived, though not because of success this time. Ships were wrecked, ships were withdrawn for convoy duty or for service in Spanish waters and, by the mid-1640s, there was once again no Armada de Barlovento.

Jamaica was occupied by the English; piracy and privateering grew to frightening new levels; but there was no permanent defensive squadron in the West Indies and, indeed, no serious discussion of establishing a new one for over twenty years. No wonder the privateers had such an easy time; no wonder that they never suffered for lack of recruits. But finally, in 1665, it was decided after long discussion that the scale of depredations was so great that something positive should be done about it.[4] A quick look at the precedents in the archives of the Council of the Indies was sufficient to show that the best thing to do would be to re-establish the Armada de Barlovento. The original plan was for a fleet of twelve ships which would operate in the West Indies as two separate squadrons – an immensely ambitious and expensive concept which reality soon whittled down to seven ships which were established as the new Armada de Barlovento under the command of Captain-General Don Agustin de Diostegui in July 1665. But a closer look at the ships, four of which were new-built frigates from Amsterdam, and a closer look at the dangerous situation closer to home in Europe convinced the authorities that such ships would be of greater value in the home fleet, and Diostegui's orders to sail to the West Indies were countermanded.

However, eighteen months later, the scale of English hostilities in the Caribbean caused the *junta de guerra* of the Council of the Indies to petition the Queen for a change of policy. The Queen gave her consent, and this time the orders were actually carried out, so that on 21 July 1667 the new Armada de Barlovento really did sail from San Lucar for Puerto Rico, its first destination. The scale of operations had been whittled down a little more, and there were now not twelve, nor seven, but five ships in the fleet, but these five – three galleons and two frigates – were powerful ships that could outgun anything that Morgan could reasonably hope to put against them. It was, then, with great hopes that the longsuffering Spanish colonists received this 'mobile garrison' which at their expense would clear the coasts of the pirates which had for so long infested them.

The winter of 1667–8 saw the new Armada at work. It split into two groups, one to patrol the coast of Campeche and the other to cruise along the coasts of Cuba and Hispaniola.[5] Diostegui reported that these were areas in which the English pirates cruised the whole year round and where no Spanish ship could sail without being taken. If this was true, the results of his first patrol must have been rather disappointing. No pirates were seen off Campeche and only one capture was made off the islands, a sloop which was reported to be sailing to Campeche to warn the pirates of the arrival of the new Armada. Nor was it all that encouraging to discover later that while Diostegui was writing his report in Havana, the capital of Cuba, Morgan was leading a squadron of privateers to land on the south coast of the same island and was soon to lead them, with no disturbance from the Armada de Barlovento, to the capture of Portobello. But no one could expect five ships to be everywhere at once, and it could be argued that, once the pirates knew a little more about the potential threat, of the Armada, they would not be so foolhardy as to risk capture at their hands. It did at least seem that the pirates left off raiding when the Armada was actually in the vicinity, and so many people were rather disappointed when orders arrived from Spain in the summer of 1668 recalling the two most powerful ships for duty in home waters and leaving the *almirante* or Vice-Admiral, Don Alonzo de Campos, to command the *trozo* or rump of the squadron which was to remain in the Indies.[6]

It was, then, as the commander of just three ships that Don Alonzo received the news of the privateers' assembly at Isla Vaca and of their determination to attack Cartagena. But these three ships were all proper warships and, once *Oxford* had blown up, probably carried a greater weight of metal than the whole of Morgan's fleet. The flagship was *Magdalena*, a small galleon or large frigate of 412 tons. Then there was *San Luis*, a frigate of 218 tons which had recently been bought for the squadron by the Viceroy of New Spain to replace another frigate which had been wrecked off the coast of Campeche. And finally there was the much smaller *Nuestra Señora de la Soledad*, a converted French merchant ship of just fifty tons. But even *Soledad*, small as she was, carried ten guns of three to four pounds' calibre and was as big as Morgan's flagship on the Maracaibo expedition.[7]

Don Alonzo had instructions to be in Vera Cruz in May 1669 in order to escort the silver fleet back to Havana and out through the Florida channel, but he felt that he had plenty of time to investigate the privateer fleet at Isla Vaca and, if possible, to destroy it. He planned to go north around the Greater Antilles to Puerto Rico, so that if the privateers had already set off to get their easting he would be ahead of them and would have the advantage of the wind.

On 19 March, nine days after Morgan crossed the Barra de Maracaibo, Don Alonzo was anchored off the port of San Juan in Puerto Rico, the windward bastion of the Spaniards in the Indies.[8] He sent a boat ashore for news, but the Governor knew nothing of the whereabouts of the privateers and Don Alonzo decided that he must have gone too far to windward. He sailed back along the north coast of Puerto Rico, through the Mona Passage, and dropped anchor in Santo Domingo on 25 March. Here he got some more positive information. A Frenchman had been captured during one of the privateers' raids ashore to round up cattle and stated, after interrogation, that thirteen English and French ships had assembled at Isla Vaca and that eight of them had sailed for Trinidad, 'planning to come and sack all the places of the Spanish Main'. The trail was getting warmer, although the *almirante*, who set sail again on 30 March to beat back to windward, was puzzled that the privateers should have sailed so far east. A few days later, he spoke to the Captain of a Dutch sloop from Curaçao who brought him much more up to date. Ten privateers who had been on the coast of Santo

Domingo had arrived at Curaçao to buy meat and had then left to sack Maracaibo. There were in fact only eight, and they had bought their meat at Aruba, not Curaçao, but the general trend of the information was very nearly accurate. Don Alonzo felt convinced that the Dutchman was telling the truth. The trail was hot. The three ships of the Armada de Barlovento spread all the sail that they could and stood for the Main.

The fleet sailed into the Gulf of Venezuela and anchored at Guaranao on the eastern side, where a party was sent ashore to gather information. They soon returned with a mestizo, the commander of a coastal watchtower, who told the *almirante* that the enemy were in the lagoon. They had sacked Maracaibo and sailed on to Gibraltar. Don Alonzo's heart beat a little faster as the implication of this information sank in. Inside the lagoon was practically the whole body of the Jamaican privateers, those insolent and heretical dogs who for fourteen years had pillaged and robbed, raped and murdered, throughout the Spanish Indies. But they had sacked their last town. There was only one way out of the lagoon and he, Don Alonzo de Campos y Espinosa, *almirante* of the Armada de Barlovento, would be there in time to block it. He could hear the cheers as he returned to Santo Domingo, his yardarms adorned with the dangling corpses of the pirates, their puny craft in his wake. Fame, wealth, promotion, glory, all would be his.

Don Alonzo burst into action. Messengers were sent to Coro, seventy miles away overland, to get pilots for the bar and to send along the coast to La Guayra, the port of Caracas, for ships and men to assist him in his glorious opportunity.[9] Letters were sent to the Governors of Maracaibo and Merida, the inland town beyond the bottom of the lagoon, advising them of his arrival and begging them to do everything they could to discommode the enemy's retreat from the lagoon. When the pilots arrived, Don Alonzo sailed to the Barra de Maracaibo, where he discovered to his joy and amazement that the enemy had left no garrison in the fort. Forty musketeers were sent ashore with powder, cord, ammunition, food and gun-carriages from the ships to see if they could put the fort back into a state of defence. The cannon were dug up from the sand where they had been buried, the nails drilled out of the touch-holes, and six were found to be in a good enough condition to use. A great cheer went up

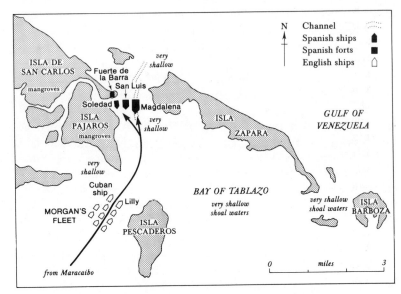

The Battle of the Barra de Maracaibo, 27 April 1669

from the ships as the repaired guns were mounted on their new carriages and the fort's readiness proved by a barrage of artillery and musket-fire. Don Alonzo drank a toast to the enemy's destruction.

He was still not completely happy with his position. His flagship, the galleon *Magdalena*, drew too much water to cross the bar and her berth outside in the waters of the gulf was not a comfortable one. Every afternoon and evening, strong north-east winds whipped up the shallow waters of the gulf into a fury which threatened to drag *Magdalena*'s anchors and cast her on the coast. The *almirante*'s anxiety was not lessened by the fact that the prevailing currents would beach them in an area inhabited by the cannibal Carib Indians. He determined to try to cross the bar. Nearly all the galleon's ballast and water was thrown out and, on 15 April, after some nervous moments, *Magdalena* was across and took up her new position off the island of Zapara in the middle of the channel. *Soledad* and *San Luis* were anchored at equal distances to starboard, while beyond them, but within easy cannon-shot, stood the Fuerte de la Barra on the eastern extremity of San Carlos Island. There was now no way out of the Laguna de Maracaibo without a fight, and a fight against very heavy odds at that. The trap was set.

Henry Morgan did not like the odds. He arrived back in Maracaibo on the same day that Don Alonzo crossed the bar and he quickly discovered from a man, so poor that he had felt it safe to stay in the town, that three Spanish men-of-war were lying in wait for him at the mouth of the lagoon and that the fort had once more been equipped with soldiers and guns. Confirmation arrived the same evening in a letter from Don Alonzo addressed to 'ye chiefe of ye English in ye Lake of Marracaia', offering him clemency in return for the surrender of himself, his men and the slaves and booty which they had seized within the lagoon. If he should refuse these terms, the *almirante* informed him that he would wait for the 'nimble frigatts' and troops that he was expecting from Caracas and then sail for Maracaibo, 'with orders to destroy you utterly and put every man to the sword. This is my final resolution: take heed, and be not ungrateful for my kindness. I have with me valiant soldiers, yearning to be allowed to revenge the unrighteous acts you have committed against the Spanish nation in America.'[10]

Things did not look too good. The channel was barred by three men-of-war which between them had five hundred men and seventy-two guns, many of sufficient calibre to blast the tiny ships of the privateers out of the water. The fort was re-armed and garrisoned with an unknown but probably large number of soldiers. Frigates and troops were on their way from Caracas. Escape overland was unthinkable. There was no way that Morgan could lead his five hundred men a hundred miles across the towering Sierra Nevada which barred the way to Rio de la Hacha or some other port where they might find shipping. There was no doubt about it; he was trapped and he had no one else but himself to blame. It was he who had led his fleet into this land-locked lagoon; it was he who had failed to leave a garrison in the fort; it was he who had allowed the privateers to spend more than a month collecting up their loot in the lagoon. But he was Henry Morgan, and maybe his luck had not run out even now.

Morgan assembled all the privateers in the market-place of Maracaibo and read out the letter, first in English and then in French. What did they want to do? Would they surrender and take their chance of the Spanish admiral's clemency? Or would they fight? As Morgan looked down on the crowd of weather-beaten white men, mestizos and mulattoes who stood before him, he could have had little doubt of their answer. Their scarred faces and the pistols and cutlasses stuck in their belts showed that they had been in many tight corners before. They 'answered with one accord that they would rather fight until the death than hand over their spoils. They'd risked their lives for it once, and were ready to do so a second time.'[11]

As the men cheered and shouted, Morgan called for his clerk and dictated a reply. 'Sir, I have seen your summons, and since I understand you are soe neare, I shall save you ye labour with your nimble frigotts to come here, being resolved to visite you with all expedition, and there wee will putt to hazard of Battle in whose power it shall be to use clemency (yours wee are acquainted with nor doe wee expect any).' He ended with the same insolent flourish that he had used at Portobello. 'Dated from His Majesty of England's citty of Marracaia this 7/17 April 1669. Farewell.'[12]

For the next week, the privateers worked from dawn to dusk in Maracaibo to prepare their ships for the approaching battle. There were spies to report on this activity to Don Alonzo. The big Cuban merchant ship which had been captured in the lagoon was being converted into a flagship. Five extra guns had been put into her, and it was reported that carpenters were doing a lot of work on the elderly ship, presumably reinforcing her for the battle.[13] It was also reported that one of the sloops was being prepared as a fire-ship, a terrifying weapon of naval warfare, but an obvious tactic to use against anchored ships. Don Alonzo took precautions. Carpenters were sent ashore to cut long booms to fend off any such menace, great tubs of water were placed along the decks of the three ships, and squads of men were directed to be instantly ready for fire-fighting duty if it should prove necessary. The *almirante* was prepared for the best that the privateers could do and he felt totally confident.

On 25 April, thirteen enemy ships appeared in sight and anchored out of range. It was clear that they would wait until the wind and tide favoured their attack. Easy to see in the van was the big Cuban ship, dressed over all and flying the English admiral's flag. The reports from Maracaibo had been accurate. Two days later, conditions were perfect and at nine in the morning the privateer fleet set sail straight for the Armada de Barlovento. Don Alonzo remained at anchor, not daring to manoeuvre in these shallow waters. Sailors were ready to cut the cables and set the furled sails should he get into any serious trouble.

The Cuban ship was leading Morgan's fleet, flanked on one side by Morgan's former flagship, the fourteen-gun frigate *Lilly*, and on the other side by another, rather smaller frigate. None of the three ships looked very frightening to the 280 men in the forty-gun *Magdalena*, which towered above these midgets. Soon the privateers were within range and an artillery duel began – a duel which the privateers got the worst of, as might be expected. But the privateers still came on, straight towards *Magdalena*, clearly planning to close and board, when their pistols and cutlasses would soon reduce the odds against them. As they approached, the three leading privateers divided, one steering for *Magdalena*'s stern, one for her bows, and the Cuban ship, guns firing and flags streaming in the following wind, aiming to hit the galleon full amidships.

As the two ships crashed, the sailors on the Cuban ship flung their grappling irons and bound the ships together. High above them in *Magdalena*, a boarding party prepared to jump to quash this insolent challenge. The Spanish sailors landed on the privateer's decks to find them clear of men. Indeed, the only men that they could see were at that moment pulling away from the Cuban ship as fast as they could paddle, as were the two privateer frigates to port and starboard. The Spanish sailors stood amazed. They had hardly expected to capture the enemy flagship with such ease. Their amazement was short-lived. Suddenly, the whole ship beneath them erupted into flames which shot up with terrifying speed and a huge cloud of smoke, up into the air and across to *Magdalena* fanned by the strong south wind. Up and up went the flames, flashing to the spars and sails, consuming the pennants on the topmasts within seconds and spreading throughout the ship with a violence and velocity which those on-lookers who survived the holocaust would not have thought possible if they had not seen it with their own eyes. Don Alonzo's booms and tubs of water looked pitifully inadequate as they remained unused on the decks. Nothing could have stemmed such a fury of flame. Within minutes the mighty *Magdalena* was a burning wreck, and those members of the crew who had not already been burned to death leaped into the sea to save their lives. Don Alonzo remained to the last, flinging planks into the sea to aid the non-swimmers and wondering how he would ever be able to explain such an appalling disaster. Who ever heard of a flagship, the most powerful and best-gunned ship in the enemy fleet, being sacrificed as a fire-ship? This was not the way that things were done at sea. Don Alonzo cursed the English as he, too, jumped and swam fully dressed towards the galleon's longboat.

Morgan's triumph had been total. Just twelve men had sailed the Cuban fire-ship into action, but to deceive the Spaniards her decks had been lined with logs of wood painted to look like men and crowned with sailor's caps. The ship had been packed with all the tar, pitch, brimstone and other combustibles that could be found in Maracaibo and her decks and spars had been treated with a similar inflammable mixture. New portholes had been cut, and through them had been stuck hollow logs to simulate the extra guns which the Spaniards would expect to grace a flagship. The logs had been packed with gunpowder and fitted with a short fuse ready for the twelve sailors to light and run as soon as they had lashed the two ships together. There had not been the slightest suspicion of the ruse on board *Magdalena* and surprise had been complete.

The first reaction of the captain of *San Luis* was to come to Don Alonzo's assistance. But when he saw the flames shoot up into the sky he realized that *Magdalena* was past help and turned towards the protection of the fort, chased by three privateer ships. Once he was under the guns of the fort, his pursuers drew away and left *San Luis* to beach herself on a sandbank as the tide fell. Her captain then ordered the crew to take all the food and weapons and to join the garrison in the fort, while he and a small party remained behind to fire the ship and so prevent it falling into the hands of the privateers.[14]

Diego de Varrio, the Sergeant-Major of the fleet, who was captain of *Soledad*, was not to be so successful. Directly he saw the flagship in flames, he, too, realized that the situation was hopeless and gave orders to set sail for the fort. The cables were cut, but when the crew went to set the sails a rope stuck in a pulley and *Soledad* drifted helpless towards land, out of range of the guns of the fort and pursued by eight privateer ships and a fleet of canoes each eager to be the first to reach this one possible prize. Most of Varrio's crew jumped overboard before the ship ran aground in a mangrove swamp, and Varrio himself had no time to fire the ship as the leading privateers leaped aboard and he, too, jumped into the sea to arrive naked and dripping wet at the fort. The privateers quickly seized *Soledad* and sailed her out to join the rest of their triumphant fleet.[15] All three remaining ships of the Armada de Barlovento which had sailed so proudly from San Lucar on 21 July 1667 were thus lost. The new Armada had lasted for just twenty-one months, and there was now once again no squadron in the Indies 'to protect the coasts from the pirates which infest them'.

The jubilant privateers, after destroying a fleet in less than two hours, were all ready to finish the job by taking the fort. But this they were to find rather more difficult. The fort's garrison had been increased by seventy militiamen from Maracaibo, who had come back down from the hills when they heard of the Armada's arrival, and by all of the 140 men from *San Luis* and a fair number of survivors from the other two ships. The one man who should have been there and was not was Don Alonzo, who had managed to get aboard *Magdalena*'s longboat but had then been chased by canoes and forced to run ashore a long way to the south. However, Antonio Camarillo, the Castellan, proved a stout replacement for the *almirante*, and when Morgan landed his men to assault the fort on the following day his repeated attacks were beaten back with ease and with considerable loss to the privateers.

The position was one of stalemate. Morgan had destroyed the Armada de Barlovento, but the fort was sufficiently well manned to prevent him leaving the lagoon to enjoy the fruits of his success. And sooner or later frigates from La Guayra and no doubt from other ports as well would come to give battle to the privateers once again. The problem was mulled over as Morgan directed the successful salvage of the blackened hull of *Magdalena*. Over 20,000 pesos of silver were brought up by divers; some of the coins had melted in the fire and had run together into great lumps of bullion. Morgan continued to ponder his problem as he led his squadron back to Maracaibo to restock with victuals for the homeward voyage.

First he tried the way of peace. The prisoners were informed that if they could persuade the commander of the fort to give the privateers a free passage, then they would be released and set ashore in Maracaibo without having to pay any ransom. If their ambassadors failed in their mission, all the prisoners would be hanged at the yardarm. Don Alonzo, who had arrived at the fort rather shamefacedly after spending three days hiding in the mountains, rejected the proposal and gave a brusque answer to the Spanish prisoners. If they had defended the fort as they should have done in the first place, the privateers would never have got into the lagoon and they themselves would never have become prisoners. 'On no account was he minded either to surrender the fort or to give the pirates any loophole of escape. On the contrary, he would send the lot of them to the bottom. The fort was his, he himself had wrested it from the enemy, and therefore he could do with it whatever he thought good for the advantage of his King and the maintenance of his own honour.'[16]

A bold speech, and all that one could expect from a man who had just lost a fleet and was hoping desperately that he might still be able to save his reputation. In any case, it is doubtful if Morgan ever had much confidence in his own proposal. What value could he have put on a Spanish offer of a free passage, even if they had made it? He did not even bother to hang the prisoners as he had threatened. But how was he to pass the fort? He had learned from prisoners that there were only six guns in working order, not many to destroy a fleet as large as his if he sailed out on a dark night. A few ships might be lost, but not all of them. He decided to share the treasure out there and then so that the risk of loss might be reduced. And maybe he could reduce the risk even more by getting the Spaniards to move two or three, maybe all, of the guns. A plan matured in Morgan's mind and he hastened to put it into action.

The Spanish garrison watched with interest as canoes full of armed men left Morgan's fleet and paddled towards a mangrove swamp some distance from the fort. The men remained concealed ashore as the empty canoes returned to pick up a fresh batch of privateers. There was obviously going to be a night assault and a large-scale one, judging by the number of men who had been ferried ashore. Don Alonzo moved some of his guns to cover the various alternative routes that the privateers might take to reach the fort and ordered his men to get some rest before the action of the night.

On board the ships, the privateers roared with laughter at the sight of the bustle of activity in the fort. It was clear that their ruse had been successful. Each canoe had really returned to the ships as full of men as when it paddled to the shore. The only difference was that, on the return journey, all but the paddlers were lying flat on their bellies in the bottom of the canoes.[17] It was an old trick, but an effective one. That night, the privateers slipped their anchors and drifted with the tide down the channel till they were level with the fort, a remarkable piece of navigation on a route that was difficult enough by daylight. They were seen, but the night was dark and, by the time that Don Alonzo had moved the guns again, the privateers had passed the danger point with little damage done to their ships. Next morning, Morgan set his prisoners ashore on Zapara Island in the middle of the bar, fired a farewell salvo to the helpless watchers in the fort and set sail for home, where he arrived on 27 May, exactly a month after the battle at the Barra de Maracaibo. Leading the squadron into Port Royal harbour was Morgan's new flagship, *Nuestra Señora de la Soledad*.

Once again the people of Port Royal lined Thames Street to welcome home the privateers, and once again the privateers filled the taverns to spend their money and enjoy their victory – a celebration which was given extra spice by the news that those ships that had deserted them on the coast of Hispaniola had met with a serious defeat. It was much better to stay with Morgan, a sure guarantee of success and a pocket full of booty. As usual, we do not really know how great the booty was. A considerable amount had been collected in ransom in addition to the plunder and slaves and the silver fished up from *Magdalena*. Exquemelin says the total was 250,000 pieces of eight, the same as at Portobello, but Sir James Modyford, who is almost certainly more reliable, wrote that the booty from Maracaibo was far less than from Portobello and his brother, the Governor, stated that the shares of the individual privateers were exactly half what they had been on the former expedition.[18] But even half a Portobello share was plenty of money, and the people of Port Royal had no reason to grumble as the pieces of eight changed hands and the wheels of commerce once more began to turn at full speed.

On his return, Morgan went to make his usual report to the Governor and informed him that the destruction of the Armada de Barlovento had been absolutely essential, since 'severall men that wee fished up assured us this fleet was intended for Jamaica',[19] a piece of information that can soon be shown to be nonsense by a quick look at Don Alonzo's orders and instructions. But this time Morgan's report was not to have its customary effect. Six days before his return, Lord Arlington had written to Modyford ordering him to put an end to all hostilities. The Governor had no choice but to obey and, on 24 June 1669, the drummers marched through the streets of Port Royal and proclaimed that Jamaica, as well as England, was now at peace with Spain.[20]

The timing of Sir Thomas Modyford's proclamation was suitably ironic. While the privateers drank up their Maracaibo money and wondered gloomily what they were going to do for a living now that no more commissions were to be issued, the galleons set sail from Spain for Cartagena and Portobello. And amongst the huge bundles of paper which the bureaucrats of Seville were sending out to colonial officials was the Queen of Spain's declaration of war in the Indies. 'I have resolved to give you notice that, on receipt of this letter, the vassals of the King my son can . . . proceed against the English in the Indies with every sort of hostility.'[21] The tables were being nicely turned. For years, Modyford and Morgan had invented or imagined every sort of Spanish hostility in the Indies. Now they were to face the real thing while their own hands were tied by the pacific orders from London.

While Henry Morgan settles down to the peaceful enjoyment of profit, plantation and marriage, we must give a little thought to Don Alonzo, who did not enjoy quite the same triumphant return to his home port as did his victorious rival. He spent quite a long time in Maracaibo trying to find a ship and, while he was there, he attempted to spread a little of the blame by bringing a criminal action against Sergeant-Major Varrio for the loss of *Soledad*.[22] Eventually, a *barco-luengo* was found concealed in the mangroves at the edge of the lagoon and Don Alonzo set off with the survivors of the Armada de Barlovento, including the manacled Sergeant-Major, on a long, dangerous, very crowded and desperately unhappy voyage to Vera Cruz. Here, on 12 August 1669, a *junta general* was summoned by the

Viceroy of New Spain to investigate the loss of the fleet. The *junta* found clear evidence of Don Alonzo's guilt and he was arrested and delivered as a prisoner to the Captain–General of the Mexican silver fleet who was about to sail for home. His orders were to hand Don Alonzo over to the Casa de la Contratación in Seville, where his case would eventually be determined.[23] The normal punishment for an officer who had failed as seriously as he had done was either death or a long sentence of *presidio cerrado*,* serving as a private and very humiliated soldier in some faraway garrison whose walls he would never be allowed to leave, and one can imagine that Don Alonzo's journey back across the Atlantic was not a happy one. When his case came to trial in Spain, the main point at issue was whether his action in challenging Morgan was one of boldness (*arrojo*) or rashness (*temeridad*), which was defined as boldness without thinking or asking advice. Don Alonzo was at first found guilty, but was later freed on the orders of the *junta de guerra* of the Council of the Indies.[24] Spain could not afford to condemn bold men.

---

* Diego de Varrio was sentenced to four years of *presidio cerrado*.

CHAPTER TEN

Don Juan Returns to Panamá

WE LAST MET Don Juan Perez de Guzmán, President of the Audiencia of Panamá and the spirited organizer of the recovery of Santa Catalina, in a very sorry predicament. He was, it will be remembered, being taken as a prisoner to Peru after having been deprived of his post by the Viceroy, the Conde de Lemos. The Viceroy seems to have been particularly vindictive towards his distinguished prisoner. Perez was thrust into solitary confinement in the castle of Callao, the port of Lima, refused all communication with the outside world and provided with no other comforts than a mat to sleep on and the clothes he stood up in.[1] No doubt Don Juan had very bitter thoughts about his tormentor as the papers which dealt with his case made their slow way back to Spain.

When the Council of the Indies came to consider his case, they decided that he had been subjected to a doubly gross injustice. Not only had he not done what the Conde de Lemos accused him of, but the Conde had also had no jurisdiction to try him, since he did not become Viceroy of Peru until he had actually arrived in Lima and been sworn in. Don Juan should be restored to his post immediately. His lost salary, all of his expenses since he had first been arrested and the full cost of his journey back to Panamá should be paid by the erring Viceroy.[2] So everything was all right for Don Juan in the end but, because he was an official in a bureaucracy whose parts were separated by thousands of miles of sea, the good news took a long time to arrive. The Council's decision was made on 14 January 1668, but the royal order for his reinstatement was delayed till 26 June and did not reach the Viceroy until 16 January 1669. Only then could the President of Panamá be released from his miserable and undeserved cell. Now the Viceroy acted promptly and obligingly in an attempt to heal the breach, but Don Juan's pride and honour were not to be easily assuaged and relations between these two key officials of the

Spanish South American empire were to remain extremely strained. Since every communication to and from Peru normally travelled through Panamá, this enmity was to have serious consequences as Don Juan regularly held up the Viceroy's mail and prevented emissaries from Spain from travelling to see him.

The Viceroy had been ordered to supply Don Juan with a ship of his choice and, on 4 February, the President set sail for the north in *Nuestra Señora de la Granada*. It is easy to forget, as one pores over small-scale maps, just how far one place was from another in this vast empire of the Spaniards in America. The direct route from Callao to Panamá is over 1500 miles and was much farther in the days of sail. It took Don Juan well over two months to sail along the coasts of Peru and Ecuador, past the great forest-clad wall of the Cordillera which barred the eastern end of Darien and so past the hilly Pearl Islands into the Bay of Panamá.

The city looked quite impressive from a distance, an orderly arrangement of white houses with red-tiled roofs stretching for nearly a mile along the Pacific shore, with the mountains and forests of the isthmus in the distance.[3] In the foreground, just behind the offices of the royal administration and the buildings of the port, stood the massive cathedral with its great rectangular tower, while beyond it could be seen the towers and cupolas of the other churches and the convents of the religious orders who owned much of the property in the city. As a ship drew closer, the first favourable impression tended to be rather blighted by the smell, since this major port had been strangely sited in a place where the sea receded for more than three miles as the tide fell, leaving the city stranded behind a vast expanse of stinking mud. Big ships anchored at the sheltered haven of Perico, six miles from the city, and passengers had to wait until high tide to be ferried to the port. Here they could step ashore, walk past the cathedral and through the great plaza with its fine shops and elegant customers to take a closer look at the houses set out along the three main streets of the city. Most visitors were surprised that, because of the shortage of stone and lime, not only nearly all the houses, but most of the public buildings and churches, too, were built of wood. Some of these were magnificent and very solid creations of the local mahogany and cedar, but most were less robust, 'being of the least strength of any place that I had entered in' as one visitor remarked.⁴ And, once one wandered off the main streets into the meaner parts of the town where the great majority of Panamá's population lived, the huts and shacks were not even made of wood, but were ramshackle erections of cane and straw, a poor protection against the city's disproportionate share of the world's rainfall.

Conditions of life were not good in Panamá. Antonio Vázquez de Espinosa, who tried to find a good word for every place in the Spanish Indies, denied the city's reputation as a death-trap, but it is difficult to find any other contemporary observer who agreed with him. The Town Council reported to the Crown in 1646 that not only was the city subject to earthquakes which often led to great loss of life, but also the excessive heat and humidity were the cause of continuous infirmity and death, while the merchants of Peru regarded Panamá with horror because of the many deaths and great sickness that they always experienced when the Peruvian fleet arrived with the silver for the galleons.⁵ The best that one could say for Panamá was that it was not quite as bad as Portobello and that the climate was a lot healthier in the dry season, from mid-December till the end of April, than it was in the almost constant rain of the rest of the year, 'when the malice of the air corrupts everything, so that even iron is consumed and destroyed'.⁶ The unpleasantness of living in such an unhealthy climate was aggravated by the very high price and often total absence of basic foodstuffs. The savannahs outside the city produced meat, and there was plenty of fruit and game in the mountains, but practically the whole of Panamá's requirements of wine, wheat, maize and beans had to be imported at high cost from Peru and Ecuador. Consignments of basic foodstuffs were few and far between, and the need to store grain for long periods in such a climate meant that much rotted and the poorer people often suffered from disease caused by bad flour.

Much more grain could have been grown close to the city if there had been people to grow it, but there were not, and this lack of people was one of the major problems of the Audiencia of Panamá, causing difficulties both for the economy and for defence. Most of the native Indians had been wiped out by Spanish hostility and by European diseases in the sixteenth century, so that by the period we are considering there were probably no more than 12,000 people in the whole Audiencia, which was roughly the same area as the modern state of Panamá. Some of these were 'wild' Indians and runaway negroes living in the mountains and jungles; some were 'Spanish' or civilized Indians living in villages such as Penonome, Cocle and Chepo; perhaps 2000 people of all races lived in the three small Spanish towns of Portobello, Los Santos and Nata; but over half of the total population of the Audiencia lived in the city of Panamá itself. The city had a population of about 6000 in 1607, of whom less than 1000 were white and nearly 4000 were negro slaves, the rest being mulattoes, mestizos, zambos and Indians. By the time of Juan Perez de Guzmán, the city had grown a bit and it is probable that the racial composition had changed, so that by 1670 there were even less whites, rather fewer black slaves, rather more free blacks and a much greater number of half-castes. The big mulatto population was the result of the shortage of white women, who disliked the climate of Panamá, and also, according to one report, because of the low morals of the Spanish men, who were 'much given to sinne, loosenesse and venery' and made 'the black-mores (who are many, rich and gallant) the chiefe objects of their lust'.[7] The zambo population of Panamá was also large, since the negroes not only found the Indian women attractive, but had also learned that under Spanish law the offspring of such unions acquired the free status of their mothers.[8]

The large number of negro slaves in Panamá – probably the biggest concentration in the Spanish Empire – reflected the city's economy. Some worked in saw-mills, on cattle ranches and on sugar plantations outside the city; some were domestic servants and labourers within; but the main function of the slaves was to provide the labour for the *trajín*, that vital carriage of goods across the isthmus which was the only reason why such a large city had grown up in such an uncongenial spot. There were negro mule-drivers and negro porters, negro boatmen on the River Chagres and negro stevedores in the ports of Portobello, Panamá and Perico. Such a large number of slaves reflected an immense investment of capital, an investment which by the late 1660s was by no means fully employed since the fleets and hence the *trajín* were only in operation every other year. But this did not mean that there was no money to be made in Panamá. Those few men who owned the slaves, the river-boats and the priceless mules imported from Nicaragua and Honduras had a complete monopoly of transport across the isthmus and they charged monopoly prices for their services. Such men were immensely rich, and there was a sizeable middle class of slave-dealers, merchants, lawyers and royal officials whom the *trajín* had made only slightly less rich. It was the wealth of these men which gave the city its reputation as 'one of the richest places in all America'.[9]

There were opportunities for the Governor of such a city to become rich, too, and there is no doubt that Don Juan, despite being intensely loyal and intensely religious, was also human and made use of his opportunities to sell offices, take bribes and generally amass a considerable fortune during his term of office.[10] However, his first thought on his return to Panamá was for the defences of the Audiencia. The loss of Portobello during his absence and the con-tinued reports of corsair activity along the coast filled him with apprehension. It did not take an accountant to work out that the two most attractive prizes for the confident corsairs were likely to be Panamá and Cartagena and, of the two, Panamá would seem to have been both the richest and the least easy to defend.

The main defence of Panamá was the isthmus itself, although this had not always been true. There had been a time when Panamá had more fear of the men who lived in the jungles and mountains behind the city and, in particular, in the wild, inaccessible area of Darien, than she had of the corsairs of the Caribbean. From early days, slaves had run away from their harsh taskmasters, and these *cimarrones* or maroons had allied themselves with the Indians of Darien to make a very effective enemy on the city's very doorstep. Raids had been made into the streets of the city to seize plunder and negro slave women to enliven the warrior life in the jungle. The passage of goods across the isthmus had become a terrifying journey for the mule-trains and their escorts, afraid that every tree might hide an ambush of the dreaded maroons. Drake and the other English corsairs of the late sixteenth century had made common cause with the maroons and Indians, who more than matched their hatred of Spaniards, and these black and Indian allies were a major factor in their successes. But, in the course of the seventeenth century, the Spaniards had eradicated most of the major maroon settlements, driving the survivors deeper and deeper into the Darien jungle, and there is no mention of danger from runaway blacks in the documents of the period with which we are concerned. There had also been considerable success in converting the Indians of Darien and, by the time of Don Juan, there were five *doctrinas*, or villages of converted Indians, in the region. These Indians still retained their fighting qualities and were available as auxiliaries under their Spanish Lieutenant-General, Don Pedro Clemente. They seem to have been especially loyal to Don Juan and, in his hour of need, over one hundred and fifty Christian Indians from Darien came out of their jungle fastnesses to give him help and die at his side.[11]

Winning the friendship of the Indians was a major factor in the policy of successive Presidents of Panamá and an important feature in the defence of the city. The terrain of the isthmus was another. It took a bold invader to brave that unmapped chaos of mountain, jungle, swamp and innumerable rivers, and the few tracks which did pass across the isthmus were deliberately kept in a poor state of repair to discourage intruders, while the entrances to the two main routes at Portobello and Chagres were guarded, as we have seen, by castles with garrisons of regular troops. Panamá itself was virtually an open city. There were some fortifications, with a few guns and fewer gunners, overlooking the port, but the rest of the city had no walls and relied for its main defence on a garrison of two regular companies with less than two hundred men. The regulars could be supplemented, as elsewhere, by the militia which was organized as at Portobello on a racial basis with companies of Spaniards, mulattoes, free blacks, mestizos and zambos. Neither Don Juan nor the interim governor, Don Agustin de Bracamonte, had any illusions about the military value of such men. None of the white officers in Panamá had a high opinion of coloured militia – an opinion which may well have been more than just a matter of racial prejudice, since the coloured population had very little in the way of possessions to protect and may well have had little interest in the Castilian obsession with military honour. Bracamonte also had a low opinion of most of the Spaniards in Panamá, considering that they only came to Panamá because they were incapable of making a living anywhere else – an opinion which also may not only be prejudice, considering what we have seen of the conditions of life in the city. Above all, the militia and indeed most of the regulars, whether white or coloured, were greenhorns who had never heard a shot fired in anger and who believed that when the day came they would instinctively fight bravely. However, Bracamonte wrote in a letter to the Queen, 'there is a great difference between saying we will fight when the enemy arrives and actually fighting when he does arrive'.[12]

Don Juan agreed with Bracamonte's analysis and his constant obsession after his return from Peru was with the Audiencia's shortage of trained soldiers. More men were needed for Portobello as a garrison for the city in addition to the garrisons at the castles. More men were needed for the castle of San Lorenzo at Chagres. More men were needed as guards and sentries at the numerous other places on the Caribbean coast where an invasion force could be landed.* If that coast could be made secure, then Panamá itself would be safe and could serve as a *place d'armes* from which reinforcements could be sent to wherever was the major threat. There was at the moment no thought of any threat from the Pacific, and Don Juan never seems to have paid any attention to the seaward defences of the city of Panamá. It was the Caribbean coastline and the threat from Jamaica which worried him. He was realistic and knew that he would never get as many men as he wanted, but he felt that at the very minimum he must have two hundred more trained soldiers for Portobello and Chagres. He must have written two or three dozen letters begging for these two hundred men during 1669 and 1670, each time pleading that the Kingdom was indefensible without them and each time pleading in vain.

He started by writing to his former gaoler, the Viceroy of Peru, whose dominions should easily have had two hundred men to spare.[13] The Viceroy's answers were slow to arrive and, when they did arrive, they were not helpful. It was quite impossible to send two hundred men. The soldiers of Peru could not be sent, because they were needed to defend Peru, while the men from the other provinces were needed to fight the Indians in Tucuman or to man the garrisons in Chile. Even if there had been men, it would have cost too much to send them. All of which may have been true, though one suspects

---

* Puerto de Naos, Buenaventura, Rio de Cocle, Rio de Indios, Veragua, Puerto Pilon.

that the mutual antagonism between the two officials had much to do with the Viceroy's refusal to send troops – a suspicion which is strengthened by the fact that, two years later when it was far too late, the Viceroy was able to send over two thousand men to the aid of Panamá.[14]

When the Armada del Sur, the Peruvian silver fleet, sailed north in the summer of 1669 to make its rendezvous with the merchants and mule-drivers of Panamá who would take the assembled treasure of two years across the isthmus, it brought further instructions for the President of Panamá. The Queen, the Viceroy wrote, had given orders for the galleons to bring reinforcements for the garrisons of the Spanish Main. If Don Juan needed men, he should apply to Manuel de Banuelos, the Captain-General of the galleons, when he arrived at Portobello. As the men of the *trajín* began to get busy, Don Juan made his way across the isthmus to inspect the defences of Portobello and to await the arrival of the galleons and his men. With him went Francisco Marichalar, a judge from Peru who had a commission to discover how the English had managed to capture the city in the previous summer and who was responsible for the disaster.[15] To help him in his enquiry, he had the results of a preliminary investigation which had been made on the orders of Bracamonte in October, the purpose of which had been primarily to ensure that the interim governor bore no blame. In this he had been successful. Bracamonte sent the papers to the Council of the Indies on 26 November 1668 and, on 16 May 1669, the Queen had issued a *cedula de gracias* completely exonerating him from any responsibility for the loss of the city, a remarkably speedy and successful piece of special pleading.[16] Now, on 30 September 1669, Marichalar got down to the real business, while Don Juan took the precaution of locking up the Mayor of Portobello and the Castellan of San Geronimo, the two survivors who seemed to him to be most likely to be guilty. They were still in the dungeon of Santiago Castle a year later and had not yet been charged with any offence.[17]

While the legal proceedings continued, the mule-trains began to arrive in Portobello after their uncomfortable journey across the isthmus and the city began to take on an air of festivity and business which completely transformed it from the cowed and beaten place from which Morgan's fleet had sailed in triumph only twelve months before. Now people could see how wise they had been to pay the 100,000 pesos ransom, as the silver piled up in the warehouses and the Royal Treasury and the visiting merchants from Peru and Panamá competed with each other to pay the astronomical house and shop rents demanded by those citizens who had survived Morgan's terror. Now, during these few days before the fleet arrived, it really would have been a prize worth taking. At last, on 24 October, the fleet was signalled and the guns of Santiago and San Phelipe saluted the seven galleons and two frigates of the 1669 Armada de Tierra Firme which sailed into Portobello Bay and anchored before the still uncompleted fort of San Geronimo.[18] The merchants and the soldiers stepped ashore to stretch their legs and the great fair of Portobello was once more under way.

Don Juan was pleased to see, among the European goods unloaded on the quay, a large consignment of arms. There were 1115 arquebuses and 499 carbines, but unfortunately none of the precious *escopeteras*, the only handguns which could successfully stand up to the humidity of Panamá. There were muskets and lances, machetes and pikes, swords and swordbelts, powder, powder-flasks and cannon-balls.[19] But where were the two hundred men for the garrisons of the Audiencia of Panamá? Captain-General Banuelos was most apologetic. Yes, the Queen had given orders for the fleet to bring five hundred extra men. He had dropped off one hundred and fifty in Cartagena and forty had been sent to La Guayra. Don Juan could have all that remained over and above the requirements of the fleet itself. But he was not sure that there would be very many left. Some had had to be left behind in Cadiz, many had deserted, many had died in hospital in Cartagena and it looked as though many would die here, too.[20] Don Juan's heart sank as he saw the wretched soldiers and sailors carried to the hospital of Portobello and heard the bells tolling for each new victim of the fevers of this, the worst of all death-traps on the Spanish Main. Four hundred and fifty men had died of fever by the time the fleet had completed loading the 5 million pesos of merchandise and the 17½ million pesos of silver coin and bullion which had been shipped up from Peru and carried across the isthmus.[21] When the fleet set sail again for Cartagena in early December, Manuel de Banuelos told Don Juan that he needed every man who had survived to protect the galleons on their homeward voyage. The best that he could suggest to the distraught President was that he round up all the men who had stowed away on the galleons and had quietly disappeared on arrival at Portobello. They might not be very good soldiers, but there were probably enough of them to fill up the gaps in his garrisons.

Stowaways! The bitter Don Juan poured his heart out to the Queen and the Viceroy. What hope was there of catching stowaways in Portobello? It was an unwalled city, open to the countryside; to catch a stowaway was 'like trying to catch water from the sea in a sieve'. And, if he did pick some up, the merchants, always short of labour, claimed that they were their servants. Where was he to get men? How was he to defend the Kingdom of Tierra Firme? 'I myself am ready to die in the Kingdom's defence, but that will not stop the enemy making war.' The flood of letters continued into 1670, as Don Juan became increasingly despondent and reports of future corsair activity became stronger and more precise.[22] On 6 June 1670, he reported to the Queen some astonishingly accurate information. He had news from spies and prisoners that the enemy intended to invade with 1500 men who would enter the isthmus by the River Chagres and so go to Panamá. At about the same time, this news was confirmed from a source in which the religious Don Juan probably had much greater faith. A Franciscan monk, who preached in the cathedral of Panamá, told his horror-struck congregation that a fellow-Franciscan called Brother Gonzalo had had a vision in which a man came from Jamaica to invade the Kingdom and the streets of Panamá ran with blood and fire. Brother Gonzalo's vision was very vivid and he commissioned an artist to represent what he had seen in a great painting which was hung on the wall of the Franciscan convent. It was a terrifying picture. English corsairs raced through the streets with pistols and cutlasses in their hands while, on the rooftops, grinning negro demons were setting fire to the city.[23]

It would be wrong to give the impression that Don Juan Perez de Guzmán was a man who did nothing but write despondent letters to his masters and listen to the sensational sermons of Franciscan monks. An old man in Panamá, who had seen fourteen presidents come and go, said that Don Juan did more for the defence of the Kingdom in the year of 1670 than the other thirteen had done in the past half-century, and this is not far from the truth.[24] When the galleons were at Portobello, a *junta* had been called to discuss the defences of the coast.[25] A new military engineer, Don Juan Betin, had been called in to make a report. One quick survey of Santiago Castle was sufficient to show that the design broke almost every rule of military architecture. Another military expert, schooled in the battlefields of Flanders, described it as the worst-designed castle that he had ever seen,[26] an opinion which Morgan would probably have gleefully confirmed. Its absurd position on the slope of a mountain meant that every bastion and every curtain – indeed, virtually the whole castle – could be overlooked by enemy sharpshooters, while the castle itself was so irregular in shape that there were numerous places where an enemy could hide himself in complete safety, while breaching the wall or raising scaling-ladders.

Great efforts were made to improve the castle.[27] Outworks were raised where the privateers had dug themselves in on the hill, and some of the irregularities in the castle were ironed out. The work on San Geronimo was also rushed ahead and improvements made to San Phelipe, the only problem being, as Don Juan reported to the Queen in June 1670, 'the very great lack of means for everything'. Fresh work was also done on the castle of San Lorenzo which stood on a cliff above the mouth of the River Chagres. An old fort had been demolished by the privateers in 1656 and work on a new and improved one had been continuing intermittently ever since. The usual problems of lack of labour and money had been aggravated by the shortage of building stone in the area, and things had not been made any easier by the fact that, for eight months out of twelve, there was continuous rain in the region. Most of these problems were to be faced once again by the builders of the Panamá Railroad some two hundred years later, but they did at least have plenty of money. The Presidents of Panamá did not, with the result that the castle of San Lorenzo was built of timber palisades reinforced with sand and earth and the quarters of the men who garrisoned it were constructed of straw and palm-leaves. Don Juan did his best to improve the defences at this key point of entry into his Kingdom, where a passage up the River Chagres could take an enemy over fifty miles into the isthmus, two-thirds of the way to Panamá. A new gun-platform was built at sea level, lest the enemy simply by-pass the castle on the cliff, and the defences at the two levels were better integrated. No one could say that the result was perfect, but Don Juan did what he could with the resources and skills at his command and the castle on the cliff certainly looked impregnable.

The President could reflect with some pride on what had been achieved since his return from imprisonment in Peru; but, as he stood in the castle of San Lorenzo and stared out to sea, he could not help but feel apprehension. None of his begging letters had produced a single extra man, and the lands which it was his duty to defend still seemed extremely vulnerable to invasion by the corsairs. The year of 1669 had seen the complete disappearance of all naval protection from the coasts of the Spanish Main. In April, Morgan had destroyed the Armada de Barlovento while, in June, the last remaining ship of any size on the coast, the *capitana* of the Cartagena coast-guard, had been reported as unable to go to sea because she made too much water.[28] A few months later, she sank at her moorings in Cartagena harbour and, since there was not enough money for repairs to be done, she was auctioned without raising sufficient funds to replace her.[29] The seas were open for the privateers of Jamaica whenever Sir Thomas Modyford might feel the time had come to reissue commissions.

It can be imagined that, with no public ships to guard the coasts and an increasing threat of the revival of English privateering activity, the governors of the cities and islands of the Spanish Indies received the Queen's declaration of war on their old enemies with great hopes. Maybe now a flood of Spanish corsairs would come forward to defend them and to take the war into the enemy's territory. The Queen's letters were received late in 1669 when the galleons arrived, but it took some time for the news to circulate. Even then, the response was a little disappointing. There were not many men prepared to risk life and fortune against a people with such a reputation for fighting as the English. But there were a few bold spirits. In 1670, after years as passive victims, the Spaniards could be said to be on the offensive.

CHAPTER ELEVEN

The Spanish Corsairs Attack

THE DRUMMER beat a tattoo and the crowd in the market-place in Port Royal looked up attentively from its private business. A group of notables, including the Governor, Sir Thomas Modyford, and the hero of the hour, Admiral Henry Morgan, were standing beside the drummer to give the occasion the solemnity it deserved. The royal standard was unfurled and the town crier read out the proclamation.

Inasmuch as the forces under the command of Admiral Morgan, with the blessing of God, have happily destroyed the fleet which the Spaniards intended against this island and since Our Sovereign Lord the King has through his Ministers of State instructed me that the subjects of His Catholic Majesty be from now until further order treated and used as good neighbours and friends . . . I, by this present proclamation, make null and void all commissions which I have previously conceded to privateers and from now on prohibit any acts of hostility against the vassals of His Catholic Majesty by whatsoever person or persons. . . .

It was 24 June 1669. After three years of private war, Jamaica was at peace with Spain.[1]

Or was she? When this same proclamation was considered by the Council of the Indies in Madrid on 23 November, the general opinion was one of extreme suspicion.[2] Sir Thomas Modyford had issued it in his own name, not in that of the King. He had made no mention of any express orders which he had received from the King, except the rather vague reference to 'neighbours and friends', and he had said nothing about the peace treaty of 1667. It was felt that the proclamation was hardly worth the paper that it was written on. It was simply a pretence and a trick.

The Council also considered a letter supposed to have been written by Modyford to the Conde de Molina, Spanish Ambassador in London, and dated 25 June 1669.[3] In fact, there is no doubt about its authorship. It bears all the hallmarks of the Modyford style. The letter was quite extraordinarily insolent, asking the Ambassador to applaud his 'justice and civility' and offering to put the Jamaican privateers at the disposal of the Spaniards to protect them from the French. He then went on to point out just how much the Spaniards needed the Jamaicans.

I know and perhaps you are not altogether ignorant of your weakness in these parts, the thinness of your inhabitants, want of hearts, armes and knowledge in warre, the open opposition of some and doubtfull obedience of other of the Indians, soe that you have no towne on this side the line, but that my master's forces heere would give him, did not his signall generosity to yours restrayne them. What we could have donn, the French will doe, unlesse these men may by your intercession be brought to serve your Master.

The final sentence could hardly be interpreted other than as a threat. 'These men will put themselves under any imployement (as most will) rather than starve. That the good encouragement your Master will give them may prevent their seeking other is recommended to your care and consideration by your very humble servant, Thomas Modyford.'

The letter was found to be 'very malicious and seeking to discredit His Majesty's vassals'. It was dismissed, like the proclamation, as of 'little account' and certainly not of sufficient importance to alter Spanish policy towards the English in the Indies. The Council then went on to discuss that policy. As usual it was felt that the best thing that could possibly be done would be to recover Jamaica, but as usual there was not sufficient means to do so. Discussion then reverted to the Queen's declaration of war of 20 April and speculation on whether the galleons had yet arrived to deliver it to the authorities in the Indies. Since they had not yet heard of any Spanish activity against the English, they assumed that the galleons were still at sea. Sir Thomas Modyford's proclamation of peace was quietly ignored.

One can understand the Council's cynicism. They had been led to believe that Spain was at peace with the English in the Indies at least since 1667, yet every action of this Governor of Jamaica made it clear that this was not so. Why should they believe the present situation to be any different? And yet, ironically, it is probable that Sir Thomas

Modyford genuinely intended to keep the peace. He had no wish to lose favour in England and was aware that such news as the capture of Portobello or Maracaibo did not meet with universal approval, especially now that his cousin and patron Lord Albemarle was ill and the hispanophile Lord Arlington was in the ascendant. He knew that negotiations were about to start for a further and more beneficial treaty with Spain that he had no wish to jeopardize. If the treaty enabled the English to trade legitimately with the Spaniards, that could only do Jamaica, and so himself, good. He thought that the Spaniards in the Indies had been so humbled by their recent reverses that there was little likelihood of an immediate counter-attack. There was no good reason not to have peace with Spain.

The only problems were the usual ones. Would peace generate enough business to fill the gap left by the cessation of war? There was now a considerable number of Jamaicans who had adopted the heterodox opinion that peace might actually be more profitable than war, that legal and illegal trading with the Spaniards would more than compensate for the ending of the gains from the privateers. Most of these people were merchants, especially slave-traders with a keen eye on the Spanish colonial market, and they now formed a party intent on the total abandonment of privateering, since Spanish trade and war with Spain did not easily mix. But, if privateering was abandoned, what was Modyford supposed to do with the privateers? It was anxiety about this which had prompted his rather ludicrous and, one must admit, offensive offer of Jamaican privateer assistance to the Spaniards against the French. Not surprisingly, it was ignored. As Lord Arlington wrote, in one of his extremely rare letters to the Governor of Jamaica, 'a proposition for the entertainment of the English privateers of those parts in the Spanish service . . . will scarce be believed a practicall one'.[4] This was true, but the problem remained.

In fact, the main problem that Modyford envisaged, that the privateers denied commissions in Jamaica would go to Tortuga, did not materialize. For the French, too, were at peace with Spain, and the Governor of Tortuga was issuing no commissions, although some of the wilder *flibustiers* accepted neither the Governor's authority nor the peace which the French Government had made with the Spaniards at Aix-la-Chapelle. They said 'that since they had not signed the treaty, had not indeed even been called to the conferences, they were not obliged to take any notice of it'.[5] Some Frenchmen also went out on 'hunting and fishing commissions', which they believed made privateering legal as well,[6] but, as far as Modyford knew, only two English corsairs had gone to join them. Some of the Jamaican privateers, too, used simple 'let passes' as commissions, hoping that the mere signature of the English Governor would give them some security. Such 'knaves endeavour to take the Spaniard and by stealth land what they get in harbours out of command', as Modyford admitted, but there were not all that many of them. On the whole, considering that he had no naval force to back up his proclamation, Modyford made a fairly good job of keeping the peace. Privateers continued to use Jamaica, but not so many nor so openly as before, and very few had fled to Tortuga. The rest officially retired from the chase, though they tended to engage in doubtfully legal activities which could very rapidly be converted to privateering if commissions were to be reissued. Several were on the Central American coast, trading with the Indians and cutting the precious logwood which was much in demand in Europe as a dye. Others were hunting in Cuba and Hispaniola, for animals not men. 'Some of the best monied', including Morgan and Collier, were building up plantations in Jamaica and apparently enjoying a settled life. It would be fair to say that, using West Indian rather than European conventions, Jamaica really was at peace with the King of Spain's subjects in the year following Modyford's proclamation.[7]

Meanwhile the galleons had arrived, bringing with them the Queen's letters authorizing hostility against the English in the Indies. The Governor of Cartagena received his letter on 27 October 1669 and seems to have been very pleased with the news. It was not long before the beat of drums was heard in the city and war with Jamaica was publicly declared.[8] There seems to have been no rush to come forward to seize this opportunity for fame and fortune. The only private ships on the coast which were powerful enough to double as privateers were the ships of the slave *asiento* and they were busy enough not to be very interested. Anyone else would have to fit out a ship from scratch – an expensive business which might well pay no return to the investor. A ship would have to be bought, its decks reinforced, cannon, firearms and food purchased, and a crew of tough or desperate men raised, before the Queen's declaration of war could be put into effect.

Only one man seems to have risen to the challenge. He was a very strange character, a bombastic and poetical Portuguese called Manoel Rivero Pardal. He received his commission on 3 January 1670 and set sail three days later with a crew of seventy men, each one of them 'a castle against the uncouth heretic'. His ship was suitably called *San Pedro y la Fama*, for it was fame and glory that Rivero sought. He wrote an extraordinary poem, an astonishingly egotistical epic, describing his exploits as he sailed across 'the wave-filled and surging sea up to the Cayman Islands where with fire I made havoc . . . and the mob all trembled at my name'.[9] He had been intending to sail for Port Morant in Jamaica where he had hoped to seize sufficient slaves to finance his expedition, but the wind was against him and he had landed at the Jamaican dependency of Grand Cayman as a poor second best. He did a fair bit of damage, all the same, burning down half the fishermen's shacks on the island and then sailing off to Cuba with a ketch, a canoe and four children who were too slow or too self-absorbed to avoid his clutches.[10]

In Cuba, Rivero heard that there was 'a thief, who was going privateering', in Manzanillo, the port of Bayamo, and set out for fresh glory. This thief was an old privateer called Bernard Claesen Speirdyke, commonly called Captain Barnard or Bart, the commander of *Mary and Jane*, who had sailed from Port Royal with letters from Sir Thomas Modyford to the Governor of Cuba, 'signifying peace between the two nations'. The message of goodwill was emphasized by the return of some Spanish prisoners from Jamaica. The Governor of Bayamo was rather suspicious of all this friendship and sent an officer aboard who searched the ship three times 'fearing she was a privateer'. Everybody then got down to business. Captain Bart had brought a cargo of European goods, and the people of Bayamo, starved as usual of such luxuries, quickly bought the lot while the Governor pretended not to notice this all too common breach of Spanish law. Captain Bart, pleased with his profit, set off to return to Jamaica.

Just as he was leaving the bay, he saw a ship flying English colours which hailed him and asked him whence he came. 'From Jamaica,' came the honest captain's reply. 'Defend yourself, dog,' boomed the voice of Captain Rivero across the water. 'I come as a punishment for heretics.' He then opened fire, and the two ships engaged in a lively artillery duel until it was too dark to see. Captain Bart had only eighteen men to Rivero's seventy, but 'the obstinate, mad heretic', as his opponent called him, was determined to continue the fight and at dawn he was ready for Rivero as he sailed down towards him to close and board. A savage battle followed in which the Jamaicans killed or wounded a third of Rivero's crew. But numbers were to tell in the end. *Mary and Jane* was on fire in two places and five men had been killed, including the 'good old captain', before the colours were hauled down.[11]

Rivero, who had a passion for self-advertisement, took the opportunity to broadcast his commission. Nine of the Jamaican crew were sent home in their boat with the message that their victor was called Captain Manoel Rivero and that 'he had letters of reprisal from the King of Spain for five years through the whole West Indies, for satisfaction of the Jamaicans taking Portobello'. Rivero then sailed home with his prize and the other four prisoners to Cartagena, where he arrived on 23 March. Such glory had not been known for some time and the city held a great fiesta to celebrate his triumph. The Governor, Pedro de Ulloa, was very pleased with this good beginning. A month later, he reported that Rivero's success had encouraged other citizens and two more corsair ships were being fitted out. In honour of his courage, Rivero was allowed to fly the royal standard in his ship, which was now to be the *capitana* of the new squadron.[12]

The cry of injured innocence that arose when the survivors of *Mary and Jane* returned to Port Royal can easily be imagined. That Jamaicans should be attacked when their governor had publicly declared peace and friendship with all Spaniards! It was too bad, and it was soon to get worse. Word arrived from Campeche that another Spanish man-of-war from Cartagena had attacked two small English ships, one of which 'did in his own defence board and take it'. Amongst the prisoners was an English renegade called Edward Browne, who reported that he had been in Cartagena when war was proclaimed at beat of drum against Jamaica.[13] Then there was the ship commanded by a certain Captain Don Francisco which took *Amity* of Bristol at the beginning of March.[14] The message was beginning to become clear to the people of Port Royal. It became totally clear when Wilhelm Beck, the Dutch Governor of Curaçao, sent Modyford a copy of a commission issued by the Governor of Santiago de Cuba to Francisco Galesio, captain of *San Nicolás de Tolentino*. The commission was dated 5 February 1670 and it included a copy of the Queen of Spain's letter of 20 April 1669.[15] This was definite documentary evidence. Spain had been at war with Jamaica for nearly a year, during three-quarters of which Jamaica had been at peace with Spain. It was outrageous.

Some Jamaicans were genuinely very alarmed. There might be only three Spanish corsairs at sea so far, but what would the future bring? The capture of English merchant ships was a lively encouragement for fresh investors. Already there were rumours that twelve ships were fitting out for the Indies on the Biscay coast of Spain, and these Biscayners or Basques were certainly rather terrifying. They had taken a colossal number of prizes during Cromwell's war against Spain in the late 1650s. At least one Jamaican planter was thinking of selling up. 'I could wish I were not so deeply engaged in planting, especially now that I see the Spaniards begin to take the right course to ruin us.' He explained their present predicament by the recent death of the Duke of Albemarle, 'that only befriended us'. That good old warrior and imperialist hawk would never have allowed the current situation to develop, 'this war, our making a blind peace, no frigates, nor orders coming'.[16]

The Jamaican privateers were certainly not frightened of a few Spanish corsairs, but they felt extremely frustrated and very angry at the death of their former comrade, Captain Bart. Modyford was told in March that 'the whole body of privateers . . . meditate revenge and have appointed a general rendezvous at Caimanos [Cayman Islands] next month'. He told Arlington that he would do his best 'to divert them or moderate their councils', but it is clear that he already resented having his hands tied.[17] A month later, he had collected a number of depositions relating to the recent Spanish depredations and was asking Arlington to give him latitude in case there was further Spanish hostility, 'with whom we shall well enough cope of our own strength, not desiring any assistance from England, unless the Spaniards send forces from Europe'.[18] But Modyford as usual got no immediate answers to his letters and, since there were no fresh attacks on Jamaicans, the whole matter died down for a few weeks.

The Spaniards, and especially their Portuguese hero, Manoel Rivero Pardal, would not let the matter die down. Rivero's blood was up after his victory over Captain Bart and, at the end of May, he set off on a second cruise.[19] With *San Pedro y la Fama* went another ship called *La Gallardina*, a former French privateer which had been captured by the *capitana* of Cartagena in 1668.[20] This time Rivero had no trouble with the wind, and the two ships appeared, flying English colours, off the coast of Jamaica on 11 June 1670. Here they sighted the sloop of William Harris, which was coming in to trade with the plantation-owners and hunters on the sparsely populated north side of the island. The two corsairs gave chase for an hour and a half, coming up close enough for the sloop's crew to recognize that their pursuers were 'all in a Spanish garbo' and to hear themselves hailed as 'doggs and rogues', but not close enough to stop Harris beaching his sloop and getting ashore with his men. The Spaniards chased them inland, but Harris and his men fired at them from behind the trees 'as long as they had any ammunition left', and eventually the Spaniards gave up. They took the sloop and a canoe that was on the beach and sailed away north towards Cuba.[21]

A week later, Rivero and his consort repeated their violation of Jamaican soil, this time at Montego Bay. They landed thirty men and 'burnt and destroyed all the settlements', before setting off back to Cuba again.[22] The reports of the landings had quickly circulated through the island, and the militia were alerted to keep a good lookout for strangers along the coasts. On 3 July, Rivero was seen again, this time on the south side of the island, only twenty or thirty miles from Port Royal itself, and some forty militiamen rode along the coast to challenge his landing. This time he had two consorts and an estimated two hundred men. Presumably, he had armed the captured sloop and picked up fresh recruits in Santiago de Cuba. Rivero stood off and on for an hour and then, not liking the look of the opposition, sailed off to sea again. But he did not go far away. Next day, he landed fifty miles farther to leeward and burned a couple of houses.[23] And two days after that it was learned that the 'vapouring captain' had landed in the night and posted up a challenge. It is a remarkable document, absolutely typical of the man who believed that 'the whole sea trembles at the name of *San Pedro y la Fama'*. It is worth quoting in full, since it is not too much to say that Rivero's naïve insolence and somewhat ludicrous heroics were a major contributing factor to the absurdly disproportionate English reprisals which are discussed in the rest of this book.

I, Captain Manoel Rivero Pardal, to ye chiefe of ye squadron of privateers in Jamaica. I am hee which this year have done that which follows. I went ashoare att Caimanos and burned twenty houses and fought with Captain Ari [Harry?] and tooke from him a ketch loaded with provisions and a canoa. And I am hee that tooke Captain Barns [i.e., Bart] and did carry ye prize to Cartagena, and now I am arrived to this coast and have burnt it, and I come to seeke Generall Morgan with two shippes of twenty gunns and, haveing seene this, I crave hee would come out uppon ye coast to seeke mee, that hee might see ye valour of ye Spaniards. And because I had noe time I did not come to ye mouth of Port Royall to speake by word of mouth. In ye name of my Kinge and Master whom God preserve. Dated 5th of July 1670.[24]

This was really too much; certainly more than Jamaica was prepared to condone. On 9 July, just three days after Rivero's challenge had been handed in at Port Royal, a full meeting of the Council of Jamaica was held at Santiago de la Vega, the old Spanish capital and still the administrative centre of the island.[25] Depositions describing Rivero's recent activities were read out, as was the commission issued to Captain Galesio by the Governor of Santiago de Cuba. Taken together and spiced with a little imagination and perhaps just a little fear, this evidence could be seen to add up to a conspiracy in the Cuban port to invade and demoralize the poor Jamaicans who were trying so hard to live in peace with their Spanish neighbours. And, in truth, it was rather frightening for the settlers on the north coast of the island. The nearest part of Cuba was only a hundred miles away and the big Spanish island almost enveloped its smaller southern neighbour. It seemed that any day the Jamaicans might find their homes and crops burned and themselves taken away into a Spanish captivity. It was almost as bad as it was for a Spaniard who lived in Campeche or Hispaniola or on the south coast of Cuba itself, places which were raided almost weekly by English and French hunters or privateers, regardless of war or peace. No one wanted Jamaica to become like that.

The members of the Council were asked to imagine what would

happen if nothing were done and enemies continued to raid the island. The Jamaicans would, of course, defeat them but, while they were away from home fighting, the economic consequences would be very serious. 'Our plantations will runn to ruine, our cattle and other stock will run wild, our slaves take the woods and wee, although by chance of warr conquerors, put to begin the world againe to our insupportable loss and most definite damage to His Majesty's service.' Fortunately, there was a solution. His Majesty, in his infinite wisdom, had given permission to the Governor, in the last article of his royal instructions, to deal with extraordinary cases in an extraordinary manner, after full consultation with the Council. An invasion of Jamaica was surely such a case and so, 'in this great and urgent necessity', the Council were happy to advise Governor Modyford that a 'commission be granted to Admirall Henry Morgan to bee Admirall and Comander in Cheif of all the ships of warr belonging to this harbour and . . . requiring him with all possible speed to draw them into one fleet . . . and to attaque, seize and destroy all the enemy's vessells that shall come within his reach'. He should also have power to land in the enemy's country in order to destroy 'the stores and magazenes layd up for this war' and to disperse the forces which had been brought together to prosecute it. In short, he should be commissioned 'to do and performe all manner of exployts which may tend to the preservation and quiet of this island, being His Majesty's cheif interest in the Indies'. To put it another way, the way that the Council must have known that the privateers would interpret it, Morgan could go anywhere he liked and do anything he liked as long as he had the smallest shred of evidence that the Spaniards who lived there had dreams of invading Jamaica. It would be nice if he started by attacking Santiago de Cuba, but this was not absolutely essential. The Spaniards could easily be taught a lesson somewhere else, so that Jamaicans might sleep safely in their beds. The Spaniards were going to rue the day that they gave Manoel Rivero Pardal a commission. As Morgan's surgeon-general was to say later, 'we doe the Spaniards more mischiefe in one hour than they can doe us in seven yeares'.[26]

Sir Thomas Modyford accepted his Council's advice, but he was very worried about the reception of his declaration of war in England. Now that the Duke of Albemarle was dead, he no longer had a powerful friend at Court to defend his more aggressive actions. The best substitute seemed to be Lord Ashley, later the Earl of Shaftesbury, very much the coming man and currently the President of the Council for Trade and Plantations. Modyford wrote to ask him for his help.[27] He admitted that it might seem 'a fond, rash action for a petty Governor without money to make and entertaine war with the richest, and not long since the powerfullest, Prince of Europe', but then pointed out his problems. The Spaniards were already on the coast of Jamaica 'with fire and sword', there was no hope of orders from the King before 'six months at least', and the privateers were his only possible protection. Suspecting that Ashley might find the cheapness and inevitable success of the privateers attractive, he expatiated on their virtues. 'And judge you, my Lord, in this exigent, what course could be more frugal, more prudential, more hopeful – the men volunteers, the ships, arms, ammunition their own, their victuals and pay the enemy's, and such enemies as they have always beaten.' He ended by begging Ashley to mediate with the King that his actions might be duly ratified.

He also, of course, wrote to Lord Arlington, reporting the decision and enclosing all the documents, and begged him, too, to try to procure 'His Majesty's ratification to what is done'.[28] He made no excuses and concealed no information, merely justifying his action by the discretionary powers given in the royal instructions. If the Spaniards made 'sharpe warre on us', there was a limit to Jamaican patience and eventually there was no option but to make sharp war on them. Modyford asked for some frigates to be sent in case the Spaniards should send 'great shippes' out from Europe to attack them and impede their trade. He had no fears of the Spaniards already in the Indies. 'On shoare we feare them not, and doe hope in time to fixe ye warre in their countrey.' This was a hope shared by the Jamaican privateers, who were naturally delighted at this termination of their unwanted holiday. The only real problem now was to determine the particular country in which it would be most profitable to fix the war.

1 and 2. THE PRIVATEERS. The frontispieces to the 1678 Dutch and the 1686 French editions of Exquemelin give a good idea of the appearance, dress and weapons used by the privateers or, at least, what European editors and engravers thought they should look like.

S^r HEN: MORGAN
Part.2. Page. 60.

3 and 4. THE LEADER AND THE LED. These illustrations are both from early editions of Exquemelin. The man below is the classic buccaneer, complete with his hunting dogs and the famous long musket.

5. (*right*) SANTA CATALIN This contemporary plan has a description of the island and of its capture by the Spaniards on the right-hand side. The primitive illustrations give a good idea of the scattered habitations of the Spanish garrison.

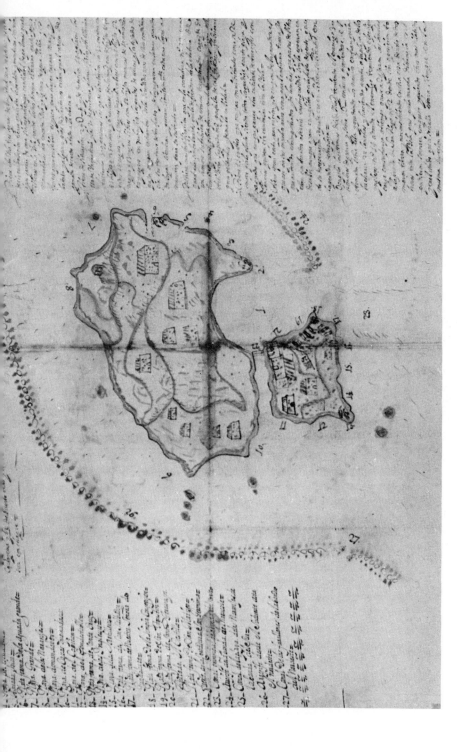

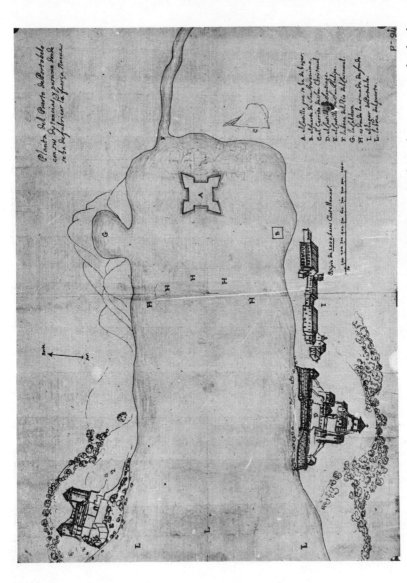

6. PORTOBELLO. This contemporary plan shows very clearly how the hill occupied by Morgan's sharpshooters overlooked Santiago castle (D). E is San Phelipe Castle, B is San Geronimo and A was a projected fort to protect the anchorage which was never built.

7 and 8. CARTAGENA DE INDIAS, richest and most populous city of the Spanish Main. The view above of the city protected by its lagoon is from John Ogilby's *America* (1670). Note the wide range of small coastal shipping illustrated, far more than would actually have been present in the harbour at the time of Morgan's depredations. The Spanish plan below gives rightful prominence to the Monastery of Nuestra Señora de Popa, the patroness of the city, on the hill in the left background.

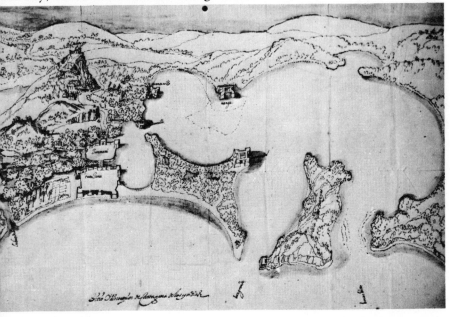

9 and 10. THE BATTLE OF THE BARRA DE MARACAIBO. These two
engravings are from different editions of Exquemelin. The lower of
the two gives a better idea of what actually happened. *Magdalena* is
blowing up in the foreground with the fireship alongside and
Soledad is being captured in the right background.

11. THE RIVER CHAGRES. This delightful illustration is from
Antonio de Ulloa's *Relación historica* (1748). It is probable that the
"canoes" described in our sources were in fact the traditional river
boats shown in the picture.

12. PART OF CONTEMPORARY PLAN OF OLD PANAMÁ. Note the
complete lack of fortifications on the landward side.

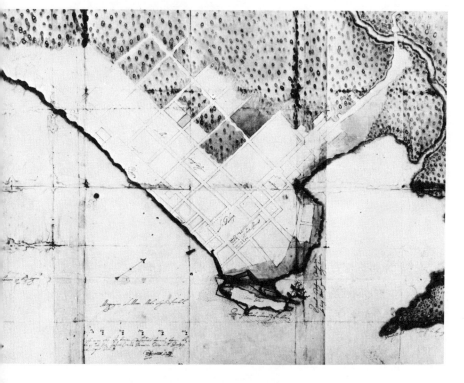

13. THE BATTLE FOR PANAMÁ. This engraving from the Spanish edition of Exquemelin telescopes all the events of the battle and much of the subsequent sack of the city into one picture.

CHAPTER TWELVE

Rendezvous at Isla Vaca

HENRY MORGAN did not receive his new commission until 1 August, three weeks after the meeting of the Council of Jamaica.[1] No doubt Modyford wanted to see if there were any fresh orders from England before finally committing himself. It was, after all, a matter of some importance to make a declaration of war against Spain, the second in his six years as Governor. The commission was worded in accordance with the Council's advice. Modyford declared the 'great confidence I have in the good conduct, courage and fidelity of you the said Henry Morgan' and appointed him Admiral and Commander-in-Chief of all the ships to be fitted out for the defence of Jamaica. The island would as usual be saved the trouble of paying for its defence. The privateers were to be 'upon the old pleasing account of No purchase, No pay and therefore that all which is gott shall bee divided amongst them according to the accustomed rules'. Morgan was given permission to grant commissions personally to the individual captains and had wide powers of discretion with regard to the many things which might 'happen in this action which cannot bee by mee foreseene'. Such matters were to be left 'to your well-knowne prudence and good conduct, referring it to you that are in ye place to do therein what shall bee needfull'.

Morgan had no doubt anticipated his commission and instructions. There was a lot to do before he could get together a sufficiently large fleet for the grand venture which was already in his mind. Many privateers were at sea, hunting, trading or raiding throughout the Caribbean from Central America and the Main to Hispaniola. Messengers were sent out to spread the good news, and the word was also passed to Tortuga. It was expected that several hundred Frenchmen would leap at this opportunity to sail against the Spaniard with a real commission, and it was hoped that some of them, especially the Protestants, would stay in Jamaica afterwards.

A general rendezvous for all the privateers was appointed at the old meeting-place of Isla Vaca off the south coast of Hispaniola.

In Jamaica itself, those privateers who had retired from the sea when commissions were withdrawn in the previous June needed to raise credit to work on their ships, some of which were described by Modyford as 'almost worn out'. Credit was not difficult to find. Most of the Port Royal merchant community were delighted at the change of policy and were only too happy to pay for ships to be recaulked, extra guns to be mounted, sails to be replaced and the hundred and one other things that had to be done before the fleet could sail. They anticipated a very high return on their investment.

Eight days after Morgan had received his commission, Sir Thomas Modyford was able to report considerable progress in a letter to Lord Arlington.[2] He had now issued commissions to ten privateers and Morgan hoped to sail from Port Royal in a fortnight. *Satisfaction* had just come in from a long cruise under 'a dull and sluggish commander'.[3] She had been at sea for eighteen months, ever since she had parted company from Morgan after *Oxford* blew up, but she was immediately revictualled and made ready to sail again. She was the biggest privateer in Jamaica, 120 tons and 22 guns,[4] and Morgan planned to make her his flagship. Then there were old colleagues like John Morris the Elder, who had stood as hostage in the ransom negotiations for Portobello and was now in command of *Dolphin*; Richard Norman in *Lilly*, the frigate which had been Morgan's flagship when he sailed into the Laguna de Maracaibo; Joseph Bradley in the 70-ton *Mayflower*; and Richard Dobson in the little *Fortune*, only 25 tons and 6 guns, but carrying a crew of 35 experienced privateersmen rounded up from their haunts in the bars and brothels of Port Royal. Altogether, when Morgan set sail on 24 August, he had 11 ships and 600 men.[5] He hoped to treble his numbers at Isla Vaca.

He had hardly left Port Royal before a sloop caught up with the fleet to recall him for a conference with Modyford. The Governor had just received a letter from Lord Arlington, dated 22 June,[6] the first for a very long time, and it was important that the Admiral know its contents before he continued with his voyage. Arlington acknowledged Modyford's letters up to 30 March; in other words, the letter contained no knowledge of the recent decisions which had been made on the island. He showed little sympathy for the Governor's problems, dismissing Rivero's unprovoked attack on Captain Bart as something 'not at all to be wondered at after such hostilities as your men have acted upon their territories', a true but not very helpful comment. He warned Modyford that this way of warring was 'neither honourable nor profitable to his Majesty' and that the King hoped to put an end to it. Indeed, he was daily expecting news from Sir William Godolphin in Madrid of the conclusion of the new treaty 'as might make them and us live like good neighbours together'. All of which was very interesting, but what Modyford wanted was some instructions, or something that looked like instructions, which he could use to justify his resumption of hostilities against the Spaniards.

He found them. Arlington had drafted his letter very carelessly, or perhaps very cunningly, and had provided Modyford with a curiously ambiguous order. 'His Majesty bids me let you know his pleasure is, that in what state soever the privateers are, at the receipt of this letter, you keepe them soe till we have a final answer from Spaine (which shall be immediately signified to you) with this condition only, that you oblige them to forebear all hostilities at land.' Modyford must have breathed a sigh of relief when he saw this. The privateers had set sail the day before and so at sea he must keep them, according to the King's own order. No doubt Morgan was equally amused when he saw the letter. Modyford told him to observe His Majesty's instructions and to 'behave himselfe with all moderation and civility possible in the carrying on of this warr'.[7] Morgan replied that 'he would observe those orders as farre as it was possible, but necessity would compel him to land in their country for food, water and provisions, or desert the service . . . Unlesse he were, by good proofs or strong circumstances, assured of the enemy's embodying in some one towne, or laying up the stores for the destruction of this island, hee would not attempt any of them.' Morgan thus neatly covered himself, quite sure that, if he did find such information of the enemy preparing to make war, the King would not wish him to 'spare such a place'. The Governor and the Admiral then bid each other farewell and Morgan returned to the fleet.

Modyford replied to Arlington's letter on 30 August.[8] 'I have with much comfort and satisfaction received your Lordship's welcome letter.' He reported that the privateers had been at sea when he received it and repeated the gist of his conversation with Morgan. He then proceeded to give the Secretary of State a few lessons in the realities of politics and warfare in the Indies. How stupid 'that reputed wise Council of Spain' had been to declare war and to issue commissions to corsairs. Had they 'suspended their resentment but two years longer, most of our privateers had betaken themselves to some other way of living, for their rigging, sails, and ships were almost worn out, and their owners disheartened for want of commissions, so that the better sort daily came on shore to settle, and the seamen who will never settle began to dispose themselves on merchant voyages'. This might well be wishful thinking, but his second point makes very good sense. 'Could the Council of Spain be well informed of their want of men to defend their large possessions in these parts, they would conclude themselves incapable of destroying Jamaica and make peace; but they are borne up with false measures of their strength and have plunged themselves into this war, and so slight the application of Sir William Godolphin.'[9] One cannot help but agree with Modyford's analysis. Spain had got the worst of all worlds by trying to make a cheap war on Jamaica with corsairs alone. There were not enough corsairs to do any lasting damage, but their very existence had predictably aroused Jamaican resentment. Modyford thought that the present campaign should be sufficient to educate the Council of Spain. 'A little more suffering will inform them of their condition and force them to capitulations more suitable to the sociableness of man's nature.' Poor Spain! Just a little more suffering!

This letter from Arlington was the last that Modyford was to receive as Governor of Jamaica, or at least the last that has survived. Nor did he receive an answer to his letter to Lord Ashley. The King, too, appears to have been silent, although there is a cryptic reference in one of Surgeon Browne's letters to the arrival in August of 'a large packet from His Majesty to Sir Thomas Modyford: what it contains is unknown'.[10] There is, however, no royal letter in the official files. Such silence is peculiar and contrasts strongly with the flow of letters from Modyford's pen, describing in detail exactly what was going on in Jamaica, complete with supporting evidence in the form of depositions. Further information was fed to leading figures at Court and to the Privy Council by Modyford's son, Charles, who acted as his political agent in London. There was a time-lag of six to ten weeks between an action in Jamaica and possible knowledge of it in London but, this apart, no one in London could plead ignorance of Jamaican affairs. And yet, during a period of delicate diplomatic negotiations, Modyford got no instructions, no order to call in the privateers, nothing.

One can only assume that London preferred it that way. With no positive orders one way or the other, no one in London could carry the blame for a wrong decision. Governor Sir Thomas Modyford could carry the blame. Already, preparations were being made by the pro-Spanish faction to remove him from office, as a sop to Spanish protests, and replace him by a man who had a very different view of Jamaica's role in the West Indies. This was Sir Thomas Lynch, old Cromwellian soldier, planter, slave-trader and hispano-phile. Lynch, who was a political opponent of Modyford, had been out of Jamaica for five years, much of which time he had spent in Spain where he had learned the language 'and to perfect it spent a whole winter in Salamanca, not talking to foreigners, learning much about the things of the Indies through his own studies and by talking to merchants and others there and in Andalusia'.[11] Such knowledge of both Jamaica and Spain made him an obvious ally for Lord Arlington, himself an *aficionado* of Spain, and the Secretary of State was ready to believe in Lynch's optimistic plans for Jamaica as a major supplier of slaves and English manufactured goods to the Spanish colonies, regardless of the fact that the Spaniards had made it absolutely clear that they would never countenance a free trade in the Indies. Such plans required peace, and Lynch was the spokesman of those Jamaicans who were beginning to think that trade rather than war should be the basis of future relations between the two nations in the Caribbean. In the autumn and winter of 1670, plans were matur-ing to replace Modyford by Lynch and they came to fruition on 15 January 1671 when Lynch received his commission as Lieutenant-Governor of Jamaica in Modyford's stead.[*][12] Modyford was told nothing about this, although he must, of course, have had a good

---

* The Earl of Carlisle was to have the title of Governor, but would remain in England, a common way of increasing the income of deserving noblemen at the public expense.

idea of what was going on from his son Charles in London. Lynch was instructed to hand his predecessor the letter revoking his commission when he arrived in Jamaica. Modyford was thus condemned in his absence, long before Morgan sailed on the expedition which finally damned him.

Modyford might have apprehensions, but he could not yet foresee his future disgrace as he finished his letter to Lord Arlington and Henry Morgan continued on his cruise. Morgan had set off west along the south coast of Jamaica.[13] He rounded the island and returned to the east along the south coast of Cuba to check on any Spanish activity and to give clear notice that a fleet now existed to punish severely any further invasions from Santiago de Cuba or anywhere else. A storm scattered the privateers and Morgan had to continue on his voyage with only eight ships, first to Tortuga where he picked up some French corsairs who were ready to sail and then round the great white cliff of Cape Tiburón, the most westerly point of Hispaniola, and so into the sheltered waters between the reef-girt Isla Vaca and the main island where he arrived on 12 September. Here he found several small English and French ships waiting for him, packed with men and eager for the chase. But Morgan was in no hurry to sail. There were still many more ships expected. Besides, it was the beginning of the hurricane season and he did not want to risk his whole fleet at sea. Those who were already at the rendezvous were sent off along the south coast of Hispaniola with their guns and their dogs for meat which could be salted or smoked ready for the expedition, while three large and three small ships were despatched to the Main to get more provisions and 'to gett prisoners for intelligence'.[14]

They set sail on 16 September under the command of Morgan's Vice-Admiral, Edward Collier, but do not seem to have gone direct to the Main, since it was over five weeks later, on 24 October, that they arrived off the coast of Rio de la Hacha, 450 miles almost due south of Isla Vaca.[15] This small port had once been famous for its pearl-fishing, but the industry was now rather decayed. The port's main function in 1670 was as the outlet for a rich area of grain and livestock farming, and it is probably for that reason that Collier selected it for attack. In 1628, the town had had a hundred Spanish residents, but the number would have been less in 1670, since Rio de la Hacha like everywhere else on the coast was in a state of economic decline. There was a fort with four guns and a small garrison, but Collier would not expect to have much trouble in taking the town. It had been captured and sacked several times previously and the population considered themselves victims rather than heroes.

Collier's ships were sighted off-shore at daybreak, and at seven he landed his men some two miles from the town and marched along the beach. Spaniards commented on the military precision with which Collier's men marched and some thought they must be regular troops fresh out from England. There was no immediate resistance. Those who were quick enough fled from the town with their belongings. The rest of the town's population 'were scared stiff at their first sight of the enemy and did not want to fight'. Some asked for quarter and others 'hid themselves under mattresses and baskets'.[16] Collier left a few men to guard the prisoners and marched on to the fort. A trumpeter was sent forward to demand surrender, since opposition would be hopeless against his overwhelming superiority in numbers.

One suspects that, normally, the fort would have obeyed the summons. But the small garrison was stiffened by the presence of some forty men from a Spanish corsair ship which was in the harbour. This was *La Gallardina*, the same ship that had been Rivero's consort during the raids on Jamaica four months previously, and her crew were no doubt extremely alarmed at the prospect of capture by the English. They did not know that the Jamaican privateers had been instructed to treat their prisoners with 'civility and humanity, endeavouring by all means to make all sorts of people sensible of your moderation . . . and loathness to spill the blood of man'.[17] If they had, they would probably have made the same reply to the trumpeter's summons. 'No,' came the answer, 'we cannot surrender because this is a castle belonging to the King. We will only surrender through force of arms.'[18] The fight went on for a day and a night until, with little loss on either side, quarter was given and the fort surrendered. Honour was satisfied, although Collier ordered two men to be killed as a punishment for wasting his time.

The privateers made their usual search for loot, torturing people to force them to reveal their treasure. Edward Collier has a much worse reputation than Morgan in this respect,[19] and three people were reported to have died as a result of his attentions. Another witness said that 'in cold blood they did a thousand cursed things'.[20] Nevertheless, the process of torture does not seem to have been very efficient, since the privateers missed 200,000 pesos which had been concealed by the lieutenant of the fort. Perhaps Collier was not really concentrating on treasure on this expedition. His orders had been to get prisoners and food. He already had the prisoners, forty-four of them shut up in the fort. He now proceeded to get the food. The prisoners were informed that they must deliver 1000 arrobas* of meat and 2000 arrobas of maize to the privateers' ships within twenty-four days or they would all be beheaded. Individuals were allowed out into the country to organize the collection of the food and the deadline was met. His mission completed, Edward Collier set sail for Isla Vaca with the meat and the maize, thirty-eight prisoners, *La Gallardina* and another smaller ship that had been in the harbour.

While Collier was counting sacks of maize in Rio de la Hacha, Morgan's numbers were increasing rapidly at Isla Vaca. Men were turning up in small open boats, canoes, even on foot, desperately keen to be part of an expedition led by so fortunate an admiral. Some men had come from as far away as Bermuda, incensed at the Spanish capture of one of the island's ships and ready to serve Jamaica 'upon any design against the Spaniard'.[21] But most of them came from Jamaica itself, from Tortuga or from Hispaniola where news of Morgan's impending voyage had spread through the forests of the north coast and brought in several of the real buccaneers wearing their stinking bloodstained garments and carrying their long muskets, their proud badge of admission to the privateering fraternity. There were so many men in such frail craft that Morgan found himself in the strange position of not having sufficient ships capable of making the long voyage to the Main, a problem which was intensified by a terrible storm in mid-October which drove every ship but *Satisfaction* on to the coast. All but three could be refloated, but the repairs necessary were considerable and Morgan did not think he would now be ready to sail till early December. Meanwhile, he was very short of shipping space and sent to Jamaica for unarmed merchantmen, anything indeed that could float and was

* These quantities were not very great. An arroba was about 11 kilos.

not too likely to break up during a 1500-mile round trip to Cartagena or Panamá or wherever else they finally decided to go. Some of the vessels that responded to Morgan's call for shipping were minute, such as the three sloops, *William*, *Betty* and *Prosperous*, which were of only ten or twelve tons' burden apiece and carried no guns. Yet, when Morgan sailed, these three were able to pack in seventy-one privateers, their weapons and sufficient food and drink for a month's voyage.

Much the most exciting arrival at Isla Vaca in October was John Morris in *Dolphin* who had the enormous satisfaction of leading in that terror of the seas, *San Pedro y la Fama*, now pacifically renamed *Lamb*.[22] Morris had been forced by a storm to seek shelter in a small bay at the east end of Cuba. Two hours later, when it was just getting dark, Rivero sailed in for the same purpose and was cock-a-hoop when he saw that he had caught the smaller Jamaican ship in a trap. He sent some men ashore to cut off any retreat and waited for the dawn to attack. But, in the morning, it was Morris who made the first move, and such was the vigour of his assault that he boarded at the first attempt and shot Rivero dead through the neck. Seeing their valiant captain fall, the Spanish and Indian crew panicked and jumped into the sea, where some drowned and the rest were killed by the privateers. A few of the crew were later discovered hiding in the hold and were taken prisoner, amongst them Rivero's Indian cook, Juan de Lao, who was to travel with the privateers in the same capacity and provides us with some interesting snippets of information.[23] A search of Rivero's cabin produced his commission, further valuable evidence of Spanish hostility, and his extraordinary poem of self-praise. One wonders how this rather absurd hero would have described his own last battle. The privateers had no doubt how to describe him. 'This is that same vapouring captain that so much amazed Jamaica, in burning the houses, robbing some people upon the shore and sent that insolent challenge to Admiral Morgan,' writes the surgeon, Richard Browne, who has left us a description of the last fight of *San Pedro y la Fama*.[24]

November saw Morgan still hard at work at Isla Vaca, seeing to the repair of the ships damaged in the storm and awaiting the return of Collier from the Main. Some important reinforcements turned up in these last few weeks – three more Frenchmen from Tortuga and another eight ships and four hundred men from Jamaica. The three biggest of these had just returned from a successful and totally unauthorized privateering voyage of their own. Led by Captain Lawrence Prince, who is described in Spanish sources as a Dutchman from Amsterdam, they had sailed up the vast Rio Magdalena in Colombia in an attempt to sack the important town of Mompos, over 150 miles inland. The attempt failed when they were checked by cannon-fire from a fort which had recently been built on an island in the river.[25] This disappointment seems to have done nothing to discourage them. Determined to 'make a voyage', they sailed in August north to Nicaragua to attempt an almost identical, and this time successful, exploit. They sailed up the San Juan river, captured the fort and then paddled in canoes up to Lake Nicaragua, where they sacked the city of Granada, a repeat of the feat which had first made Morgan's name in 1664. When the three captains reported to Modyford, he reproved them for daring to attack the Spaniards without a commission, but thought it prudent not 'to press the matter too far in this juncture' and ordered them to go and join Morgan, 'which they were very ready to do'.[26] Prince seems to have been a desperado in the best or worst tradition of the privateers. The Spanish report said that when he sacked Granada 'he made havoc and a thousand destructions, sending the head of a priest in a basket and saying that he would deal with the rest of the prisoners in the same way unless they gave him 70,000 pesos in ransom'.[27] Morgan was so impressed with his new recruit that he made him third in command after himself and Collier. This was the sort of fighting captain that he needed.

When Governor Modyford wrote to Arlington on 10 November, he was able to report that Morgan's force could not be less than 2100 'well-seasoned and experienced men', the largest concentration of privateers that the West Indies had ever seen. He had done his duty, as he saw it, and had provided for the defence of Jamaica. But would Jamaica be worth defending? During the summer, some very disturbing rumours had arrived in the island. Modyford had seen letters from English merchants to their agents in Jamaica saying 'that this island was to bee sold to ye Spainard or att least that there was a working to that purpose'. The merchants had advised their agents 'not to plant, for as one lately expressed, it's not a place for you to live long in nor to get an estate in, as affairs now stand betwixt ye Crowne of England and Spaine'.[28] How was a governor supposed to develop a new colony with rumours like that going about, rumours which were, as we have seen, quite accurate? Letters from England to Spain had indicated that many at Court would be only too happy to get rid of such a troublesome possession, and the Conde de Peñaranda had certainly broached the matter with Sir William Godolphin.[29] Godolphin had dismissed the idea, but Modyford did not know that because nobody in England bothered to tell the Governor of Jamaica anything relevant to his difficult task.

It is when one considers the uncertainty under which Modyford had to govern the island for the King that one has much sympathy for the often misjudged man. After all, if he had heard about the possibility of the island being sold, he had almost certainly got wind of the discussions in Spain about the *empresa de Jamaica*, the plan to reconquer Jamaica. We know that this plan collapsed, but it was still being seriously discussed at almost every meeting of the Council of the Indies during the winter of 1670/71, the very period when Morgan and Modyford were preparing their own 'Grand Design'. One can suspect their motives; both men stood to make plenty of money out of making war on Spain. One can easily agree with the verdict of Sir Richard White, an Irish double-agent who was in Spain at the time and was to comment on the actions of the Governor and his Admiral: 'It is not credible that those few prizes and that burning can have been the occasion or the true motive, since the vengeance is infinitely unequal. It is clear that the main reason for the events was the ambition . . . of the Governor and those thieves who seek under such pretexts to satisfy their vile and unjust desire for the gold and silver of the Indies of Spain.'[30] This rings true enough but, for all that, one cannot completely write off the reasoning that lay behind their decisions, specious though it might seem after the event. Jamaica *was* potentially threatened and the English Court, far from being prepared to do something about it, such as sending frigates to protect the island, seemed to be trying to sell the island behind the backs of the planters and merchants who had invested so much time, effort and money in its development. Modyford begged Arlington to press the King to proclaim that Jamaica did indeed belong to the Crown of England and that he held 'himself obliged to protect his subjects there as amply as in any other his dominions'.[31] But, as usual, the Governor of Jamaica got no answer to his letter.

So, Jamaica had to defend herself, in the only way she could, with her privateers 'under the auspicious conduct of so brave, prudent, and noe less valiant as successful a commander as Admiral Henry Morgan'. Surgeon Browne, waiting at Isla Vaca for the day of departure, got wind of another, more favourable rumour in October. Prince Rupert, with twenty-five men-of-war and five thousand soldiers, was coming to the Indies in February. He thought that they would be able to 'overrun and conquer all . . . and adde a very splendid diamond to his most sacred majesty's crowne'. But he was not sure that they would be able to manage all that well without the assistance of Morgan and his 'old privateers', for they were a very special breed. 'The privateers of these parts, theire bodys are habituated to this country, they knowe each place and creeke, know the mode of the Spaniard fighting, townes being never so well fortyfied, the numbers never so unequall, if money or good plunder be in the case, they will either win it manfully or dye coradgiously.'[32] Many Spanish governors would have ruefully concurred in this assessment of their enemies. The privateers themselves, eating their *boucan* and waiting restlessly in their rendezvous at Isla Vaca, were absolutely certain that it was true.

CHAPTER THIRTEEN

Bad News along the Main

'GOD free us from so many thieves and look after Your Excellency.'[1] Simon Barranco, Governor of the small port of Santa Marta, heartily reciprocated both sentiments as he finished reading the second of the two letters which he had just received describing the English capture of Rio de la Hacha. The letters had been written, four days after Collier's arrival, by citizens who had been allowed out into the countryside to organize the collection of the maize and meat demanded as ransom, and had then taken a further week to travel the hundred mountainous and inhospitable miles between the two towns. No doubt Barranco felt pity for his fellow-countrymen in Rio de la Hacha, but his first thought was probably one of relief that it had not been his turn this time. Santa Marta had been sacked enough times in the last twenty years as it was and needed a long period of peace to recover some of its lost economic vitality. But this was no time for complacency. He called for his scribe and dictated a letter reporting the news to Pedro de Ulloa, Governor of Cartagena, the next city along the Main.

The news seemed very bad. As usual the privateers had been quite incapable of holding their tongues, and Barranco had received a tolerably accurate estimate of the enemy's total numbers and intentions. It looked as though the attack on Rio de la Hacha was no more than a preliminary to the biggest raid that the longsuffering Spanish Main had ever known. The privateers had said that fifty big and small ships were gathering in Jamaica and Isla Vaca and that they planned to attack either Cartagena or Panamá by way of the River Chagres. Various estimates were made of the numbers of the privateers, but none was less than two thousand, and some of the men were said to be regular soldiers fresh out from England. Some said that the Duke of York was behind this enormous concentration of the enemies of Spain. Opinion was divided on whether Panamá or Cartagena was the most threatened, but the majority view was that 'it is for Cartagena (may God save Your Excellency)'.

Barranco's letter, with its enclosed copies of the correspondence from Rio de la Hacha, took a further five days to travel the slightly longer distance to Cartagena, so that it was not till 9 November that the Governor, Pedro de Ulloa, was informed of Collier's landing. The news had taken seventeen days to travel just over two hundred miles, a good indication of the problems of communication on the Spanish Main. Letters would have travelled far faster by ship but, of course, the whole problem was that the privateers were masters of the sea and very few Spanish ships sailed along these coasts any longer. This humiliating indication of the effectiveness of the privateers made communication and mutual defence very difficult, and reinforced a naturally selfish and insular attitude amongst the governors of the particular cities, especially since the prevailing wind and current meant that, once ships or men had been sent to leeward (that is, to the west), it was very difficult to get them back again.

It can be imagined that, in these desperate days, the Spanish empire in the Indies was alive with rumour of privateer activity. Hardly a letter was written which did not report some news of an imminent threat, and colonial governors could not afford to treat every one of these too seriously. If they had, they would have found themselves on full alert practically all the time – a state of affairs which would have meant not only an almost complete cessation of business but also an unacceptable pressure on public resources, since if the militia were called to arms they were supposed to be paid. Ulloa's reaction to Barranco's letter was therefore fairly mild. The opportunity was taken to send letters to the Presidents of Santa Fé and Panamá asking for money for his regular troops, who had not been paid for thirty months. The people of the surrounding districts were warned to be ready with their arms to come to Cartagena's assistance at short notice, and the farmers on the coast were ordered to move inland with their grain and their herds in case of enemy raids.[2] Such precautions were not too disruptive and had the added advantage that they cost the Government nothing. However, on 17 November, Ulloa received another letter from Barranco enclosing a communication from the lieutenant of the castle of Rio de la Hacha. This did little more than repeat the news which had already been sent along the coast, but it seems to have been sufficient to persuade Ulloa that an English invasion really was imminent and that Cartagena was the privateers' main target. Next day he called a *junta* and got down to the serious business of putting the city in a proper state of defence. Cartagena might rely mainly for its protection on the good offices of Nuestra Señora de la Popa, who watched over the citizens from her commanding position on a mountain high above the city, but there were still a few things that mere men could do.

The records of the *junta* make it quite clear why Ulloa liked to be quite sure of the facts before taking positive defensive action, and incidentally show why Spanish colonial defences were nearly always in such an appalling state. The problem was quite simple. Defence cost money and, since it was public defence, this meant public money. The rules developed by an untrusting central government for the spending of public money on defence were laid down by a royal *cedula* of 1633, and they are worth quoting, since they give a good idea of the difficulties under which colonial governors laboured.

I order that from now onwards none of my governors nor other ministers can take any money from my royal coffers . . . with the excuse that it is to be used to provide preparations for war . . . unless . . . it is truly and probably held as a certain and evident thing that there are enemies on the coast. Before anything, can be spent, a *junta* of the officials of my Royal Treasury must be held and then only exactly what is necessary must be taken . . . on pain of paying four times as much as has been taken for any transgression of these instructions.'[3]

In other words, nothing could be spent on defence until the enemy was almost at the gate, and this was the most important port on the Spanish Main, a city that was only four days' sail from Jamaica with the winds prevailing at this time of year, a city that was described as 'the jewel that the pirates most seek in these parts'.[14]

Ulloa complied with the *cedula*. A scribe was ordered to read out Barranco's letters and all the enclosures. The members of the *junta* heard the evidence and agreed that there 'truly and probably' were enemies on the coast and then got down to seeing what they could do about it. There was a lot to do. Cartagena was a big city and its garrison of four hundred regular troops was bigger than those of Panamá and Portobello together. The city's castles and gun-

platforms were equipped with fifty guns. But none of this meant that
the city was ready to resist invasion. The garrison, as we have seen,
had not been paid for thirty months and 'soldiers cannot feed
themselves without pay'. The soldiers were said to be so hungry that
they would be unable to defend the city. This was a serious matter,
but there were plenty of other things wrong. A wall was broken in
one of the city's three castles; a large number of gun-carriages had
rotted and had to be repaired or replaced; all the castles needed militia
reinforcements and stocks of food to stand a siege; and, as usual,
there was a very great shortage of gunners. 'All those people who
were good at handling guns, whether they were foreigners or citizens, whether they were in the city or in ships in the harbour', were
to serve at the bastions as the Governor directed.

The English obligingly did not attack while Ulloa put his city into
a state of defence but, as November and December went by, he
continued to receive disquieting confirmation of the enemy's hostile
intentions. On 29 December, a Dutch sloop arrived at Cartagena*
with a bundle of letters from Curaçao, Venezuela and Puerto Rico.
All told the same story. The English and French were massing at Isla
Vaca for a descent on the Main. There was very specific information
from Don Franco Lomellin, the Genoese slave agent at Curaçao,
who wrote that a ship had recently arrived at the Dutch island after
trading on the north coast of Hispaniola.[5] Her captain had reported
that many of the cattle-hunters had gone to Isla Vaca, where twenty
ships and three thousand English and French pirates were already
gathered 'to make some surprise in the Indies'. Most people thought
that Cartagena was the target. When the captain had left Hispaniola
on 31 November, it was said that the pirates were expected to be
sailing any day.

Lomellin also reported some other interesting news. In a letter
from Amsterdam, dated 9 October 1670, he had learned that peace
had been concluded between the English and the Spaniards in the
Indies, 'news which I judge to be correct since it is confirmed by
many other people'. The news was correct. Godolphin and
Peñaranda had worked hard in Madrid that summer, and a new and
specifically 'American' treaty had been drawn up which satisfied

* From Curaçao; the journey had taken only eight days.

most of England's demands and was to remain the basis of Anglo-Spanish relations for over forty years.[6] This time there was none of that silence on the question of the Indies which had characterized the 1667 treaty and had enabled the English to assume that there was still no peace beyond the line. Spain had at last agreed to recognize all the English possessions in America, including Jamaica, and England had agreed to bring an end to all hostilities against the Spaniards in the Indies and to recall all privateering commissions. Both sides agreed to forget all past hostilities, which were to be buried in oblivion as if they had never occurred. There was no mention of reciprocal trade between the peoples of the two empires in the Indies, but Godolphin had managed to have inserted the 'wood and water' clause by which English ships in need or distress could call at Spanish ports for supplies or repairs. This was assumed – incorrectly, as it turned out – to be almost as good as an open admission that the English could trade at Spanish American ports.

The Treaty of Madrid was signed by Godolphin on 21 July, a fortnight after Modyford had unilaterally declared war on the Spaniards in the Indies. The Treaty was then sent to London for ratification, which had to be done by 28 November, and a further eight months were allowed for its publication in the Indies. The letter of the Treaty thus allowed for hostile acts to be excused up to July 1671. However, the spirit of the Treaty was obviously for there to be peace in the Indies from the moment of signature, and there could be no possible excuse for an English attack on the Spanish Main if it could be proved that the English knew of the existence of the new treaty. Whether they did know officially is still a matter under discussion. Communications were slow, and official correspondence was subject to delays due both to bureaucratic procedures and to deliberate policy. Unofficial news of the treaty reached Curaçao in the middle of December and Cartagena on 29 December. But no one had to believe unofficial news. The Queen of Spain's official letter to Pedro de Ulloa, sending him a copy of the Treaty and ordering him to bring an end to hostilities with England, was written on 28 October, but it did not reach Cartagena until the arrival of an advice-ship from Spain on 12 February 1671, ironically the same day as Ulloa heard of the sack of Panamá.[7]

The news from Curaçao certainly did not bring an end to Ulloa's feverish efforts to put Cartagena in a state of defence. That would have been very unwise, for, as Lomellin pointed out, 'you cannot trust these people who always plan to rob when such occasions of peace make it least suspected and, the affair succeeding, excuse themselves by saying that they have not received the news'. This was an opinion with which Ulloa fully agreed. Indeed, he was certain that the news of peace would make the English more, not less, hostile. 'They will want to make some great coup between the war and the peace, so we must be very careful.'[8]

Pedro de Ulloa felt certain that Cartagena would be the object of that great English coup, but he had, of course, passed all the news along the coast to his equally threatened colleague, Don Juan Perez de Guzmán in Panamá. The letter reporting Collier's attack and the English assembly at Isla Vaca was sent on 19 November. In order to avoid any pirates who might be hanging around outside Portobello or Chagres, the letter was sent by canoe two hundred miles across the sea to Darien and then overland through the jungle to Panamá. The officials in Cartagena thought the journey would take twelve days, but in fact it took over twice as long, and so Don Juan did not receive the news of the imminence of attack from the privateers until 15 December 1670, just three days before Morgan sailed from Cape Tiburón.

Don Juan did not have much time to prepare his defence, but he certainly made energetic use of what time he had. He had been anticipating an invasion from Jamaica ever since his return from prison in Peru, eighteen months previously, and he was just as certain that Panamá was the target as Ulloa had been certain it would be Cartagena. Don Juan could feel that he was already in quite a strong position since Spanish horror at the loss of Portobello had called forth funds to spend on defence and, as we have seen, the fortifications of both Portobello and Chagres had recently been much improved. Preparation was therefore mainly a matter of placing his very limited numbers of men in the places where he thought that they could do most good and ensuring that they had food to eat and arms to fight with.[9]

In the absence of any naval forces, Don Juan saw the protection of Panamá as dependent on three separate but interconnected areas of defence – the coast, the isthmus and the city itself. It was possible for an enemy to land at several places on the Caribbean coast of Pánamá and, with the aid of experienced local guides, to make his way across the isthmus. However, Don Juan thought it almost certain that an invasion force as large as the one that was reported at Isla Vaca would attempt to use one of the two normal trading routes across the isthmus, either landing at Portobello and making their way along the mule-trail through the mountains or landing at Chagres and travelling up the river to the head of navigation at Venta de Cruces and so overland to Panamá. All Spanish thinking on the defence of the isthmus was based on this assumption and, as a result, the only fortifications on the coast were at the beginning of these two routes: at Portobello and at San Lorenzo at the mouth of the River Chagres. Don Juan hoped that these fortifications, whose improvements he had been supervising during the previous year, would be sufficient to prevent the enemy from advancing into the isthmus and he decided to put nearly all his best men into their garrisons.

Portobello was already a rather different proposition from the city so easily captured by Morgan in 1668. The alterations to Santiago Castle had made the approach to the city very much more difficult and, within the city, the fort of San Geronimo was now virtually completed. The regulars and militia companies were also closer to full strength, and there were some three hundred armed men to defend the city. Don Juan hoped that, by increasing the garrison, he could make the city virtually impregnable and hence ensure that the mule-trail to Panamá was denied to the enemy. As soon as he got the news from Cartagena, he gave his orders, and the trail became very busy as two hundred extra men, including nearly all the regular soldiers in Panamá, marched to reinforce Portobello's garrison and a large consignment of salt meat, maize, rice, gunpowder and bullets was sent across the isthmus to enable them to sustain a long siege. Arrangements were made that, at the enemy's approach, the whole population of the town should retreat with all their valuables to the three castles, where a two-month supply of food had been laid in.[10] Don Juan had learned from a correspondent that the Duke of York had written to Henry Morgan and asked him why he had not hung on to Portobello after capturing it. Morgan was said to have replied that, if he was sent sufficient men and provisions to sustain himself, he could go back there any time he liked.[11] Don Juan thought this to be pure conceit and rather hoped that Morgan would go back to Portobello, for he considered it now to be the strongest part of all his defences. But most people thought that an English invasion would be directed not at Portobello but at Chagres – a route which looked very attractive to a maritime people because of the ease of transporting men and weapons two-thirds of the way across the isthmus by river.

It was said afterwards, even by hostile witnesses, that Don Juan had done everything possible to reinforce the defences of the Chagres river, and this seems to have been no more than his due. The normal garrison of the castle of San Lorenzo at the mouth of the river was 160 men. Don Juan more than doubled this to 360, sending the fifty remaining regular soldiers from the Panamá garrison and seventy Spaniards and eighty mulattoes and free blacks from the militia companies of the city. He also sent some specialists, including a 'very skilled gunner', and made sure that the garrison had plenty of food and arms. All the boats and canoes on the river were requisitioned to send biscuit, meat, ammunition and handguns to the castle. The Castellan, a distinguished old soldier called Don Pedro de Elizalde, reported that the castle had everything that it could possibly need for its defence and that 'all the people were in good spirits'. He was totally confident that he could repel anybody who might come against him. 'Even if all England were to come,' he wrote to Don Juan, 'they would not capture the castle.'[12]

Just in case the Castellan's confidence should be misplaced, Don Juan also garrisoned the river itself. Francisco Gonzalez Salado, a former Castellan of Santiago and a man in whom the President had great confidence, was made the captain of the river and was given some four or five hundred militiamen, nearly all of them Indians, negroes and half-castes, for the defence of the Chagres. Many of these men were locals who knew their way perfectly through the bewildering chaos of mountain and jungle that surrounded the river. Gonzalez made his base at Venta de Cruces, the head of navigation where there was a custom-house and warehouses used by the merchants who transported goods up and down river.[13] He also prepared four strongpoints down-river,* each of them with

---

* Barro Colorado (or Santissima Trinidad), Tornomarcos, Caño Quebrado and Barbacoas.

stockades high enough to protect their defenders. The lowest down the river and the strongest of these stockades was at Barro Colorado, which is now an island in the huge lake formed when the River Chagres was dammed during the construction of the Panamá Canal. In 1670, Barro Colorado was where the river began to get quite narrow, about halfway between San Lorenzo and Venta de Cruces. Downstream from Barro Colorado, Gonzalez had lookouts and canoe patrols and an advance guard at Dos Brazos, some twenty miles up-river from the castle.

Finally, in the unlikely event of an invading force not only taking San Lorenzo Castle but also managing to get past the stockades erected by Gonzalez, Don Juan had to think about the defences of Panamá itself. He had sent all of his regular troops to reinforce the castles on the Caribbean coast, so he had to rely entirely on militia for a garrison, although he had quite a few experienced old soldiers such as himself to command them. Everyone in the city had left off business and begun to prepare themselves for defence when the news arrived from Cartagena. It hardly seemed possible that mere pirates could get together three thousand men to invade the isthmus but, if they did, it was best to be ready for them. We have seen that the majority of the population of Panamá was slaves, and not many of these could be trusted with arms. The city had also been stripped of just under a thousand free men to man the defences of the isthmus and the coast. However, by the end of December, Don Juan was able to muster a thousand men in Panamá who could be sent where they might be needed and he was expecting more from the town of Los Santos and from the province of Veragua. He could feel little confidence in this backstop of his defences, except perhaps for the two hundred cavalry whom he had managed to get together. Few of the infantry were Spaniards, most were poorly armed, if they had arms at all, and nearly all of them were untrained greenhorns who could not be expected to stand for long against men of the calibre of the privateers. However, Don Juan did not anticipate that these reserves would be needed, for he had been assured by his officers 'that the forts on the river as well as the castle were all impregnable'.[14] When he went to the cathedral to seek that divine assistance without which all human efforts were but empty gestures, he prayed that his officers' assurances might prove accurate.

CHAPTER FOURTEEN

The Privateers Sail

HENRY MORGAN was a little anxious as he scanned the southern horizon from his anchorage at Isla Vaca. Where was Edward Collier? It was now the first week of December 1670, and his Vice-Admiral had been gone for eleven weeks. Could he have suffered a defeat? Morgan badly needed Collier's four hundred experienced men, a fifth of his total manpower, if he was to take some great city. He also badly needed some prisoners from the Main to provide him with the justification for an invasion, in accordance with the conditions of his commission, which gave him permission to land and attack any 'place belonging to the enemy where you shall bee informed the magazenes and stores for this warr are layd up or where any randezvouz for their forces to imbody are appointed'.[1] Given the prisoners he would soon get the information he required, but he dared not wait at Isla Vaca for Collier and his prisoners very much longer. It had been something of a miracle to gather so many of the very independent privateers together in one place as it was. Inaction would soon determine some of the more impetuous captains to go off and make war on their own.

There was also another very good reason for wanting to be gone from his well-known rendezvous at Isla Vaca. The day before, a sloop had arrived from Jamaica with a message from Modyford, instructing Morgan to 'hurry up with what he was planning since he had heard that there was peace between Spain, England and the Englishmen that were in the Indies'.[2] The sloop's arrival had not been unexpected. Morgan had already received the news from a ship direct from England which had given him the same message: 'Hurry up and seize some place from the Spaniards.'[3] Morgan could hardly wait much longer at Isla Vaca and pretend that he had never heard of the peace, nor could Modyford pretend much longer that he had been unable to inform Morgan of the new conditions. He could pretend once, as he did on 28 December when he wrote a letter to Lord Arlington reporting that he had sent a ship to Morgan with a copy of the articles of peace with Spain, 'intimatinge that though I had them but from private hands and not any orders to call him in, yet I thought fitt to let him see them, and thereon to advise him to . . . be careful to doe nothinge that might prevent the accomplishment of his Majesty's gracious and peacable intentions'. This letter, with its typical Modyford ambiguities, arrived at Morgan's rendezvous as we have seen, but Modyford pretended that it had not. 'But that vessel', he wrote to Lord Arlington, 'retourned with my letters, missing him at his old rendezvous.'[4] Don Franco Lomellin in Curaçao had been accurate in his prediction that the English would 'excuse themselves by saying that they have not received the news'.[5] But they could not do so for much longer.

It was, then, with considerable relief that, on 8 December, Morgan heard the lookout shout that he could recognize the topsails of Collier's flagship on the horizon. As the rest of the fleet came into sight, he could see that there were two more ships than had sailed in September, a sure sign that the expedition had achieved some success. There was a great cheer from the assembled Frenchmen as they recognized the larger of Collier's prizes as *La Gallardina*, the Tortuga corsair which had been captured with its entire crew by the *capitana* of Cartagena five years previously. Better still was the discovery that the captain of *La Gallardina* had a privateering commission from the Governor of Cartagena and had been in consort with Rivero during his raids on Jamaica earlier in the year. It seemed a good omen, and Morgan promised that the ship should be returned to the French, who were short of shipping for the buccaneers, who were still arriving in small parties from their hunting-grounds in the north of Hispaniola.

The maize and meat that Collier had brought from Rio de la Hacha were a very welcome addition to the provisions that had been collected in Hispaniola. Feeding two thousand hungry men was a real problem for an admiral with no commissariat. Morgan divided the food 'among all the ships according to the number of men that were in every vessel' and then got down to the job of interrogating the prisoners that Collier had brought from the Main. Richard

Browne, a surgeon who served with Morgan, tells us how this was done.

The first designe when we are abroad is the getting of a prisoner, which when we take we make him say and subscribe under his hand and seale that either at Carthagen, Porto Bell or other maritime townes they are mustering of men, fitting a fleet for sea to invade Jamaica. Some through torments, confesse what wee please. Other more ingenious and stoute will not be drawne to speake or subscribe what they know not, who are then cutt in peices, shott or hanged.[6]

One man who was hanged 'for not speaking and subscribing what they suggested' was Manuel Fernandez de Acosta, the Spanish captain of *La Gallardina*, who had been given quarter at Rio de la Hacha. The captain's courage caused delay but nothing else, for it did not take long to find two 'pityfull spirited Spainards' who were prepared to say what the English wanted them to. Their depositions were solemnly taken down by Morgan's secretary, John Peake, to provide the necessary pretext for an invasion of Spanish territory.[7]

Marco de Luba was the master of *La Gallardina*, a Canary Islander who declared that 'he did see the people of Carthagena listed and all in arms offensive against the English'. Since the last time he had been in Cartagena was before the English attack on Rio de la Hacha which initiated the alarm along the Main, this was clearly a lie to save his skin. By the time that he gave his testimony, the people of Cartagena were, of course, all 'listed', but this was in arms defensive, not offensive, and was a direct result of the news of Morgan's fleet at Isla Vaca. Luba also said that the Spaniards on the Main had been given great encouragement against the island of Jamaica by the President of Panamá, 'and the more by reason of a fleet fitted out of old Spaine for those parts under the command and conduct of one Don Alonzo'. This, too, is quite clearly a figment of a tortured man's imagination, and it looks suspiciously as if, in his desperation, he was thinking of the Armada de Barlovento under its commander, Don Alonzo de Campos, which Morgan himself had destroyed the previous year. We have seen that the Council of the Indies would dearly have loved to send a fleet against Jamaica, but such a desire had never been anywhere near translated into reality and no word of such an invasion had been sent to encourage Don Juan Perez de Guzmán or anyone else on the Spanish Main.

Luba and his colleague, Lucas Perez, a seaman from Majorca, did provide some accurate information in their depositions. Both men said that corsair ships were fitting out in Cartagena against the English, which was quite true. What they did not say, because they were in no position to know, was that there was at that date only one corsair ship fitting out and that even that one ceased to make preparations for war directly the news of the peace with the English arrived in the port.[8] Luba and Perez also said that the President of Panamá had 'granted severall commissions against the English', an admission which Morgan was very keen to obtain, since there seems little doubt that, from the beginning, he had the invasion of Panamá as top of his priorities. There is, however, no evidence that Don Juan issued any privateering commissions at all, although he was, of course, quite entitled to do so by the Queen's orders of 20 April 1669. No ship was ever captured with such a commission, and there is no indication of any Spanish corsair using Portobello, the only Caribbean port in the President's jurisdiction, as a base. Such facts were of little interest to Morgan and his captains. What they wanted were depositions signed by Spaniards saying that men and ships were being prepared for an invasion of Jamaica, and they did not care how much 'they scrued and extorted' to get them. After a little persuasion, Marco de Luba and Lucas Perez had provided them with just that.

Now that Morgan's fleet was complete and he had provided himself with the necessary stores and evidence of Spanish hostility, he was ready to sail. The motley collection of ships which surrounded Morgan's flagship in the waters off Isla Vaca would have been a joke to anyone schooled in the great fleet actions of the Second Dutch War, but they were a terrifying sight to the Spanish prisoners on board. Who could ever have believed that there were so many pirates in the Indies? There were thirty-eight ships in the fleet, the largest assembly of privateers that had ever been seen in the West Indies.[9] The ships varied enormously in size. The biggest was *Satisfaction*, Morgan's flagship, with 22 guns and 140 men. Then there were twelve other ships with ten or more guns, carrying an average of seventy-five men apiece. The other twenty-five ships in the fleet were very small and many had no guns at all, but they were just about seaworthy, and in the absence of the fish and turtles which were their normal cargoes they could pack in a fair number of the hardy privateersmen who thought nothing of travelling a thousand miles in an open boat, if there was a promise of plunder at the end of the voyage. The presence of Morgan provided that promise, and he had had no problem in getting men to come to fight for him. Estimates of Morgan's total numbers vary, but they were certainly less than the three thousand that was being bandied about on the Spanish Main. The official figure was 1846,[10] but it seems probable that the actual figure was over two thousand, of whom about one-third were French and the rest English. Such a number, which again seems minute by the standards of European warfare, was huge in the context of the seventeenth-century West Indies – twice as many men as Morgan had managed to assemble at his last rendezvous at Isla Vaca before *Oxford* blew up, four times as many as the numbers with which he had taken Portobello and Maracaibo. Such figures mean that Morgan had been able to get together under one single command nearly every English and French privateer in the West Indies – a remarkable tribute to his leadership and reputation. The Governors of Jamaica normally reckoned that there were between 1200 and 1500 privateers based on the island, while the Governor of Tortuga reported in 1671 that there were about a thousand privateers (*flibustiers*) and a hundred hunting buccaneers (*boucaniers*)* in Tortuga and Hispaniola, so that something like eighty per cent of the available manpower had flocked to Morgan's flag at Isla Vaca. According to Juan de Lao, the Indian cook who had been captured in Rivero's ship, there was also one woman who travelled with the two thousand men in Morgan's fleet. 'She was small and old and English and it was publicly said that she was a witch whom the English had brought along to prophesy for them and through her diabolical arts to advise them what they should do.'[11]

There is no evidence that this old lady was present at the great council of war which Morgan held in the cabin of *Satisfaction* on 12 December 1670, though some of his thirty-seven captains were certainly superstitious enough to have welcomed the advice of a

---

* Many *boucaniers* had become *flibustiers* in the previous few years.

witch and they would all have been glad to know what the future was likely to bring. Morgan started proceedings by issuing commissions to those captains who had none and by arranging for a new set of articles of association, or *chasse-partie* as the French called it, to be drawn up. These were similar to those drawn up before the Portobello expedition, with elaborate arrangements for the division of the booty, provision of compensations for those who were maimed or blinded and a scale of premiums for the brave, 'such as being the first to tear down the flag on a fort and run up the English colours. This would earn an extra fifty pieces of eight, while a man who brought in a prisoner when intelligence was needed would have an extra 200. As for the grenadiers, they were to receive five pieces of eight extra for every grenade they threw into a fort.'[12] Grenadiers were to prove very important on this campaign, a fact which Morgan had anticipated, and there were plenty of hand-grenades, fire-bombs and other explosive missiles on board the ships.

Once such important administrative details had been settled, the captains could get down to the most serious business of the council of war. Where should they first attack? Morgan had no doubt decided where he wanted to attack already, but he needed to be very careful not to offend the fiercely independent captains who sat round the great table in the cabin before him. In particular, he had to be careful not to offend the large French contingent, a third of his men, who were never prepared to accept dictation by an Englishman and would have stormed out of the cabin and sailed their ships away at the first display of any arrogant authority. So Morgan conducted the council in a spirit of true democracy, arranging for everything to be translated for the benefit of his French colleagues and agreeing to be bound by the decision of the majority.

There was no doubt in anybody's mind that this great concentration of ships and men was a unique conjuncture which must not be wasted on anything petty, especially since the news of peace meant that this would probably be the last privateering expedition for most of the English present. They were agreed that they must make 'some good coup between the war and the peace', as Pedro de Ulloa had anticipated. Only four targets were seriously discussed. Santiago de Cuba, the second city of Cuba whose powerfully defended port on the south coast of the island was only 150 miles from Jamaica, had been specifically mentioned as a target by the Council of Jamaica and in Morgan's instructions. The city had been captured by the privateers in 1662, so many of those present knew it well, but no one was at all keen to venture there again. The only entrance to the port was through a narrow slit in the cliffs which was guarded by a powerful fortress. Such a target promised too much danger for too little potential gain, and Morgan had already abandoned any idea of attempting it. Vera Cruz, the port of Mexico, was more attractive, a rich city protected by an island fortress a musket-shot from the shore. But was it rich enough to make a prize big enough to be shared between two thousand men? Vera Cruz was rather like Portobello, a ghost town except when the silver fleet was in port. In any case, they had no nicely signed and sealed depositions stating that Vera Cruz was arming against the English, so this target, too, was abandoned. This left Cartagena or Panamá and, after lengthy discussion, it was unanimously decided that Panamá was both the richest and the least well defended of the two despite its awkward position seventy miles across the isthmus on the Pacific. None of the privateers had ever been to Panamá, and it retained its legendary reputation as a city flowing with silver and gold and with all the good things in life ready to be seized by bold and determined men like themselves. Panamá! The privateers liked the sound of the name as they drank a toast to their success.

Morgan got his secretary to draw up a declaration which was signed by the captains.[13]

Wee, having seriously considered of what place may prove most advantage-ous for the safety of the English and more especially for the security of his Majesty's island of Jamaica to prevent the invasions of the Spaniards . . . doe all of us conclude that it stands most for the good of Jamaica and saftey of us all to take Panama, the President thereof having granted severall comis-sions against the English to the great annoyance of the island of Jamaica and our merchantmen – as by the oaths of two Spaniards hath been made most evidently appeare.

This declaration was filed with his commission, the Governor's instructions and letters and the two Spanish depositions, all ready to be produced as necessary to demonstrate the complete legality of his actions. The captains then got down to a detailed discussion of just how they should take Panamá.

On 18 December, Morgan inspected his fleet and gave the order to set sail. Just before his departure into the unknown, he wrote a last letter to Sir Thomas Modyford in Jamaica, reporting that he was 1800 strong 'and that he was that day due to sayle to make further discoveryes of the enemye's intentions, haveinge by prisoners and the depositions of two Spanish captains beene informed that about Cartagena, Porto Bel and Panama, soldyers were listinge to be ready against the galleons came to be transported against this island'.[14] He was careful not to mention which one of the three towns was his target, so that Modyford might feel that any further failure to discover the privateer fleet and report the news of the peace was not his fault. The Admiral was a very considerate man.

Morgan's fleet had the wind behind them, and they logged over a hundred miles a day as they sailed south-west through the deep channel between the Roncador and Serrana Banks towards their initial target, whose rugged hills were a familiar sight for many of the privateers. For Morgan and his captains had decided that, since it was on the way to Panamá, they might as well recapture the 'King's antyent propriety' at Providence or Santa Catalina island.[15] It was the early morning of 24 December when they dropped anchor off the island – Christmas Eve for the Spanish garrison and the Frenchmen from Tortuga, who used the new-style Gregorian calendar, but just ordinary 14 December for the old-fashioned English.

Santa Catalina had reverted to its usual lethargy after the murder of its gallant conqueror, José Sanchez Ximenez, in 1668. The commander of the garrison was now Don Joseph Ramirez de Leyva, who had been captain of the troops from Cartagena during the recapture of the island. Ramirez was not the man that Sanchez had been and he was unable to create a very high morale in his lonely command, especially as he stood accused of embezzling the men's pay and reducing them to poverty.[16] He had less than two hundred men – 'a very small number compared with what the enemy brought'[17] – and, since they were unpaid and rather hungry and many of them were convicts, it is not surprising that he viewed with some alarm the sight of thirty-eight ships bearing down on the island.

Morgan sent two ships round to face the port and prevent anyone leaving to warn the people on the Spanish Main and landed a thousand men at Aguada Grande on the west side of the island. By two in the afternoon, he had taken possession of the whole of the main island with no resistance. Ramirez had retreated with all his men to Isla Chica which, as a result of the efforts of Smith and Sanchez, was now considerably better fortified than it had been when Mansfield invaded the island in 1666. There were eight cannon in the fort of La Cortadura between the two islands, twenty in the main fortress of El Castillo and another twelve in the batteries of San Matheo, San Agustin and Santiago overlooking the port. As the privateers approached La Cortadura, the drawbridge was raised and they were met with heavy fire which, although it did not do them any harm, was sufficient to force them to retire. It was raining and they were hungry and had already taken a strong dislike to the island, which looked particularly miserable in the driving rain. The situation was very similar to that facing Sanchez in 1666, although Morgan, of course, had nearly ten times as many men. He must win in the end, but he might lose quite a few men before he seized the fortresses on Isla Chica if there was any real resistance. Morgan did not want to lose any men on this preliminary target, nor did he want to lose any time – sentiments shared by the privateers, who, after a night spent sleeping on the soaking ground without any supper, were extremely fed up and wanted to go to Panamá and had no wish to hang about a minute longer than necessary in Santa Catalina.

For what happened next we have to rely on the unsubstantiated word of Exquemelin, which I have been reluctant to do in this book. Morgan simply reported that he sent 'a summons to the Governor to deliver the little island, who willingly submitted so that hee might have good quarter and transportation to any part of the Maine which was granted and duely performed',[18] while there is virtually no Spanish evidence relating to this second English capture of the island. Exquemelin's story is certainly amusing and worth repeating.[19] On the morning after he landed, Morgan sent a canoe over to the Spaniards, under a white flag, summoning them to give up the island and threatening to give no quarter if they did not surrender. Ramirez asked for two hours' grace while he consulted with his officers. The privateers sat around in the rain, trying to keep their muskets and powder dry, while the garrison deliberated. At last a canoe came back from Isla Chica carrying two Spaniards to arrange the terms of capitulation. Ramirez was quite willing to surrender the island but, mindful no doubt of the ten years' *presidio cerrado* to which Governor Ocampo had been sentenced after his surrender of the island in 1666,[20] he begged Morgan to join with him in a mock battle to save his reputation. The privateers should cross the bridge joining the two islands at night and storm the fort of La Cortadura. Meanwhile the ships should sail into the harbour as if they were about to attack the main garrison at El Castillo.[21] Men should be landed at the San Matheo battery who would capture Ramirez as he made his way from La Cortadura to El Castillo and force him to surrender the fortresses. Everything should be done as noisily as possible, with heavy firing on both sides, but the muskets and guns should be fired in the air or loaded with blank. Morgan agreed to the proposals on the one condition that, if any of his men were killed or wounded, the garrison would be slaughtered to the last man. That same night the mock battle took place. The privateers and the Spanish garrison played their parts with great gusto and the island was surrendered at midnight.

Some evidence that something like this really did take place comes from the deposition of Juan de Lao, the Indian cook who was on board one of the privateer ships. He later escaped from his captors and told his version of what had happened at Santa Catalina to the Governor of Cartagena.[22] The first part agrees with Exquemelin. The English sent a message to the Spanish Governor telling him to surrender or they would put everyone to the sword. 'Later I heard several cannon fired and knew and understood that the English and French were winning possession of the island's fortresses. They took the whole garrison and everyone that was there prisoner and they did not kill a single one of them.' Lao said that this strangely low casualty-list was due to an agreement made by the Spaniards and the French members of Morgan's forces not to spill blood on Christmas Day – in its way as nice a story as that of Exquemelin. Whatever the truth, the island was certainly surrendered without the loss of a single man on either side.

Morgan now proceeded with the second stage of his campaign. 'Understanding the Castle of Chagres blocked our way, I called a

Councell of all the cheif captaines where it was determined that wee should attacque the Castle of Chagres and forthwith there was dispatched 470 men in 3 shipps under the command of Lt. Col. Joseph Bradley.'[23] This was a small number to undertake the capture of such a powerfully situated castle which had a garrison nearly as big as Colonel Bradley's assault force. But Morgan clearly did not wish to let the people of Panamá know how strong he was, and trusted to the experienced Bradley's skill and the almost proverbial luck of the privateers to win the day. Bradley's three ships sailed on 30 December, while Morgan remained on the island to round up the slaves, whose number was variously estimated at sixty and a hundred, and to gather together some £500 worth of plunder. He also completely destroyed the island's fortifications, deciding that he could not afford to spare the men to garrison his new conquest for the King. All the guns were spiked and thrown into the sea, the gunpowder and munitions were divided amongst his ships and everything that could be burned, except the church, was razed to the ground. Finally, he carried out what had been the main object of the invasion of the island. The prisoners were rounded up and questioned to find out if there were any convicts familiar with the passage of the Chagres and the road to Panamá. Volunteers were promised their freedom, a share of the booty and a passage to Jamaica. Not surprisingly, several men stood forward, amongst them an Indian from Panamá called Antonillo who knew the river well.[24]

When Morgan set sail a few days after Bradley, he was heavily laden. The population of Santa Catalina had to be transported to the Main for the second time in four years. But this was a small chore for such an easy success, and Morgan felt very confident as he made his way to the south-west, his passage slowed by contrary winds. He had the men, he had the guides; soon he would have Panamá. The fact that, in Panamá, there was a proud President and a proud people who felt equally confident that they were quite safe behind an impregnable castle, a well-defended river and a chaos of mountain and jungle did not disturb him.

CHAPTER FIFTEEN

San Lorenzo

In the still air of noon, the sound of trumpets and martial music could be heard quite clearly as it carried across the forest to the castle of San Lorenzo.[1] No one who heard it could be in any doubt what the strange barbarian fanfares signified. The pirates were landing. How often had the days of boring garrison service been interrupted by a false alarm as enemy ships sailed uncaring down the coast? But this time there could be no doubting that it was the real thing, and every man in the garrison knew that today he would face the test of fire. All day they had had a running commentary from the lookout high up in the watchtower of the castle, itself high up on its great cliff above the mouth of the River Chagres. At dawn, he had reported Bradley's three ships anchored in El Portete de Naranjos ('The Haven of the Oranges'), some four miles north of the castle. He kept a tally as the canoes were launched and the privateers were ferried to the beach. By midday, he reckoned that the six canoes had made fifteen trips between them and had landed three or four hundred men who could now be seen drawn up on the beach, their banners limp in the hot noon sun. By one o'clock, the privateers had vanished, lost in the morass of undergrowth, forest and ravine that lay between the beach and San Lorenzo de Chagres. The garrison waited. Three or four hundred men did not sound too dangerous. It was no more than they had themselves behind the walls of their well-equipped and well-armed castle. Rumour had said that the pirates would come three thousand strong. The garrison of San Lorenzo began to look forward to the fight.

The lookout's information was confirmed by Joseph de Prado, a negro captain whose scouting party of twenty-five archers and lancers had made their way across the rough, broken country between the castle and the beach and had watched the English and the French land from close to. His runners were able to report in detail on the enemy's numbers, disposition and arms. The Castellan, Don Pedro de Elizalde, was pleased with the information. It seemed as though the English shared the Castillian love of precedent and were going to approach the castle by the same route as they had used in the course of their last invasion in 1656. He ordered Captain Prado to set an ambush in a narrow defile through which the enemy would have to come and then sat down to write to his Captain-General, Don Juan Perez de Guzmán.

Señor, I give you notice that today, the Feast of the Epiphany, the enemy has disembarked his people with flags and trumpets in Portete de Naranjos, little more than one league from this castle. . . . I expect them within two or three hours at nightfall or at dawn. The reports say that there are some three hundred men but, even if there were many more, they would be well punished. May God keep you for many years. Here's a scourge for these infidels![2]

Colonel Bradley had in fact appeared off the mouth of the river two days previously and had stood off and on in full view of the castle, in order to get a good look at his objective. He had not liked what he had seen. The River Chagres was quite wide here at its mouth and could be seen stretching inland between wooded banks towards that faraway goal, the city of Panamá. The right-hand or south bank was low and densely forested but, on the left, the land rose in three steep and rocky peninsulas. On top of the first peninsula and dominating the whole mouth of the river was the castle of San Lorenzo with four bastions commanding the landward side and two more facing the sea. Below the castle was a tower, mounted with eight cannon, which guarded the river's mouth, and beyond it were two more gun-platforms ready to fire at anything which should get past the tower. Connecting the castle on the cliff and the batteries at the water's edge was a stairway cut out of the cliff. In the distance, beyond the riverside fortifications, could be seen the warehouses and huts and shacks of the village of Chagres itself. It was clear to Bradley that there was no hope of a passage up the river unless he captured the castle, after which the batteries by the water should fall with no trouble. It was equally clear that there was no way that his men could climb the almost sheer cliffs that rose from the sea and from the river to the castle. His only hope was to anchor farther down the coast and approach San Lorenzo from the landward side.

The Castellan and Captain Prado had misjudged their enemy's intentions and speed across rough ground. The privateers took only two hours to cover the four miles from Portete de Naranjos, and they went most of the way along the beach and so avoided the negro captain's ambush. It was still very heavy going, especially the last part of their approach as they climbed up from the beach, sweating and cursing as they hacked their way through thick undergrowth with their machetes and clambered up tumbled heaps of boulders. By two in the afternoon, they reached the summit of the peninsula and could see the castle ahead of them. They could also see that their assault was not likely to be easy. Directly they broke cover from the woods where they stood waiting, they would come out on to a broad *campaña* or open stretch of land where all undergrowth had been cleared to give the defenders a wide field of fire. Beyond the *campaña*, just in front of the castle, the summit was split by a deep gully, La Quebrada de las Lajas ('The Ravine of the Slabs'), which made a natural ditch behind which the walls and bastions of San Lorenzo rose up into the sky. The walls themselves were built of double rows of wooden palisades, packed with sand and earth, which were covered with a roof made of woven reed and palm-leaves to protect both the garrison and the walls themselves from the rain which made life in the castle such a misery. It had been discovered that, in the wet season which lasted eight months of the year, the constant rain rotted the wooden palisades and, if there had been no roof, the fortifications would have fallen apart.[3] But now, in the first week of January, it was the dry season and the defenders were glad of this protection from the glare of the afternoon sun as they waited with cannon loaded and muskets primed for the privateers' assault. The privateers had no cannon and no siege equipment. It would have been an impossible task to haul guns up from the ships. Bradley's men were armed with just the usual weapons of the privateer – musket, two pistols and cutlass or machete – while his grenadier sections carried, in addition to their personal weapons, an assortment of hand-grenades and fire-bombs ready to lob into the castle if they could get close enough.

Bradley, who had assaulted many Spanish fortresses in his day, and had a low opinion of the courage and staying power of their defenders, determined to assault the castle immediately. He left a reserve in the woods, divided the remainder of his men into two squadrons and advanced out of the shelter of the trees into the open ground of the *campaña*. He was greeted at once by heavy and fairly accurate cannon-fire and musket-fire and a hail of arrows from the Indian archers, but his men drove on, stopping every now and then to take a steady shot with their long muskets. A few of the defenders fell at their posts, but much more damage was done to the privateers as they crossed the exposed ground. 'One could not see the *campaña* for the dead bodies of the enemy,' wrote a Spaniard later with pardonable exaggeration.[4] The slaughter was certainly sufficient to check the privateers' progress, and Bradley was forced to sound the retreat and retire to the woods.

An hour later, the privateers, determined not to be beaten by mere Spaniards, returned to the attack, showing a coolness and discipline under heavy fire which regular front-line troops might well be proud of. But, once again, the Spanish fire was too well sustained and too accurate for Bradley's men even to reach the ravine, let alone the castle. As the privateers turned and ran back to the shelter of the woods, the Spaniards danced on the beaten earth of their walls, shouting insults at the 'English dogs' and chanting 'victoria, victoria, victoria'. And a victory it certainly seemed, as the privateers looked out from the woods at the bodies of their dead and wounded lying on the *campaña* and at the untouched walls of the castle beyond.

Now was the time for Colonel Bradley to show his qualities of leadership. The privateers were not used to such losses, especially for the sake of a castle which probably had no loot; but they, too, had their pride, and their leader was able to persuade them to return to the attack one more time, lest they be disgraced in the eyes of their fellows in Santa Catalina. As the sun fell low over the coastline ahead of them, all the survivors of Bradley's four hundred men advanced once more into the *campaña* and, ignoring those who fell beside them, raced forward and dropped into the deep ravine beneath the castle walls. In order to divide the enemy's attention, the attack was launched at two different sections of the palisade. The main body, under Colonel Bradley himself, concentrated their fire on the men who defended the curtain wall between the bastions of San Francisco and San Joseph, while an independent company engaged the Spaniards who were defending the bastion of San Antonio, nearer to the cliff edge overlooking the sea. Now, as the *campaña* was shrouded in darkness, it was difficult for the defenders to distinguish the privateers in the gully and their aim was no longer as true as it had been earlier in the afternoon, although they were still able to do considerable damage by dropping explosives on the privateers' heads. The defenders themselves were silhouetted against the after-glow of the sunset, making an easy target for the long muskets of the English and French sharpshooters. Several Spaniards fell and the remainder were forced to keep their heads down, lest they fall in their turn.

Now, as the enemy fire wavered, was the moment for the grena-diers to earn their bonus money. Lighting the short fuses of their grenades and the cotton stoppers of their fire-balls,* they crept up from the gully and lobbed their explosives high up into the air, aiming to drop them on top of the reed-and-palm thatch that pro-vided a roof above the defenders' heads. Several grenades hit their target and the dry thatch burst into flames, illuminating the de-fenders, who struggled to free themselves as the burning palm-leaves fell amongst them. One large section of the roof collapsed and fell down behind the parapet where it set fire to a store of swords, lances, shields, loaded muskets and gunpowder which had been kept in reserve for the men on the walls. Other sections fell on the wooden palisades, which caught fire in their turn. The grenadiers were assisted in their fire-raising by the musketeers, one of whom demonstrated to his colleagues an effective method of spreading the fire. An Indian arrow had pierced him in the shoulder. 'In a fury he wrenched it out, took a wad of cotton from his pouch, tied it to the arrowhead and set fire to it. When it was well alight, he stuck the arrow in his musket and shot it into the palm-leaf thatch of some houses within the fortress walls.'[5] There were plenty of arrows in the gully, and other musketeers did the same, finding the fire-arrows particularly effective when they stuck quivering in the palisades. Soon the whole curtain between San Francisco and San Joseph was a wall of flame.

---

* Pots containing combustibles.

Bad as things were for the Spaniards, they were not yet lost. While the walls still stood, there remained a chance of extinguishing the fire, and the Castellan had organized a bucket-chain in an attempt to do so. However, at this moment, just after seven in the evening, there occurred one of those unlucky accidents which so often seemed to dog Spanish efforts against the privateers. The main defence of this curtain wall was a big bronze cannon which had continued to inflict heavy casualties on the English and French. Suddenly, and for no apparent reason, there was a terrific explosion as the cannon blew up, ripping to bits the palisades below it and collapsing a long section of the wall to either side. The Castellan and the Spaniards, still equal or even superior in numbers to the privateers, who had lost many men on the *campaña*, stood to the breach and there was no question as yet of an immediate assault. But the damage was considerable and, now that it was impossible to hold the privateers back from the line of the ruined wall, the grenadiers could get up much closer to throw their bombs, protecting themselves behind the mounds of earth which had spilled out as the palisades collapsed. One grenadier, with a particularly strong right arm, managed to lob a grenade far into the interior of the castle, where it landed on the roof of the quarters of the Castellan, once again covered with the very inflammable thatch. Soon the whole house was on fire and, with another huge explosion, practically all of the garrison's reserves of arms and most of the castle's gunpowder were blown into the sky. The interim President, Don Agustin de Bracamonte, had been right when he criticized the wood-and-thatch construction of San Lorenzo Castle.[6] It might be all right in the wet season but now, tinder-dry and so easily set alight, it was a recipe for disaster.

Fire and death soon had an effect on the morale of the garrison. 'The soldiers were frightened, seeing themselves without defence and so many dead and wounded.'[7] By midnight, a long line of men, many of them wounded or hideously burned, could be seen creeping down the steep stairway on the river side of the castle to escape from the holocaust in the canoes which were moored at the water's edge. Spanish sources state that a hundred and fifty men took this easy, but dishonourable, way out. Many others had already been killed or burned to death by the explosions, fires and muskets, and so there were possibly just another hundred and fifty left to hold the breach in the curtain wall and to watch the privateers' other point of attack at the bastion of San Antonio. The Spaniards had no powder left, but sword and lance were probably better for close-quarter fighting and there was no question of the courage of the Castellan and of the men who elected to stay with him to the end. As the fires continued to rage, there was a lull in the fighting and both sides tried to get a little rest before dawn.

The privateers attacked at first light. Twice they charged and twice they were driven back with great loss, the men who attacked San Antonio suffering particularly heavily from a cannon loaded with musket-balls which was fired at them from point-blank range. The privateers regrouped and, for this third assault, the position of honour was given to the Frenchmen from Tortuga and Hispaniola. There was no need now for the buccaneers' long muskets. In they went, pistol in each hand, and then the cold steel of cutlass and machete. The Spaniards wavered and broke, and the men who were fleeing up the river by canoe could hear the French sing as they burst into the castle – 'victoire, victoire'.[8] And still it was not all over. The Castellan, Don Pedro de Elizalde, rallied the survivors inside the castle and, surrounded by seventy men, refused quarter and prepared to sell his life dearly. Not a man survived. One by one they fell, the Chaplain, the Lieutenant and finally the brave Castellan himself, who refused quarter once again and gave the privateers 'no choice but to shoot him dead'.[9] But, as these last defenders of the castle of San Lorenzo fell, they took many of the heretic dogs with them. The privateers had never before fought such a desperate action.

The news of the fall of San Lorenzo travelled quickly up the River Chagres and reached the President in Panamá the following day. Don Juan was sick and had been in bed for four days, very feverish and with boils bursting out all over his body. The surgeons were worried. He had been bled three times and given a low diet, but he still seemed very ill. There was talk of calling for the priest.[10] The news of the loss of the castle hardly improved the President's health, but he did not despair. He had put nearly all his best men into the garrison and now they were all dead. The way lay open into the isthmus, but the isthmus itself was well defended. There were still many men left and he still had hopes of that divine assistance for which he had so often prayed. Ignoring the surgeons' advice, he got up from his sick-bed and could be seen, a sick man but still radiating confidence, as he walked or rode about Panamá, inspecting those few defences which the city had and leading his people in devotional exercises in the great cathedral. The enemy might come, but it would never be said that he had neglected any necessary precaution, sacred or profane. On the morning after he received the news, he wrote a reply to the letter which Pedro de Ulloa had sent him through Darien warning him of the enemy's intentions.[11] He apologized that he, too, had no money to pay his troops and so could not help the poor soldiers of Cartagena. Then, bluntly, he told his colleague along the coast the terrible news. 'The enemy has taken the castle of Chagres which was garrisoned with more than 350 men. . . I have 400 men on the Chagres river. I am with the rest, about 1000 men, waiting for news of the enemy's movements, in order to go out to meet him, when we will do everything possible up to dying.' He begged Ulloa to send any ships which were in Cartagena to come and attack the privateer fleet – a hopeless request, as we have seen. The letter closes with a prayer, a prayer which came straight from Don Juan's pious and courageous heart. 'God, who watches us with eyes of pity, give me victory over these heretical dogs.'

That heretical dog, Colonel Joseph Bradley, was lying in San Lorenzo Castle, dying of the wounds that he sustained in the assault. Many more of the seventy-six other wounded privateers were also destined to die, as their wounds festered in the fly-blown heat, and thirty men had been killed outright in the fight. Casualties of over a quarter in their first action boded ill for the survivors who still had to fight their way up the river and into the city of Panamá itself, before they could hope for any plunder. But it was no good having morbid thoughts. There was still no sign of Morgan, and so his old colleague, Captain Richard Norman, styled 'Major' for this land-based campaign, took command of the castle. There was much to do. The privateers would have to garrison the castle and garrison it well, lest it be retaken and their passage home from the isthmus blocked. But, first, a considerable part of the landward side of the castle had to be rebuilt. The fit privateers laboured alongside the slaves they had brought from Santa Catalina or captured in the village of Chagres.

San Lorenzo

Fresh timbers were cut to replace the burned-out palisades and the earth was again packed between them, but the privateers thought it wise not to replace the palm-leaf thatch that had once sheltered the walls from the sun and rain.

The work was nearly completed when, on 12 January, five days after the capture of the castle, the main privateer fleet was signalled. The thirty-three privateer ships, with *Satisfaction* in the van, were a welcome sight, and the castle's new garrison cheered as they sailed in towards the mouth of the river where Bradley's three ships now lay anchored near the waterside fortifications. The incoming privateers cheered in their turn as they saw the English flag flying in the stiff breeze and their colleagues lining the walls. As the ships drew closer, the watchers waited to see which side they would sail round the Laja Reef which lay in waiting, covered by a few feet of water, just outside the river's mouth. To their horror, *Satisfaction* came straight on and hit the reef with an almighty crash which brought her masts and yards tumbling down and flung several of those standing waving on the deck into the choppy sea. Four more ships followed *Satisfaction* on to the reef, before the sixth ship in the line saw the danger and put her helm down. Two ships had already been lost on the reefs of Santa Catalina, and such incidents make one wonder just how competent the seamanship of the privateers was. They certainly knew their way around the Caribbean; every creek and rocky cove seems to have been familiar to them. They certainly knew how to navigate, despite the enormous difficulties of determining one's longitude before the invention of a reliable chronometer. But they seem to have been very careless, despite the presence on board of many qualified seamen, and one wonders sometimes if they were not particularly interested in the ships which they acquired so easily from the Spaniards and which they only used to transport their men from place to place, so that they could exercise their martial arts on firm ground. The results of Morgan's 'ill fortune to be cast away', as he put it,[12] had no real effect on the success or otherwise of his campaign. None of the five ships was recovered. The wind was blowing hard across the reef, and they were shattered to pieces. No doubt the privateers thought that they could soon find other ships if they needed them. The important thing was that most of the stores and nearly all the men were saved. But ten men were drowned, 'ye sea running very high', and so was the only woman in the fleet, if we can believe our Indian cook.[13] Morgan would have to make do without a witch from now on.

Morgan spent a week at San Lorenzo, putting the finishing touches to the restoration of the defences which had been begun by Norman. He had been informed that a large contingent of Spaniards was making its way overland in an attempt to retake the castle and he would have been foolish to expect anything less. Norman was left in command of three hundred men to garrison the castle and look after the ships, while Morgan prepared to venture into the interior with the remainder, whom he said in his report were 1400 men but were probably rather more. On 19 January 1671, he set off up the Chagres with seven of the smaller ships from the fleet, packed with men and guns, and thirty-six boats and canoes. Norman watched them as they sailed up the first broad, straight reach of the river and then lost sight of them as they turned round a bend and vanished into the forests of the isthmus of Panamá.

CHAPTER SIXTEEN

The River Campaign

THE MAN whose job it was to stop Morgan coming up the River Chagres was Francisco Gonzalez Salado, a forty-year-old native of Cadiz and a former Castellan of Santiago Castle.[1] He had been captain of the river during Morgan's capture of Portobello and was the obvious choice for the same post when his new threat to the isthmus became imminent. He had organized the construction of four stockades on the banks of the river and had just under four hundred men with which to garrison them, in addition to another company in reserve at Venta de Cruces, the head of navigation. This might seem a small number with which to check the advance of some 1500 privateers, especially since Gonzalez' men were poorly armed, having only 210 firearms, 114 lances and 69 bows and arrows between them. However, the nature of the country could well make up for small numbers. Nearly all of Gonzalez' men were negroes, half-castes and Indians who knew the jungles of the isthmus well and were thus well equipped to take advantage of the numerous opportunities for ambush in the densely forested, and in places nearly impenetrable, country through which Morgan would have to travel. A small, well-led force might well check the privateers' advance and make life so unpleasant for them that many, if not all, would lose heart and turn back to rejoin their ships. Crossing the isthmus of Panamá was a difficult enough task for strangers even when they faced no determined opposition.

Gonzalez was at his advance post of Dos Brazos, well down-river from all the stockades, when he first heard the sound of cannon-fire at San Lorenzo and realized that the enemy had landed. He sent fifty men forward to see if they could reinforce the garrison but, on the way, they met the wounded fleeing from the castle and returned to Gonzalez at Dos Brazos, who sent a report to Don Juan in Panamá, telling him what had happened. Gonzalez then retired upstream to

Barro Colorado, the first and strongest of his stockades, where he was when he received the news of the final fall of the castle. He left Captain Luis de Castillo in command and retired farther upstream to Barbacoas, the last of his stockades, telling the men at each stockade as he passed to go down to Barro Colorado, which he had decided to reinforce with all the men under his command. The other posts could be filled up with men whom he hoped that the President would send across country to help him. Gonzalez himself remained at Barbacoas, a long way from his men and even farther from the enemy. Barbacoas, he said, was a convenient post for distributing orders and people.

When Don Juan first heard of the loss of San Lorenzo, his immediate reaction was to take his whole army down to Venta de Cruces, link up with Gonzalez and fight the privateers on the river. This was what the President of Panamá had done the last time that the English had captured San Lorenzo, and it seemed to many people that such a precedent was as good a reason as any to do it again. However, the President was persuaded against this scheme by people who knew the river well and pointed out that it would be perfectly feasible for the privateers, who were almost certain to have good guides, to by-pass the main river by turning off at Dos Brazos and coming up a tributary called the River Gatun, from which they could easily get to Panamá and sack the city behind Don Juan's back. Don Juan agreed that this was a risk that he dared not take and ordered that just two companies should go down to Venta de Cruces to serve under Gonzalez, while he with the rest of the Panamá army would shortly march to Guayabal, a high plateau some ten miles from Venta de Cruces from which he could cover the enemy's advance whichever way he chose to approach Panamá.

Don Juan was, however, reluctant for his men simply to stand and wait for the enemy. All that he knew at the moment was that the English had landed, three or four hundred strong, and had then lost a lot of men in capturing the castle. It seemed quite possible that a strong and determined relief force could retake it. As his counsel was to say later, 'they expected there to be the same men in the castle who had taken it. No one expected that a pirate, by himself alone, would have been able to bring such a numerous army.'[2] Three captains, two mestizo brothers and a negro, who were in Panamá gaol on an unknown charge, volunteered to lead this relief force to clear their names. All three men were natives of the Chagres river and so could be expected not to get lost. Don Juan accepted their proposal and arranged for a lieutenant who had formerly served in San Lorenzo Castle to accompany them. They took 150 men from Panamá and their orders were to go across country to the river, collect 150 more men from Gonzalez' command and then march down the river, where they were either to engage the enemy as he was coming up or, if he had not yet made a move, to go on down to San Lorenzo and attempt to regain the castle.

Henry Morgan had only the vaguest idea of the dispositions of the enemy as he set off up the river from San Lorenzo on 19 January 1671.[3] His fleet of small ships, boats and canoes had little trouble the first day as they sailed and paddled up the broad tree-lined river and anchored at Dos Brazos for the night. Many men went ashore here to forage, but found the Indian huts and plantation houses deserted. The population had fled before them, taking all their possessions. Morgan's scouts failed to notice the relief force from Panamá who had halted just outside Dos Brazos and had watched with amazement as the huge flotilla came into sight round a bend in the river. No one had told them that there would be 1500 or 2000 privateers to fight. It was a time for discretion.

Don Juan reported their reaction. 'They met the enemy coming up the river at Dos Brazos (which is six leagues from the castle) and they neither fought with them nor did more than flee to the mountains, without trying either of the two things that they had promised.'[4] *Alferez* Marcos Salmon, who was a member of this force, understandably saw things in a different light. Their sentries reported that the enemy was coming up the river and, since they had orders to get ahead of the enemy and make an ambush, they paid an Indian guide to take them through the mountains across a bend in the river, so that they could get well upstream of the privateers. But, unfortunately, 'he misled them by a bad path and they were detained'.[5] Whatever the truth – and one suspects that Don Juan had it – they struck no blow at the enemy and their wanderings in the mountains removed three hundred much-needed men from the defence.

Henry Morgan had no knowledge of the mental anguish that his very presence was causing to the leaders of the relief force. He set sail next day quite oblivious of the fact that he had even been seen by the enemy. Progress was now slower, and Morgan began to realize that the dry season, which had made the firing of San Lorenzo so easy, might cause some problems on the river. His guides told him that the water was low, and he could see for himself the exposed roots of mangroves under the banks and huge snags of rotting tree trunks which had been washed down in the previous rains and now made jagged and dangerous barriers, stuck into the mud and sandbanks in the middle of the river.

Still, progress could be made and, while the helmsmen laboured to avoid the snags and sandbanks, those privateers who were interested in such things could admire the scenery of the valley of the River Chagres, scenery which has now vanished for ever under the waters of the lake formed by the making of the Panamá Canal.[6] Dense forest stretched away into the distance on either side of the narrowing river, the monotony of the greens and browns occasionally enlivened by the sudden burst of colour of the gorgeous scarlet passion-flower, now in full bloom. The forest of palm and bamboo, mahogany and lignum-vitae was dominated by the huge cedar-trees from which the Indians made their dugout canoes, their trunks soaring up without a branch for a hundred feet and supporting canopies of foliage often fifty yards in diameter. Wildlife was abundant – schools of monkeys swinging and chattering through the trees, the brilliant plumage of parrots and humming-birds, the alligators and iguanas, the sudden dive as a heron saw another fish. Nearer to hand were less pleasant things, for the Chagres is a terrible river for mosquitoes and sandflies, while in the woods were all sorts of nasty creatures – tarantulas and scorpions, wood-ticks and jiggers, huge red and black ants, snakes and centipedes – ready to make life miserable for any man who went ashore to scout for ambushes or forage for food. The forest and the river were a riot of colour, noise and life. The only creature who was rarely seen was man. Occasionally, an Indian would peer out from the river bank and glide away again through the trees. But there were no soldiers, no bullets – nothing to stop the privateers' progress but the river itself.

On the morning of the fourth day, 22 January, their guides warned them that they were close to Barro Colorado, the first of the Spanish stockades. Morgan sent a strong party ashore to test the strength of this barrier to their further progress. The privateers crept through the undergrowth to the clearing in front of the stockade and then, with a great cheer, rushed up to the chest-high wooden palisading which they swarmed over, only to discover that there was no one there to defend it. 'The enemy had basely quitted it and sett it on fire.' No food, no weapons, nothing of any interest at all had been left behind. Judging by the embers, the enemy had been gone for two or three days. Where had they gone? Where was Captain Luis de Castillo and the men who had been left to guard this vital advanced defence post?

The men at Barro Colorado had been very miserable when Gonzalez left them and retired up-river. Their numbers had been considerably reduced in order to bolster the abortive relief force, and there were only 216 men, thirty of whom had succumbed to the endemic malaria of the river. They had no cannon and only 130 firearms between them and, although they were protected by stockades, they felt very vulnerable. Captain Luis de Castillo had been given command simply because he was the first captain to arrive there. He does not seem to have been a man of great resolution and, from the beginning, resented his exposed position so far down the river. On several occasions he sent letters up-river to Gonzalez, reporting that his men were extremely 'discontented' and asking permission to retire. Gonzalez replied that on no account must he retreat from his post, but he never came down to give the men the moral support that they so badly needed. Finally, Captain Castillo took matters into his own hands. His sentries and canoe patrols reported that the enemy had now begun to ascend the river and that they had two frigates, two river-boats, two launches with artillery and twenty-seven or thirty canoes with a very large number of men. Understandably, Castillo, with just 216 men, lost his nerve. At midnight, he called a *junta* of the other officers at the stockade – an action totally contrary to Spanish military law. A captain had no right to call a *junta*. He had no right to 'do anything except obey the orders of his superior officer'.[7] But Spanish military law meant very little to Captain Castillo and his brother officers at dead of night in the middle of the jungle with the privateers moving rapidly up-stream to overwhelm them. They were quite simply scared stiff. The *junta* decided to burn the stockade, their huts and all the stores that they could not carry and retreat at dawn. They informed Gonzalez of their agreement and he made no attempt to stop them.

The Spaniards might have decided not to impede the privateers' progress, but the river was not so kind. It was now so cluttered up with snags and so low in places that the seven small ships could go no farther. From now onwards, most of the men would have to take 'to the wild woods' and walk, while the lighter-draught canoes would be all that was available to carry 'necessaries'. It was difficult to know just what was necessary for the journey of unknown duration and unknown hardship that lay before them. Morgan took all the weapons and ammunition, of course, but in order to lighten the men's loads he left the food behind with Captain Robert Delander, who was to remain at Barro Colorado with a guard of two hundred men for the ships. Food seemed no problem to Morgan. They had come about a third of the way to Panamá. There was only another fifty or sixty miles to go. The jungle and the Spaniards would supply them with the food they needed.

Marching through the wild woods was no fun. There was no more of the easy and pleasant, if slow, progress of the first three days. The jungle which had looked so attractive from the river was no pleasure at all on close inspection. There were 'no paths for 24 myles but what wee cutt'. Most of the privateers tried to keep close to the river and the canoes, hacking their way through bramble and thorn, cane-brakes and mangroves, and through great enshrouding webs of creepers, sometimes so dense that they formed a huge roof over the forest, underneath which individual trees could not be seen through the close-woven webs. Other men soon tired of the endless bends of the river which travels two or three times as far as the direct route. They tired, too, of the endless tributaries, each with its plank bridge broken by the retreating Spaniards. They tried to find overland routes across the bends, only to get lost in the impenetrable undergrowth or find their way barred by swamps. Progress was very, very slow.

Such labour made men hungry, but where was all the game that they had been able to see from the river? Where were the wild hogs and deer, the grouse and wild turkey with which the forests and mountains of the Chagres valley were said to abound? Where were the monkeys whom they had seen swinging through the trees and whose flesh was supposed to be so delicate, even if they did look rather like little boys after they had been skinned? Where were the iguanas, so 'eagerly sought for by the natives for its flesh which is tender and delicate as a chicken'?[8] The privateers saw none of these delicacies. The noise they made, as over a thousand men crashed and hacked their way through the never-ending undergrowth, had driven all the game away for miles around. They were left in the ironic position of nearly starving in a game-rich jungle, they who were the best shots in the West Indies and had spent much of their lives hunting in the forests of Jamaica and Hispaniola.

Sometimes the going was easier and the privateers were able to march on both sides of the river, six abreast through high grass between the trees, with their colleagues in the canoes paddling between them. But there was still no food. The privateers now looked forward eagerly to the possibility of an ambush. Only then would they have food. Each time they got to one of the stockades, their hungry hopes rose high and they 'got ready for the fight with as much zeal and joy as if they had been invited to a wedding feast'.[9] Their eyes lit up at the thought of the banquet of Spanish provisions which would follow the fight. They came to Tornomarcos and then to Caño Quebrado and finally to Barbacoas, but each time it was the same. The privateers raced forward to seize the post, only to find it deserted, the stockade and huts burned down and not a scrap of food or drink to be found.

Gonzalez had decided that his men were incapable of defending the stockades and had ordered Castillo to burn them as he marched up the river and then join him at the upstream post of Barbacoas. When they arrived, Gonzalez promptly called another *junta* at which it was decided to retreat still farther to the head of navigation at Venta de Cruces. Here they would make a stand. Gonzalez wrote to Don Juan justifying his decision on the grounds that his men were 'useless, discontented and afraid',[10] epithets which one fears are as easily applied to himself. Don Juan wrote later that there was no other reason for the decision of this second *junta*, 'except the fear that oppressed them'.[11] In some sort of attempt to redeem himself, Gonzalez remained at Barbacoas with three priests and four comrades for a couple of days. But, on the second night, an Indian patrol came in and reported that the enemy would be at Barbacoas the next morning, 'and so, seeing that he could make no resistance, he retreated to Venta de Cruces, a place marked out by the President as one where they could make a stand'.[12] Before we condemn Gonzalez and Castillo too much, we should perhaps consider the opinion of Don Antonio de Córdoba, a former Lieutenant-General of Horse in the Army of Flanders, who inspected the whole terrain of the Panamá campaign a year later. 'The river is very wide and the enemy was able to march on both sides with their boats in the middle, in such good order that even the most experienced soldiers would have had a job to resist them.'[13] Gonzalez and Castillo were certainly not experienced, nor were any of their men, but one still feels that they should at least have made a token resistance to the privateers' advance.

Cowardice and fear might be the motives for the rapid Spanish withdrawal, but it did have considerable military value. As Morgan's men were drawn into the centre of the isthmus, they were getting hungrier and hungrier and so less able to engage in the ferocious fighting for which they were famous. They did what they could to find food, but the Spaniards had been very thorough. In one place they ate some empty leather provision-bags which had been left behind. In another they found a small barn which a careless planter had left full of maize when he fled. 'At once the barn was demolished, and each man took all the maize his hands could hold and devoured it on the spot.'[14] Such desperate rations did not go very far and, by the end of the second day after they left their boats, the privateers were already getting weak with hunger, weak and exhausted from the labour of cutting their way along the river bank. These carnivores were now reduced to eating grass and leaves, their clothes plucked to ribbons by the grasping thorns and creepers, their boots and feet a constant reminder of the harshness of the going and a happy haven for the ticks and jiggers of the forest. They were no longer a fearsome sight, more like a rabble struggling to keep going, some already beginning to curse Morgan for bringing them this way, some silent and plodding, still keyed up inside by the thought of Panamá and loot. But still there was no one to oppose them or even to observe them, except the occasional Indian patrol on their flanks.

On Sunday, 25 January, the third day of the march and the sixth

The River Campaign

since they had left San Lorenzo, they had nearly got to the normal head of navigation at Venta de Cruces. Here they felt certain that they would find resistance and, after they had defeated it, food. Their anticipation was further aroused by their first ambush, which they encountered just outside the village in 'a very narrow and dangerous passe'. The enemy were easily driven away by the vanguard, but it seemed that Venta de Cruces was to be defended and the privateers prepared for the assault, cleaning their weapons and 'firing off their muskets to make sure they would be in good order when they went into action'.[15]

Their hopes were to be dashed once more. When they got close to the village at midday, they could see great plumes of smoke rising and, as they rushed in, they found that all the buildings had been fired except the King's custom-house and stables, which no one had dared put to the torch. Venta de Cruces, where the captain of the river, Francisco Gonzalez Salado, had planned to make his great stand against the enemy, had been deserted on his orders the previous night. Gonzalez and his men were masters of the scorched-earth policy and, if he had only taken advantage of the enemy's weakness, one would have nothing but admiration for his strategy of continuous retreat. He had left very little in Venta de Cruces, but what he had left was absolutely perfect if he had planned to turn Morgan's once remarkably well-disciplined army into a desperately weak and disorderly rabble. There was no food, except for a few stray dogs which the privateers shot and ate. But, in the royal custom-house, there were sixteen jars of Peruvian wine, which Morgan's men immediately broached and began to drink. The effect on men who, for three days, had eaten either nothing or a revolting mixture of leather, leaves and raw maize was predictable. Some got drunk, but most got very sick and decided that the Spaniards had poisoned the wine.

Morgan must have had doubts about the success of his venture as he looked at his miserable men, reeling and puking in this 'very fine village', some two-thirds of the way across the isthmus. It had taken him six days to cover some fifty miles, six more days for the Spaniards to prepare an army which must be standing to arms somewhere ahead of him. Would his men still be able to fight? But there was really no turning back. He must press on, now leaving the narrow, shallow river to his left, and march the remaining twenty-five miles along the well-used mule-track to Panamá, hoping and praying that he would be able to find some food on the way. He rested his men for the remainder of that Sunday and set off the following morning, having sent all the canoes back down-river, except for one which remained at Venta de Cruces to provide a means of communication. There was no way for the faint-hearted to retreat.

The country had been getting hillier ever since they left the ships at Barro Colorado, with several high peaks visible above the trees on the left-hand side of the river. Now, as they left the river, the scenery became more dramatic with lofty conical mountains on both sides. The road went through rolling, luxuriant woodland and occasionally through deep ravines between the hills. A perfect place for ambushes, and ambushes there were to be in plenty during the morning of Monday, 26 January as the privateers, still sick and hungry, marched on. Don Juan had sent over four hundred men to ambush this road, three hundred Indian archers, including a hundred of the faithful Darien Indians who had volunteered to come and die for their beloved President, and a hundred musketeers under the command of Joseph de Prado, the negro captain from the castle of San Lorenzo.[16]

This 'invisible foe', hidden behind the trees and rocks, seemed far larger in number to the privateers and caused them some trouble with their 'ambuscadoes and small partys'. In the worst place, where the road was 'so narrow that wee could but march 4 abreast and such a deep hollow that the enemy lay over our heads',[17] they lost three men killed and six or seven wounded but, on the whole, as Don Juan later admitted, the ambushes were not very successful. The privateers might be in a very poor physical condition, but they were still aware that they were marching through a very dangerous part of enemy country. The men kept going and there were few stragglers, and Morgan was able to maintain extremely good discipline. Two hundred of the fittest and best-equipped privateers scouted ahead as a skirmishing line with their eyes open for Indians and likely spots for ambushes. Behind them, the rest of the army marched, with a wing of skirmishers on each side who were able to cut off each ambush as they came to it and force the Indians and musketeers to retreat with little damage to themselves. One band of Indians did stand their ground and fight, until at last their chief fell wounded. 'Yet even then he tried to rise and run a privateer through the body with his spear – but was shot before he could land the blow, and fell amid three or four other Indian dead.'[18] But such bravery was exceptional, and the privateers made much faster progress than they had along the river, despite the occasional skirmish. At noon they were out of the woods and came on to the grassland of the savannah where there was less danger of surprise attack. Morgan marched three miles farther 'and then took up our quarters to refresh our men and thank them for that daye's service'.[19] Refreshment still did not include food. The privateers had now marched for four days without a meal, and as they sank down to rest themselves they must have wondered if they would ever eat again.

On Tuesday, 27 January they started early to avoid the worst of the sun, which was much hotter now that they had crossed the watershed of the isthmus. Spanish horsemen watched them as they marched across the savannah, but gave them no resistance. At nine, the vanguard breasted a hill and, to their joy, 'saw that desired place, the South Sea'. They could still not see the city, but in the bay towards Perico they could see a galleon and five or six coasting craft and they knew that at last they were near their goal. The joy increased still further when they descended the hill on the other side and came out on a plain covered with horses and cattle which the Spaniards had failed to drive away. 'I commanded a general halt to bee made,' reports Morgan, 'and our men did kill horses and beefe enough to serve them all.' Exquemelin describes the break of their enforced fast more dramatically. 'At once they broke ranks and shot down every beast within range. All got busy: while some hunted, others lit fires to roast the meat. One gang of men dragged in a bull, another a cow, a third a horse or a mule. The animals were hacked up and thrown, dripping with blood, on to the fire to cook. The meat scarcely had time to get hot before they grabbed it and began gnawing, gore running down their cheeks.'[20] Leaving this herd of cattle on the savannah was the worst mistake that the Spaniards made. Gorged with the rarest of rare beef, the privateers needed a couple of hours for digestion and then they were ready to fight. Morgan let them rest through the midday heat and then, about four, they were fit to march off again, now in the very best of tempers with their goal so near before them.

Soon they could see the tiled roofs and spires and the great square tower of the cathedral of Panamá itself. Between them and the city was a small problem, 'the enemy where hee lay in battalia'. But would the Spaniards be able to stop them now? They had conquered the jungle and the river. They had conquered and then assuaged their hunger. Now all they had to do was to fight to win their prize. 'They gave three cheers and threw their caps into the air for joy, as if they had already gained the victory. It was decided to sleep there, and march down on Panamá in the morning. They pitched camp on the plain, and began to beat the drums and blow the trumpets and wave their flags, as if at a celebration.'[21]

CHAPTER SEVENTEEN

The Defence of the City

THE FEAST of San Pablo Ermitaño, which fell on 10 January, was always an important day in the social and religious life of Panamá.[1] It was the anniversary of the defeat of Sir Thomas Baskerville, Drake's lieutenant, who had led the last attempt to capture the city in 1596 and had been gloriously defeated. Now, seventy-five years later, the fiesta was celebrated with particular solemnity. Once again, the English pirates were on the attack. They had already captured the castle of San Lorenzo and could soon be expected to begin the ascent of the River Chagres. Don Juan prayed hard for guidance and inspiration and wished that he had in his service those reinforcements from Peru which had made such a difference in 1596. He prayed, too, for an improvement in his health, lest purely human weakness should hamper him in the performance of his duty. But his prayers were not answered, and soon he was back in bed again. The bad news and the efforts that he had made to awaken a spirit of optimism in the city had taken their toll, as the doctors had predicted, and his condition was now much worse. A very painful erysipelas developed – St Anthony's fire, as it was often called – and a large tumour broke out on his right breast. The President's temperature was very high, and the doctors shook their heads as they bled him three more times.[2] Don Juan, unable to walk a step, remained in bed.

The President was still in great pain, very weak and feverish, when on 20 January he received the news that the enemy had begun to sail up the River Chagres the day before. Now he knew that he was needed in person and insisted on getting up. Better that he should die facing the enemy than in his bed. He paid for masses to be sung for success in war and arranged for there to be a solemn procession of monks and nuns, who progressed around the city with their holy images and relics while the whole penitent population followed devoutly behind them. Don Juan then mounted his horse and rode out of the city, followed by every able-bodied man who could bear arms. Many men were already ahead of him, on the stockades of the river, in Venta de Cruces or engaged in the abortive relief force which had gone down towards San Lorenzo, but he managed to muster another eight hundred men, mainly Indians, negroes and half-castes, but including practically all the Spaniards left in the city, ready to do again to Morgan what their ancestors had done to Sir Thomas Baskerville. Lawyers, scribes and merchants rode alongside their President and Captain-General as the sick man struggled to stay upright on his horse in the van. In the rear trudged three hundred negro slaves who were brought out with their over-seers to do any hard work which had to be done, such as digging ditches and building palisades.

Don Juan pitched camp at Guayabal, sixteen miles from Panamá and ten from Venta de Cruces, a village where he believed he could intercept the privateers whichever way they came and described by a witness as 'an elevated place and a suitable site to give battle'.[3] Don Juan remained here for three days, a period during which he received nothing but bad news. First, he heard of the failure of the relief force which he had sent down-river under the three former convicts. Then he heard of the desertion of the stockade at Barro Colorado by Captain Castillo and his garrison, and then of the desertion of all the other stockades in rapid succession. The President was very upset. Don Juan de Aras, the Chaplain of the Audiencia and a man who was also, rather surprisingly, an expert in fortifications, had inspected the stockades and had assured the President that the river was so well provided with ambushes and defences that 'it would not help the enemy to enter the castle, since in the river we would be certain of victory'.[4] When Gonzalez and Castillo came to Guayabal to report in person, they got very short shrift. Castillo was immediately put on a charge for retiring from his post without orders, while Gonzalez, who had asked to be relieved of his command because of illness, seems to have been completely cold-shouldered by his former patron.

No one yet had very definite information about the enemy's strength. The defenders of the river had retreated long before they had a chance to find out. But, on Friday, 23 January, the first day of the privateers' struggle on foot up the river bank, Don Juan began to get much more definite but not totally accurate information. Gonzalez' *ayudante* and namesake, Don Simon Gonzalez, reported that he had gone down-river with an Indian patrol and had seen the enemy marching by land with their canoes beside them in the river. He told Don Juan that the enemy would sleep that night in Barbacoas and would be in Venta de Cruces the following day – a slight exaggeration of the privateers' rate of progress. It was not one day but two days later that they got to Venta de Cruces. Later, on that same Friday, there arrived a letter from the negro, Captain Prado, saying that the privateers were marching up the river with over two thousand men – an exaggeration of about one-third in their actual numbers. Since none of the patrols had taken a single privateer prisoner, Don Juan was not able to discover anything about the enemy's morale. If he had known how hungry they already were, and if his imagination could have conceived how hungry and weak they would be by the time they reached Venta de Cruces, the whole campaign might well have taken a very different turn and there might have been a new day to celebrate in the Panamá church calendar.

Don Juan's immediate reaction when he heard that the enemy was clearly committed to coming up the main course of the River Chagres was to go straight over to Venta de Cruces and wait for them. It was obvious that he was going to have to fight Morgan somewhere and, as the Treasurer of Panamá put it, 'we could do more in an hour on the river than we could in a whole day anywhere else'.[5] But there were not many who agreed with this opinion. The rich and important citizens who had ridden out of Panamá with the President were worried about their property. They were worried that, even now, the enemy might cut them off from the city and sack it before they had even had a chance to fight for it. What the army should do was to retire to Panamá and fortify the city against the privateers' attack. The rank and file of Don Juan's army had no property to protect. The main trouble with them was that the news of two thousand battle-hardened pirates coming up the river had filled them with fear and they were beginning to look around for ways to slip off without their officers noticing.

That evening a *junta* was held to discuss the situation. Don Juan spoke eloquently for either staying where they were or advancing to

Venta de Cruces to face the enemy. Panamá was an open city, he
said, and impossible to fortify in the short time available. Some men
agreed, but the majority were determined to retreat to look after the
wealth that they had managed to accumulate during their service in
America. The final decision was shelved for the night but, in the
morning, Don Juan found that it had been made for him. The army
of Panamá had voted with its feet. Only a third of the eight hundred
men were left in the morning, nearly all of whom were coloured
militia. Practically all the Spaniards had fled back to Panamá in the
night. 'When Saturday, 24 January dawned,' wrote Don Juan ruefully in his report, 'I found myself with two-thirds less men through
the fear which had infested them, so that I *had* to retreat to Panamá.'[6]
All that he could do was to arrange for some of the troops, who were
still out in advance of the remnant of his army, to set ambushes on
the road between Venta de Cruces and the savannah. Everyone else
was ordered to return to Panamá to defend the city. The whole,
well-tried policy of engaging an invader as far as possible from the
city had collapsed. Don Juan remounted and rode sadly back to
Panamá, where he arrived that Saturday night to find that the
citizens were already attempting to improve their defences with
flour-bags and wooden barricades across the streets.

Don Juan still thought it was hopeless to try to barricade himself in
the city. There were no walls and very few guns. Many of those
which were usually in Panamá, together with all the best gunners,
had been sent to reinforce San Lorenzo. The only way left to protect
the city was to fight and win a battle on the level savannah outside it.
They should have fought on the river or at Venta de Cruces or at
Guayabal. But fate and the weakness of men had been against them.
Now, with their backs to their city, the citizens of Panamá would at
last have to fight, and their President would inspire them with the
courage to do so.

On the morning of Sunday, 25 January, Don Juan went to Mass in
the cathedral where he received the Communion with great devotion. He then went out into the plaza and, before a great crowd, read
out a proclamation. 'That all those who were true Spanish Catholics,
defenders of the Faith and devotees of Our Blessed Lady of the
Conception should follow my person, being that day, at four o'clock
in the afternoon, resolved to march out to seek the enemy and defend

her purity until we lose our lives. And that he who should refuse to follow me should be held as infamous and a coward in so basely slighting so precise an obligation.'[7] Don Juan had correctly judged the mood of the citizens of Panamá. The proclamation so moved the people that everyone came out into the great plaza to cheer the President and swear that they would follow him into battle.

As an earnest of his devotion, Don Juan now shared out all his worldly wealth between the churches and convents of the city. It was a truly noble gesture and, to the cynic, an interesting reflection of the fortune that a relatively poor man could accumulate in a few years as President of Panamá. The total paid out for jewels, vestments, masses and other types of devotional expenditure, according to his defence counsel and the accounts scrupulously kept by the religious houses, was 28,450 pesos, some £7000, a very reasonable fortune in 1671. The major recipients were the nuns of the Convent of Our Lady of the Conception, the patroness of the city, who received 9000 pesos in jewels, rich vestments, payments for processions, sung masses and masses to be said for success in war. The vestments were of silk or cloth of gold or of the finest white wool and linen embroidered with flowers made of gold thread and hemmed with silver and pearls. The jewels were equally magnificent – a huge pectoral pendant of diamonds, a necklace of diamonds and rubies, an imperial crown of beaten gold. The other convents were not neglected. The Dominicans received a massively rich necklace of Colombian emeralds worth 1500 pesos and a great chain of gold for the Virgin of the Rosary to wear on the days when the images were taken out in processions. The Franciscans received diamonds and jewels worth 1200 pesos and a large sum for masses. No one was forgotten. Even the Jesuits received a diamond ring each for San Ignacio and San Miguel Arcangelo and a staff with a gold head set with diamonds for St Michael to carry in processions.[8] Thus did the President seek 'the favour of God by means of his Saints'.[9] If Morgan could have seen what Don Juan handed out that day, the day that his men were recuperating from the effects of the wine in Venta de Cruces, he would have had no doubt that he was doing the right thing in pressing on to Panamá. It was a paradise for a robber.

At the appointed hour of four in the afternoon, Don Juan went again to the cathedral and, kneeling before the now beautifully bejewelled and robed statue of the Virgin, he swore to die in her defence 'and everyone else did the same with great fervour and devotion'.[10] He then donned his arms and rode out of the city to a place called Mata Asnillos, about a mile outside, where the road from Venta de Cruces crossed a broad plain. Here he made camp and awaited the arrival of the privateers. In the city behind him, preparations for defence continued. The streets were barricaded as well as they could be and the few guns were placed facing the road by which the enemy would come if the trial by battle were lost.

On Monday the city began to empty. Most of the men were with Don Juan at Mata Asnillos, while the women and children, nuns and other religious, made preparations to leave by sea. With them went their recent gifts of jewels and vestments and much of the private wealth of the city. Don Juan had been reluctant to give permission for this evacuation, which clearly had an appalling effect on the morale of his army. 'If the city had been walled, he would never have given the citizens permission to take out any silver at all,' pleaded Don Francisco Jaymes, the President's defence counsel at his later trial, 'but because it was indefensible and because everything had to be ventured on the moment of peril of one battle, it would not have been good policy to obstruct the citizens in getting their wealth away'.[11] Down at the port of Perico, people were getting ships ready to sail if the city fell. Amongst them was Francisco Gonzalez Salado, the rapidly retreating captain of the river, who claimed later that he spent a thousand pesos out of his own pocket buying food for the nuns. There, too, was Antonio de Silva, Don Juan's secretary, taking the President's papers to safety. They had orders to seize all the boats from the city and from the bay in order to prevent the enemy from taking to the sea if he should capture Panamá.

Out at Mata Asnillos, Don Juan's chosen site for the battle, there was a mood of anticlimax after the drama of the dedication in the cathedral and the march out of the city. There was also some dissension. There were those who said that the army should stand on a hill which rose on the right of the plain where the President had made camp. Otherwise there was a danger that the enemy might outflank them. But Don Juan insisted on remaining on the plain. He now had four hundred cavalry, the only real advantage he had over the privateers, and he thought that they would be very much more effective on level ground. There was also another reason. His infantry were desperately inexperienced and needed to be on the plain so that, at all times, they might see their leader on his horse in the vanguard and so be encouraged that they had not been deserted. Then there was the question of the artillery. Panamá had just three guns that were suitable for use in the field. Should they not be brought out of the city? Some said that, if they were brought out, the enemy would see them and attack from another direction. Some pointed out that they had only two competent gunners. Some fainthearts declared that, if the enemy captured them, the guns would do more harm to the Spaniards than they could ever do to the enemy. So, in the end, Don Juan's army had no artillery at all.

The army waited at Mata Asnillos through Sunday night and all of Monday and Tuesday. The numbers were rising all the time as latecomers arrived from the various abortive missions on the river and from farther afield. There was a great cheer as two hundred and fifty men of the militia of Veragua came in, led by their Governor, Juan Portuondo Burgueño, who was given command of the right wing. Other contingents came in from the scattered villages of the President's jurisdiction and soon it began to look quite an impressive army, in numbers if not in arms or military experience. There is no denying that morale was rather low, despite the dedication of so many people to the service of the Virgin. The continuous retreat since the loss of San Lorenzo had not been a very good idea.

Nevertheless, most men in the army were cheerful enough when the privateers first arrived in sight on the Tuesday evening. They did not look very prepossessing. The advance guard were only six hundred strong and they seem to have managed to bring some of that Peruvian wine with them in their flasks. They were not really very frightening as they capered about and sang drunken songs. 'Don Gomez,' said one Spaniard in a voice loud enough to be heard by the militiamen all around him. 'We have nothing to fear. There are no more than six hundred drunkards.'[12] Perhaps they were to be heroes after all. Perhaps they would be able to honour their pledge to the Virgin. But, as the rest of the privateers, more than as many again, marched in to join their comrades, hearts began to sink. Don Simon Gonzalez, the *ayudante* from the river, was heard to say that he had two good horses ready to fly and he advised everybody else to get their mules ready for the same purpose. Don Juan leaped up to restore morale. Don Simon, he said, was 'a chicken and an enemy spy'. He had discouraged everyone on the river and now he wanted to do the same on the battlefield. An officer was ordered to take Don Simon's sword, and he was escorted off the field to the public gaol, where he was put in irons.[13] But the damage was done. Too many people agreed in their hearts with what Don Simon had said, and the night of Tuesday, 27 January was not a happy one in the Spanish camp as the part-time soldiers waited fearfully for what the dawn would bring.

CHAPTER EIGHTEEN

The Battle for Panamá

THE DAY dawned fair on Wednesday, 28 January.[1] There was not a cloud in the sky as the sun came up behind the hills gently rising on the left of the privateers' camp and, although there was quite a stiff breeze blowing across their front, it promised to be a very hot day. First light showed that the enemy had not moved from their position of the night before. A great oblong of infantry, several men deep, was stretched across the plain, with horsemen before them and on their flanks. The road to Panamá stretched away to the south-east through the Spanish centre, and beyond could already be seen the roofs and towers of the city, just a quick battle away. Morgan's men had eaten before dawn, gnawing on the cold remnants of the beef they had slaughtered the day before, and they were in good heart. They had come a long way for this moment and, as Morgan reviewed his troops 'and a little incouraged them', he could see that these 'well-seasoned and experienced men' were not too bothered by the thought of the first pitched battle which most of them were to experience. What difference did it make if they did their fighting on a field of battle or in a city street? These men before them were only Spaniards and would soon run as their countrymen had so often run before. They stuck the remains of their meat in their pouches, patted their muskets, ran their fingers lovingly along the keen edges of their cutlasses and machetes, and waited for the order to move forward.

About seven o'clock, the privateers began their advance in four squadrons, one behind the other, their red and green banners and flags clearly visible to the Spaniards who awaited them on the plain a couple of miles away. Each squadron comprised three hundred men, according to Morgan, though the Spaniards thought their opponents' army was rather bigger, most estimates putting their numbers at about two thousand in all. The vanguard was led by Lawrence Prince and John Morris, two men whose recent exploits had left them full of confidence. Behind them came Morgan in command of what would become the right wing of the main body when they formed up in line. Then came Edward Collier in command of the left wing; and finally the rearguard, which was commanded by a newcomer, Colonel Bledry Morgan, 'a good old soldier' who had come out to Chagres in a sloop from Jamaica with a message for his namesake* from the Governor. We do not know what was in that message, but it is possible to guess that, apart from good wishes, it included a further admonishment to the Admiral to get a move on before diplomatic interference spoiled his grand design. We are at least assured by Henry Morgan's secretary that the letter 'gave no countermand at all'.[2] Jamaica still wanted its supposed enemies destroyed.

Don Juan had drawn up his army in what seemed the best formation to receive a frontal assault, in line across the road to Panamá with a hill on the right to protect his flank. He had about 1200 of what could politely be called infantry, in that they did not have horses. These men were divided into two 'double squadrons', the right commanded by the Governor of Veragua and the left by Don Alonzo de Alcaudete, an experienced soldier from the Portobello garrison whom Don Juan had asked to come and help him in his hour of need. The squadrons in fact overlapped in the middle, so that the effect was of a continuous formation of infantry, six deep and some two hundred yards long. Commanding the centre was the septuagenarian Sergeant-Major of Panamá, Juan Ximenez Salvatierra.

All Don Juan's army, with the exception of a few of the officers, were inexperienced militiamen. There were two or three hundred Spaniards and all the rest were black or coloured, 'people who never in their lives have seen bullets'.[3] Nearly everyone, except a few of the richer citizens who had their own weapons, was very poorly armed. Only about six hundred of the men had any firearms at all, and these were mainly arquebuses which could fire only about half the distance of the privateers' muskets, while those militiamen who were designated as 'pikemen' – in other words, anyone who had not got a gun – were armed with halberds, lances and bows and arrows. Don

---

* No relation, apparently.

Juan did the best that he could with the equipment to hand, putting the men with the better weapons on the flanks and in the centre and attempting to make sure that all the arquebus men were protected by pikemen. His instructions to the men were very explicit. No one was to move at the enemy's approach and then, when he was within range, 'the first three ranks should fire on their knees, and after this charge they should give place to the rear to come up and fire and that, although they should chance to see any fall dead or wounded, they should not quit their stations but to the last extremity observe these their orders'.[4] To expect untrained men to stand still under fire was rather optimistic, but Don Juan knew that, if they did not stand, there was only one way they were likely to run.

Don Juan reported later that, as the privateers approached, 'the army all appeared brisk and courageous, desiring nothing more than to engage',[5] but he himself probably had most confidence in his four squadrons of cavalry, comprising some four hundred horsemen altogether, who were guarding his flanks and waiting for the order to charge. The privateers had no pikes and, of course, no cavalry of their own, and a cavalry charge might well be able to break up their ordered advance and give even the most inexperienced infantry the encouragement to come in for the kill. In order to make the confusion of the enemy complete, Don Juan had prepared a secret weapon, 'a stratagem that hath been seldome or never heard of'. As the cavalry broke up the enemy vanguard, two great herds of oxen and bulls driven by fifty negro cowboys were to be stampeded into the privateers' rearguard and so force their main body on to the arquebuses, lances and bows and arrows of the Spanish infantry. Don Juan himself was a prominent figure as the enemy approached, an upright, proud leader on horseback, riding up and down the front of his army 'as if he had not been ill at all', encouraging his men and exhorting them to remember his orders and their vow to defend the Virgin or die in the attempt.

As the privateers got closer to the army of Panamá, Henry Morgan was able to make a better assessment of the situation. He was not to know that he was facing 'an army of greenhorns who have never seen the face of the enemy nor come to grips with him'.[6] For all he knew, these might be regular, well-trained troops. It was obvious that, even if a frontal assault was successful, he would lose a lot of men and might even be swept off the field by the cavalry, who looked very menacing with a whole plain in which to move. He could not afford to lose men, here on the shores of the Pacific with seventy miles of hostile jungle and mountain between his army and their only means of escape from the isthmus. However, it looked as though a frontal attack would not be necessary. The hill, which Don Juan thought was protecting his right flank, seemed to Morgan to be almost completely undefended. If he could once gain it, he could attack the flank of the army of Panamá on a narrow front where their cavalry and the bulk of their infantry would be of no value to them. The fact that he would then be facing west would be an added advantage, since both the wind and the early-morning sun would be in the enemy's eyes. He ordered the vanguard to wheel to the left, where they vanished into a gully from which they very easily captured the small hill. The other squadrons followed the vanguard at a short distance.

When the privateer vanguard re-emerged on to the right flank of Don Juan's army, they were temporarily isolated from Morgan's main body. Seeing what seemed a good opportunity, the two squadrons of cavalry on the Spanish right charged, only to be broken by the very accurate fire of the French sharpshooters in the vanguard. Each man picked off one of the leading horses, forcing the remainder to wheel to their right out of danger, where they galloped off harmlessly in the direction of Panamá. Only the cavalry commander kept coming, so violently and so fast that 'his careere could not be stopt till hee lost his life in the front rank of our vantguard'.[7]

This cavalry action was over in a moment. The Spanish infantry had still not moved from their positions. Suddenly, the men on the left wing of the Spanish army, some two or three hundred yards away from the privateers, started to break out of their ranks and rush forward across the front of the rest of the army. What had happened was that they had seen Morgan's men wheeling into the gully out of sight and had assumed that they were running from the field. 'Advance, advance, they are fleeing,' came the cry from the left, and nothing that Don Alonzo de Alcaudete could do would stop them breaking ranks in their excitement. As they ran forward, shrieking abuse and waving their lances and arquebuses in the air, they were totally out of the control of their officers, and Don Juan had no choice but to order the right wing to attack as well and try to make the most of the excitement. At least they were running towards the enemy – the first time that this had happened since the fall of San Lorenzo. Don Juan mounted his horse and, raising his staff of office high into the air, he cried out: 'Come on, boys; up and at them! There is no other remedy now but to conquer or die. Follow me!'[8]

Nothing could have suited Morgan better than a wild attack by untrained, poorly armed men totally out of control. The two squadrons of the main body, commanded by himself and Edward Collier, were now coming down the hill to join the vanguard. With the advantage of height, sun, wind and superior weapons, they made no mistake with their first volley, killing about a hundred of the first men to approach the hill and turning the Spanish attack into a rout. One volley was enough. 'Hardly did our men see some fall dead and others wounded,' reported Don Juan, 'but they turned their backs and fled and it was not possible to stop them.'

The President continued to advance slowly on horseback, his staff raised high as a sign that he was still in the field, a few faithful servants and a priest all that remained to assist in his final gesture of defiance and despair.

I found myself alone, but nevertheless went forward towards the enemy to comply with my word to the Virgin, which was to die in her defence. I held my staff high, like a mast, beside my face and they struck it with a bullet. God permitted them to kill many that were sheltering themselves behind my horse but, although no person ever passed through such a great number of bullets, God our Lord let me stay alive to endure the torment of giving Your Majesty the account of so great a disaster.

The priest, who had stayed with Don Juan, begged him to flee and save himself, as the battle was already lost. Don Juan twice sharply reprimanded him for seeking to prevent him from fulfilling his vow to the Virgin. 'But the third time he persisted, telling me that it was mere desperation to die in that manner, and not like a Christian. With that I retired, it being a miracle of the Virgin to bring me off safe from amidst so many thousand bullets.' As Don Juan rode despondently away, he was met by his surgeon, who had been amazed that he had been able to ride a horse at all. He, too, thought it was a miracle when he saw the President leave the field with the bullet which had struck his staff in his hand as a melancholy souvenir of the battle of Mata Asnillos.[9]

The army of Panamá was no more. The Spanish commanders had tried to stop the flight by shooting down some of their own deserters, but it was no good. A few men turned their faces to the enemy again, 'but they were so closely plied by our left wing, who could not engage at the first by reason of the hill, that the enemy's retreat came to plain running'.[10] Even the bulls and oxen proved to be of no value. Don Juan had given the cowboys the order to stampede the herds at the same time as he advanced against the enemy. But they were easily turned by the privateers and soon all that could be seen on the field of Mata Asnillos were men, horses, bulls and cattle running towards the city or the mountains with the privateers in close pursuit, slashing with their cutlasses and machetes at the laggards, killing, killing, killing men and even priests in the mad bloodlust that followed the excitement and the tension of the battle. By the time they had finished, some four or five hundred Spaniards, negroes, Indians and half-castes lay dead or wounded upon the field, a quarter of Don Juan's army. Just fifteen of the privateers had fallen. It was a very easy victory.

When asked the cause of such a terrible defeat, most Spanish witnesses said quite simply that it was 'the will of God and the greater strength of the enemy'. No individual was to blame. The latter point was elaborated by the distinguished soldier, Don Antonio de Córdoba. 'When the enemy arrived, sword in hand, with more than two thousand men, all of them soldiers and in sight of such a rich prize, it could easily be seen what the outcome would be.'[11] He may have exaggerated Morgan's numbers but we, who have followed the privateers' progress and seen the quality and nature of the Spanish defence, can hardly disagree with his verdict.

A rich prize! Indeed it was, and one that had been valiantly earned by Morgan and his men after their epic journey across the isthmus. They had succeeded where so many had failed. They had conquered where Baskerville and Drake had been defeated. The city of Panamá, 'one of the richest places in all America', lay open and undefended before them. Their bloodlust satisfied, they wiped their cutlasses and marched forward to claim their prize.

Don Balthasar Pau y Rocaberti was the Captain of Artillery of Panamá. He had not joined in the battle, for the simple reason that Don Juan's army had no guns. Instead, he had remained in the city and waited anxiously for the outcome. He had verbal orders from the President which would require a delicate sense of judgement to obey. If the army was defeated, he had been told, and if there was no hope of saving the city, he was to blow up the powder magazines and spike the guns.[12] Panamá would not provide Henry Morgan with the means to do any more damage. Don Balthasar waited, his fuse ready to be lit, the nails in the touch-holes of the cannon ready to be hammered home. When the moment came, he had no doubt of his duty. One look at the first desperate men fleeing from the field with the privateers in pursuit and he lit his match. Six miles away, in the port of Perico, the President's secretary heard the explosion and looked at his watch. It was nine o'clock in the morning, just two hours after Morgan had set out from his overnight camp.[13]

Morgan's men were pressing hard on the heels of the fugitives as they swarmed over the Matadero Bridge at the west end of the city and so past the Mercedarian convent into Panamá itself. There was some resistance in the three main streets, where barricades defended by guns had been set up. But most of the guns had already been spiked on the orders of Captain Pau and the explosions that the privateers heard were of a different kind. Two hundred barrels of gunpowder had been placed in houses throughout the city and these were now touched off one after the other in a riot of noise and flame. The scene was one of total confusion. Privateers broke into bars and quenched their thirst from the broached wine-barrels. Privateers rushed into houses to prevent the citizens getting away with their more portable valuables. Privateers ran through the streets mopping up the last signs of resistance at the west end of the city and then pushed their way through towards the great square behind the port.

The citizens fled before them, some shrieking 'Burn, burn; that is the order of señor Don Juan.' Soon, new fires started as negro and half-caste militiamen raced from wooden house to wooden house with flaming torches in their hands. The vision of Brother Gonzalo was coming true, and the streets of Panamá were running with blood and fire. Damian Guerrero, the *alferez real* of Panamá, who had fled from the field with three hundred men, had a job getting out of the city on the eastern side because there was already a belt of flame barring his way. The plaza itself, where some men had hoped to make a stand, soon emptied. When Gabriel de Urriola got there, he found just a boy and an old man and a few negroes. The President had already ridden out of his burning city, his vow forgotten now, a beaten man crying out that all was lost.

Antonio de Silva, the President's secretary, reported later what he could see and hear from the safety of the islands in the bay.[14] After the explosion of the powder magazine at nine in the morning, he heard intermittent gunfire in the city, muskets, arquebuses and some artillery, until noon when the city fell silent. During the morning, he had also been able to see continuous fighting on the beach where the privateers were struggling to prevent the last few remaining boats from being burned. At three in the afternoon, Silva heard a salvo of guns, first two, then three, then five, which he took to be the signal that the enemy had finally mopped up all the resistance and had taken possession of the city. At about the same time, he was supervising the embarkation of the last of the nuns in the very crowded ship, *La Naval*, which was anchored at the island of Taboga. Many ships had already sailed, including the large cargo-vessel, *San Felipe Neri*, which had left two days before. In it, and without a very good excuse, was that bastion of the river, Francisco Gonzalez Salado.[15] Antonio de Silva himself travelled in the last ship to leave the bay, *Nuestra Señora del Buen Suçeso*, which sailed at four in the afternoon. As the sails filled and they tacked out towards the Pearl Islands, he looked back towards the place where he had made his home for several years. The setting sun behind the city could hardly be seen through the pall of smoke. The whole of Panamá was in flames.

Night fell, but for the privateers there was no orgy of drink and women to celebrate their victory. Ever since three o'clock, when they had gained 'quiet possession of the city', they had laboured to put out the fire and so save for themselves some of the fabled wealth of Panamá. Buildings were blown up to prevent the fire spreading, but sparks were easily carried by the easterly breeze which had continued to blow all day. They carried on long into the night, but it was hopeless. At midnight, they gave up. The whole of the centre of the great wooden city was alight and would soon be burned to the ground. All that remained were a few public buildings, which were built of stone, such as the offices of the Audiencia and the Governor's house behind the port, and the great square tower of the cathedral which stood out alone amidst the smoking ruins of the city. Some of the negro shacks in the suburbs were also saved, as were two stone convents on the outskirts of the city which provided lodging for the exhausted privateers. Here, in the rooms so recently vacated by the nuns, those men who were not needed for guard duty lay down to rest after fighting a battle and trying to save a city in the eighteen hours since dawn. It had been a hot day.

CHAPTER NINETEEN

No Help for Don Juan

DON JUAN was a broken man after the battle, still very unwell, defeated and in despair at his failure to honour his vow to the Virgin. He made no attempt to organize resistance in the city, or to reassemble the more stalwart of his men. He did not even arrange a rallying-point for the men to regroup and hopefully return to interfere with Morgan's depredations in the countryside around Panamá. Many witnesses claimed later that they had no idea where the President had gone – a rather disgraceful state of affairs and an indication of the complete collapse of Don Juan's leadership and initiative in the immediate aftermath of the battle. His enemies were to put the matter more harshly. The President, they said, slept with his mules ready saddled, still being frightened that the enemy would capture him, though he was over a hundred miles away.[1]

This was a slight exaggeration. Don Juan in fact stopped running at the small town of Nata, seventy miles south-west of Panamá on the Pacific side of the isthmus. Many people thought that he should have gone in the opposite direction, over the mountains to Portobello, where he could have organized resistance from that stronghold. But Don Juan said later that he had sent the wounded Alonzo de Alcaudete back to take charge in Portobello and that, by going west along the isthmus towards Veragua, he had a good chance of picking up fresh contingents of people still making their way towards Panamá. It is true that most of the larger villages under his jurisdiction were in this direction, and he did in fact meet a few small parties on the road who were rather surprised to see their President riding fast away from his city with his servants and friends, on less good horses or on foot, straggling in his wake.

Don Juan was not, of course, the only man to flee in panic after the battle. His whole army and all the population of Panamá fled as fast and as far as they could to escape the privateers, most of them not stopping until they had put at least twenty miles between themselves and the burning city. They fled in two main directions, some going the same way as Don Juan and ending up in various places on the Pacific side of the isthmus, the majority fleeing towards the mountains in the centre of the isthmus, where they hid themselves 'in places where they could never be got out'[2] and led a desperately deprived existence. No one had any further interest in fighting the privateers. It was now a case of every man for himself. Vows to the Virgin, pride in a shared Spanish heritage, all had been forgotten.

Once in Nata, Don Juan seems to have pulled himself together a little and at least made a show of organizing fresh resistance to the privateers. On 4 February, a week after the battle, he issued a proclamation which was read out in the small town with its mixed Spanish and Indian population. In the preamble, he said that it was the duty of Spaniards to defend themselves and their faith, and all the more so since the present enemy were heretics. 'All those who live in this city of Nata and its jurisdiction', read out the Mayor, 'whether soldiers, officers or whatsoever person capable of bearing arms should come immediately to defend the city of Nata, carrying their arms. . . . Those who fail in such an honourable action and in their duty, which is to defend their homes, will be regarded as cowards and men deprived of honourable sentiments and will bear the infamy and stain for ever.'[3]

This was rather more like the old Don Juan, but it did not do much good. Five days later, a muster was held to see the effect of the proclamation and 298 men turned up, most of them soldiers from Panamá who had fled with their President. This was better than nothing, but hardly sufficient to dislodge a confident Morgan. Don Juan stayed in the same area for the next month, moving between Nata, Los Santos and the Indian village of Penonome. Fresh proclamations were issued, but the musters that resulted became smaller and smaller as Morgan's men spread out farther from Panamá in their search for prisoners and as captured shipping began to raid on the Pacific coast. On 25 February, a notary made an inspection of Penonome on the President's orders. 'At noon, I went to the houses of the said village to see if there were in them some of the men from the militia companies . . . but there was no one there.'[4] The President never did get a relief army together.

If Don Juan could get no help from the men of his own jurisdiction, he would have to look elsewhere. He could not just stay in Penonome or Nata and do nothing. It seemed probable that Morgan intended to stay in Panamá and use the city as a base for further conquests. There was talk about a prince whom the English had brought with them to crown as King of Tierra Firme[5] – presumably a reference to Prince Rupert who, as we have seen, was rumoured to be coming to the Indies with five thousand men. This was all nonsense, but it did not seem nonsense to a defeated people. They thought that Morgan's next move would be to invade Peru, possibly in conjunction with the French, who it was rumoured were planning to seize the port of Realejo on the Pacific coast of Nicaragua and move in two thousand families in order to give themselves a permanent Pacific base. It was feared that Morgan would go south from Panamá, which was Don Juan's main justification for ordering the city to be burned. It seemed impossible that a pirate could set out with such a huge expedition without a commission from the King of England to seize the whole Indies. The city had been burned to deprive him of arms and powder and of the iron, nails, canvas and timber with which a fleet could have been built to sail to Peru.[6] It must have seemed a very reasonable precaution, although it was difficult to convince the citizens of Panamá after the event. They were more interested in the ruins of their uninsured property.

Don Juan did not act very fast for a man worried about a possible invasion of Peru. It is perhaps an indication of his muddled and despairing state of mind after the defeat of his army that he did not write his first letter asking for help until 9 February, twelve days after the battle. This was a rather confused letter of self-justification and near-despair addressed to his old enemy, the Conde de Lemos, Viceroy of Peru. He described at length the various disasters which had afflicted his well-planned defences one after the other and ended with a statement of his current position. 'I am without arms, powder, cord, ball or money and all the people of this kingdom so frightened that only God could give them courage.'[7] Nowhere in the letter did he give the Viceroy any of the important information which would be necessary if he was to send a relief force. He does not discuss the present disposition and numbers of the enemy, does not say how many soldiers would be necessary to defeat him nor which ports would be open for a relief army to come ashore.[8] It is really rather a helpless letter. Don Juan simply was not thinking like a soldier.

He was even slower in sending official news of his plight to Portobello, a city under his own jurisdiction and the only place in the Audiencia which still theoretically had the military strength to do anything to dislodge Morgan. His first letter seems to have been written on 16 February and was passed on to Cartagena, where it was received on 5 March, providing the Governor with his first knowledge of where Don Juan had gone after the battle.[9] Once again the letter is one of despair and does not comprise any useful military thinking. He grumbles that he has been unable to get two hundred men together to disturb the enemy, 'despite all the trouble that he has taken and the rewards that he has promised. Fear has conquered all the inhabitants of this kingdom, so that every Englishman seems to them to be a powerful squadron in himself by which means the enemy succeeds in most of his designs.'

On 19 February, Don Juan wrote to the Queen, reporting the three-weeks-old disaster and recounting what he had done since Panamá was lost.[10] He was less than honest. 'I proceeded to seek help from the Governor of Cartagena and the Viceroy of Peru . . . but up to date I have not had news of the arrival of my letters.' This is hardly surprising since the first letter to Peru had only been sent ten days previously. There is no record of any letter going directly to the Governor of Cartagena at this time. He then once again goes into the problems of rebuilding his army. 'It is impossible to get men together to face the enemy, because fear has so entered into their hearts that, throwing away their arms, they have saved their lives (on the pretext of going to look after their wives) in the most impenetrable of the mountains.' He took this opportunity of repeating an old plea. 'This will always happen, so long as Your Majesty does not order old soldiers and paid troops to be sent.' He concluded by saying that he would stay in Penonome, 'to be near Panamá', to wait for help to come from Peru, Cartagena and Mexico. In other words, Don Juan had given up all hope of doing anything to stop Morgan raping the province of which he was President and Captain-General.

The news of the fall of Panamá had, of course, reached Portobello a long time before the President's letter. After the battle, Don

Alonzo de Alcaudete and his officer colleagues who had fought alongside him went straight back across the mountains, having heard that twenty enemy ships were attacking the city. This turned out to be a false alarm, although five big privateer ships had appeared off the port shortly after the capture of Chagres.[11] Everyone had stood to arms and the castle guns had been fired to show the enemy that they were well prepared. The gesture seems to have been successful and Portobello was not threatened again during Morgan's Panamá campaign, though the whole coast between Portobello and Chagres was invaded time and time again by the men whom Morgan had left in San Lorenzo Castle.

The citizens of Portobello wrote to the Governor of Cartagena on 31 January, reporting the loss of Panamá.[12] They suggested that he send ships and men to join with them in attacking the twenty-nine ships which the privateers were said to have on the River Chagres. With help from Cartagena, it would be 'easy to defeat and destroy this enemy that has been so formidable for this kingdom'. They felt that Portobello itself was safe, now that the fortifications had been improved and arrangements made for the whole population to retire within the castles if the city were attacked. Portobello would be kept for Spain. Their only real problem was food, which was getting very short and which was soon to get shorter, 'since every day some families arrive from Panamá with what they can save'.[13]

The messenger from Portobello was delayed at sea and did not reach Cartagena until 12 February, the same day that an advice-boat arrived from Spain with a copy of the peace treaty and orders from the Queen to carry out the terms of the treaty 'in blind obedience, keeping good correspondence with the English nation'.[14] The Governor, Pedro de Ulloa, felt certain that the news from Panamá must cancel out the Queen's pacific instructions, but did not feel that he could do much to help either Panamá or Portobello. It was with 'great grief and distress' that he found himself without sufficient ships or people to oppose or destroy the enemy, but his first duty was to his own city. It was absolutely necessary to reinforce the garrisons of the castles of Cartagena with people from the militia of the city's hinterland and so preserve a port to which ships bringing relief from Spain could come.[15] There would be no military assistance for the Kingdom of Tierra Firme from Cartagena, and the

privateers would be able to keep their ships in the River Chagres
with no fear of any attack at all.

Governor Ulloa did manage to send a cargo of salt meat and fish,
cassava, rice and honey which successfully ran the gauntlet of the
privateers and was delivered to the hungry people of Portobello. The
only other thing he did to vent his frustration at being unable to
bring a relief force to Panamá was to write a letter to the privateer
admiral in the hope that, despite all appearances, he might have some
sense of the niceties of international law. It was a very well-informed
letter. [16]

Señor General Enrique Morgan. It is a long time now since I first heard of the
ships and men that you were bringing together at Isla Vaca to invade these
coasts and ports of Tierra Firme. . . . I have heard for certain* that while you
were in Isla Vaca . . . a ship arrived from England with news of the peace
signed in Madrid between our two crowns on 18 July, a peace which relates
also to the Indies. . . . But you, lacking public faith and the obedience that
you owe to the majesty of your king, went out with your fleet, despite that
news, and went to the island of Santa Catalina which you sacked, making
prisoners of the Governor and Spanish garrison, dismantling its forts and
throwing its guns into the sea. From there you passed to the coast of
Portobello and the castle of Chagres which you captured on 6 January,
killing most of the garrison, and afterwards went with most of your troops
to the city of Panamá, carrying all with blood and fire, and defeated the
President of that kingdom who opposed you in just defence. . . . You have
no pretext of ignorance, since you knew about the peace so early and . . .
you should give satisfaction for the very serious damage that you have done
and restore everything that you have robbed. It occurred to me to write this
to you, enclosing a copy of the peace, in order that you might observe it as
you should and, if you do not, I will have to give an account of all to the King
my Lord.

We do not know what Henry Morgan made of this letter with its
feeble concluding threat, or even if he ever received it, but it is not
difficult to imagine the reaction of the victor of Panamá to such a
piece of paper. But that was the best that the Governor of Cartagena
could do to help his poor, beleaguered colleague, Don Juan Perez de

---

* From the Indian, Juan de Lao, who escaped from the privateers after the capture
of San Lorenzo. See above, p. 185.

Guzmán. Panamá would get no assistance from the Spanish Main.

The only hope of fairly speedy help that now remained was that which might be provided by Don Juan's former gaoler, the Viceroy of Peru. The news of the English invasion was taken south by the refugees who left Panamá by ship on the afternoon of the city's capture. They had a good run to the Gulf of Guayaquil in Ecuador and arrived at the port of Santa Elena on 12 February, only fifteen days after the battle.[17] Their news caused consternation in Ecuador, not just for its own sake, but also because the people there had just learned that there were twelve English ships off the port of Valdivia in Chile. It seemed as though the English had planned and carried out an extremely well-timed pincer movement for the conquest of Peru, with simultaneous invasions from north and south to split the Viceroy's forces. Never had the Spanish empire in the Indies seemed in so much danger, with Panamá and the isthmus lost and several thousand English soldiers and sailors loose in the Pacific.[18]

The Viceroy's communications system, and his nerves, were stretched to the limit in the first three months of 1671 and he emerges from the ordeal as a man to be admired, a man who earned the praise with which a colleague honoured him when he died two years later. 'He was a señor of rare virtue, zeal and justice, and of very great understanding of the business of these kingdoms . . . one of the greatest Governors that these vast provinces have had.'[19] Don Juan might not agree with this assessment of his old enemy; the thought of those two hundred men who never turned up might still rankle; but even he would have to admit that the Conde de Lemos did as much as was humanly possible to help him, once he learned that Panamá had fallen. Once again, we have to appreciate the enormous distances with which he had to cope before we can fully understand the Viceroy's problems. It is well over two thousand miles from Lima to Valdivia in Chile, over fifteen hundred from Lima to Panamá and eight hundred from Lima to Guayaquil in Ecuador. Communications, whether by land or sea, took weeks. Once the Viceroy had committed troops in any one direction, they were lost to him for months, so to be faced with two simultaneous invasions at the extreme ends of his jurisdiction, 3500–4000 miles apart, was the very worst thing that could happen.

The Viceroy first received the news of the twelve English ships off

Valdivia on 24 January in a letter from the commander of one of the Chilean watchtowers. The news, which was already over six weeks old, was confirmed two days later in a despatch from the Governor of Chile, who was in the field with his army fighting the Indians. The ships had been seen by Indian fishermen, and the Governor had immediately sent 270 regular soldiers and 500 Indian auxiliaries south to help the garrison of Valdivia. No current Spanish official had ever had to deal with a problem of this kind, but they knew what to do. Many lessons had been learned by their predecessors during Dutch raids into the Pacific in the 1620s.

The Viceroy leaped into action on receipt of the news from Chile. Messengers were immediately sent to every port along the coast, so that people could prepare themselves for defence against the enemy fleet. There was no predicting where the attack would be. Callao was put on full alert, and orders were given for the militia of Lima to muster with their arms and horses. If he heard that Valdivia had actually been captured, the Viceroy planned to attack by land and sea, but for the moment he sent just 270 experienced men overland to assist the Governor of Chile. Meanwhile the usual religious precautions were taken. Masses were sung in the cathedral of Lima and in all the convents, and a series of holy processions were arranged in an attempt to gain divine assistance against the threat of invasion.

Three weeks later, on 14 February, when the whole Pacific coast of South America was in a hubbub of excitement and preparation, the Viceroy received another letter from Chile. It turned out that the Indian fishermen had been mistaken. There were not twelve English ships off Valdivia; there was only one. It was later discovered that this ship was *Sweepstakes*, the Royal Navy vessel which the Duke of York had provided for the voyage of exploration undertaken by Admiral Narborough and Carlos Henrique Clerque in the summer of 1669.[20] They had lost their consort, probably through mutiny, off the coast of Patagonia and had then sailed alone through the Straits of Magellan to arrive off Chile late in 1670, very short of food and arms. When they had appeared off Valdivia, on 15 December, they had first claimed to be from Spain, but the badly pronounced Spanish of their linguist had given them away. They then admitted that they were English, claiming that they came in friendship and that, by the terms of the peace, they had the right to call at any port in the South Sea if they were in distress. They asked to be allowed to anchor and to buy food and arms.

No foreign ship had been seen in these waters for twenty-five years, and the Chileans treated them very cautiously, especially when they started to ask questions about the strength of the garrison and whether there was gold and silver in the interior. Eventually, they managed to take four of the crew, including a lieutenant, as hostages and informed the Admiral that they would only sell him food if *Sweepstakes* was anchored under the guns of the castle. This was one place that Narborough did not want to be and he sailed away, leaving the hostages behind to be taken as prisoners to Lima, where their fate was to be a matter of diplomatic interest for a long time into the future.[21]

By the time that he realized the truth about the English ships, the Viceroy of Peru had managed to muster six or seven thousand men for the defence of the South American coast and still had plenty left to defend Lima itself. He was naturally delighted to discover that the English invasion had turned out to be a false alarm, especially as the news arrived on the first day of a novena for the Virgin of the Rosary, the patron of arms of the kingdom. He was, however, still worried that an English ship should be in the Pacific at all, and the ports were told not to relax their watch. One ship could still do a lot of damage. He was also worried that the English had once again learned how to sail to the west coast of South America. He felt certain that they would make use of the information. Next summer, he expected the Pacific to be swarming with English ships and feared that his defences would be insufficient to protect the coast. How could you protect over three thousand miles of coastline without a proper naval squadron? He begged the Queen to send out some well-armed ships from Europe; otherwise he feared that the Indies would be lost, 'a terrible thing to happen, to lose in a few days what has cost so much in Spanish blood and to have heresy introduced where our holy Catholic faith is so well established, followed and venerated'. The Viceroy was right to be alarmed. The English and French did use the information provided by Narborough to sail into the Pacific, although it was to take them a little longer to realize the potential of this new theatre of privateering than the Viceroy had anticipated.

The Viceroy had barely had time to relax following the good news from Valdivia, when he received a letter from Don Juan Perez de Guzmán reporting the capture of the castle of San Lorenzo de Chagres and asking for men and arms. The Viceroy, of course, had men and arms ready and, within five days, he had found shipping and had despatched four hundred soldiers and some money to pay the troops of Panamá. This party had only got as far north as Payta, the port on the border of Peru and Ecuador, when they received the further news that the English had captured Panamá. This put a rather different complexion on things. Four hundred men might have been sufficient to put some stiffening into Don Juan's forces, but they were hardly enough to reconquer Panamá from a victorious enemy. Hernando de Rivera, the commander of the relief force, decided to stay in Payta and wait for the Viceroy's further orders.

People in Lima could not believe the news. For years they had had to read panicky letters from Panamá about the danger from corsairs, but nothing ever actually happened. Now they felt certain that it was impossible for an enemy to capture Panamá by an invasion up the River Chagres. This was just another annoying rumour. They were fed up with standing to arms. But the Viceroy believed the news and was disgusted to hear that two thousand Spaniards had fled in terror before six hundred Englishmen, for that was the information which he received. He now acted extremely quickly to try to restore the situation.

He first heard of the fall of Panamá on 8 March. Fifteen days later, five fully armed ships sailed from Callao with a thousand men, weapons, ammunition and food for eight months. They were to link up with the advance force in Payta and then go on to Guayaquil to pick up three hundred more men from Ecuador and all the fugitives from Panamá who were fit to bear arms. In his report to the Queen,[22] he said that, by 7 April, twelve ships and more than two thousand men should be in Panamá ready to restore the Kingdom to Spain. He had already sent a fast ship ahead with a letter to Don Juan, advising him of the approaching relief force and asking him to get as many of his own men together as possible. He also wanted to know what the present situation was and where his men could land.

The relief of Panamá went more or less as planned, although almost inevitably it did not arrive quite as quickly as the Viceroy had hoped. There were delays while the fleet waited for the *almiranta* of the Armada del Sur and another five hundred men whom the Viceroy had decided to send at the last moment. There were delays in Payta and further delays in Guayaquil, where the men from Ecuador and the fugitives from Panamá embarked. Francisco Gonzalez Salado, sadly aware of the dishonour of his flight first from the river and then from Panamá itself, took this opportunity to attempt to redeem himself. He begged the *corregidor* of Guayaquil to be allowed to serve with fifty men at his own expense and paid four thousand pesos into the Royal Treasury for this purpose. But it did him no good. He was arrested the moment he set foot in Panamá[23] on 22 April,[24] fifteen days later than the Viceroy had hoped. But at least they had arrived. One hopes that there was a cheer from the miserable citizens of Panamá as the 2400 men of the relief force disembarked, together with their arms and artillery, ready to drive Henry Morgan from the isthmus and to save the Indies for the King of Spain and the holy Catholic faith.

CHAPTER TWENTY

Henry Morgan Returns

'THUS was consumed the famous and antyent citty of Panama,' wrote Morgan in the report which he later delivered to the Council of Jamaica, 'the greatest mart for silver and gold in the whole world, for it receives all the goods into it that come from Old Spaine in the King's great fleet and likewise delivers to the fleet all the silver and gold that comes from the mines of Peru and Potazi.'[1] Now it was no more. What should have been the richest prize in America lay smouldering in ashes at its melancholy conqueror's feet. Henry Morgan's achievement had been the dream of generations of Englishmen. He had succeeded where Sir Francis Drake had failed, but where was the joy of conquest if there was no plunder and no pay?

Henry Morgan was not the man to remain melancholy for long. Panamá might be burned, but there would still be treasure in the ashes. The citizens might have fled, but some of them would not have fled far enough. The privateers set to work, each man eager to find for himself some of that silver and gold that had given them the strength to perform such epic feats. The storming of San Lorenzo, the march across the isthmus and the battle for Panamá would not be for nothing. Some men remained on guard, lest the Spaniards recover their nerve and come back to attempt to recover their city. The rest set out on a systematic search of the province of Panamá. If there was treasure, they would find it.

There was something to be found in the ashes of the city itself, and the privateers spent a week picking them over. Not all the buildings had been burned completely to the ground, and there was plenty of food to be found in warehouses and cellars behind the port. Shops full of silks and cloth might have gone up in flames, but some things were indestructible. Hiding-places in the wooden walls of houses,

237

once safe from prying eyes, were now exposed by the fire. Wells and cisterns had dried up in the intense heat, making easy access for the privateers who climbed down to find their hidden treasures. The churches and convents had been emptied of their portable wealth by the priests and nuns when they fled from the city, but some things were too heavy to move. Legend has it that a great gold altarpiece in one of the churches was painted to look like wood, a ruse which fooled the looters. But, if the legend is true, there were many other pieces of gold and silver plate which were discovered, reduced by the fire to shapeless lumps of metal. Shapeless or not, they were precious and were added to the pile, ready to be divided man for man when the time should come. This pile soon became quite impressive, though not too much when it had to be divided between some two thousand men – 'a fair amount of silverware and silver coins which the Spaniards had hidden in their cisterns', according to Exquemelin; 'some inconsiderable things', according to William Frogg.[2] This was poor reward for the labour they had endured to capture the city, and the privateers seem to have taken a vandalistic revenge on the man who had ordered Panamá to be burned and so deprived them of their rights. The President's house had remained untouched by the fire, but when he at last returned he was to find his home in ruins. Beds, mirrors, desks and priceless pictures lay in a great smashed heap, while his most valued possession, a library of five hundred books, had been torn to pieces by his illiterate enemies.[3]

The privateers were to have more success in their search for treasure outside the ruined city. The very richest treasures and much of the city's silver and gold had been got safely away on the three big ships which sailed to Ecuador. Most of the nuns and priests and the wives and children of the richer citizens had also sailed south. But the citizens themselves had fought in the battle and so did not have the chance to flee by sea afterwards, while many people had not been able to afford the panic rates charged for goods and passengers travelling to Ecuador and Peru. Many citizens, therefore, had arranged for their families and portable wealth and, if possible, themselves to be taken to the islands in the Bay of Panamá, assuming that these would be safe from the privateers since the President had ordered all boats that remained on the mainland to be burned. The privateers had anticipated this, and a search for shipping had been

one of their first priorities when they broke into the city. Some of the
fiercest fighting had been on the beach below Panamá where
fishermen were accustomed to keep their boats. The privateers had
little success here, but made up for it farther down the coast at La
Tasca, where they found a barque which had come in from Darien
with a cargo of maize the day before the battle and had then got
stranded by the tide. Her crew had tried to burn her, but the English
were too quick and put the fire out. By next high tide, the barque had
been unloaded, repaired and armed with a few guns and a strong
party of privateers who went aboard to search the many islands of
the bay.[4]

Once they were mobile, the privateers were able to make a clean
sweep of the defenceless islands and, according to Spanish witnesses,
most of the silver seized by Morgan in the Panamá campaign was
taken from Perico, Taboga, Taboguilla and the other small inshore
islands.[5] That first barque soon captured others and, within a few
days, the privateers had a flotilla of three armed barques and a
brigantine with which to cruise. Some of the shipping captured had
fairly prosaic cargoes – soap, cloth, biscuit and sugar – but every
ship had some silver hidden away and there were hundreds of
prisoners to be taken, each of them clutching his most precious
possessions. Exquemelin tells us that the privateers only just missed
the biggest prize of all: 'a galleon, loaded with the King of Spain's
silver, together with all the jewels and treasure of the foremost
merchants in Panamá', whose boat crew were captured when the
ship anchored at one of the islands to take on water. The privateersmen reported the news to their captain, but he 'had been more
inclined to sit drinking and sporting with a group of Spanish women
he had taken prisoner, than to go at once in pursuit of the treasure
ship'. By the time he had finished enjoying himself, the galleon had
sailed and their delayed pursuit was unsuccessful.[6] This is a nice
story which could possibly be true. The last two big ships to leave
Panamá only sailed on the afternoon following the battle, and they
might well not have had time to take on their full complement of
water. The ship with the biggest treasure of all, *San Felipe Neri*, had
sailed two days earlier and would have been unlikely to be still
hanging around the islands.

The activities of the privateer squadron in the Bay of Panamá and along the Pacific coast were complemented by a massive quest for prisoners on the mainland. Every day 'our men marched out in parties', wrote William Frogg, 'sometimes 100, sometimes 40, sometimes 10 in a party, and took prisoners every day, but never saw an enemy to face them'. Morgan reported that these search-parties went twenty miles out into the mountains to the north and north-east of Panamá, and he confirmed that there was absolutely no resistance by Don Juan's defeated men. There was not 'as much as one gunn shott at us in anger'. Spaniards grumbled that the privateers wandered about their country with as much freedom as if they were in England.[7]

The privateers were very efficient at flushing out the hidden fugitives from their pathetic lairs in the mountains, gleefully noting the plume of smoke, the trampled undergrowth or the cry of a child which gave their victims away. Stealthily, they would encircle the spot and pounce. A quick search and the threat of torture soon revealed the hidden treasures, the bag full of pieces of eight, the few pitiful jewels, the rosaries and the holy pictures which were all that could be carried in the flight from the city. Each day saw more half-starved men, women and children marched back to Panamá, where many of them would be forced to endure further horrors. In all, Morgan claimed to have taken the staggering total of three thousand prisoners from the battlefield, the city, the islands and the mountains. Most of these would have been men and women of little substance who were released after a perfunctory search, but those who looked as though they might have something to hide, those who looked as though they might have relatives to ransom them, those with smooth hands or fancy clothes were subjected to the full privateer treatment.

Surgeon Browne later claimed that the reports of atrocities on the Panamá campaign were a great deal worse than the reality. 'What was in fight and heat of blood in pursuit of a flying enemy I presume pardonable. As to their women, I know or never heard of any thing offered beyond their wills. Something I know was cruely executed by Capt. Collier in killing a friar in the field after quarter given, but for the Admiral he was noble enough to the vanquished enemy.'[8] Well, maybe the Admiral was noble. He could probably afford to be. His men certainly were not, and there are more Spanish complaints of torture and particularly of death from torture on this campaign than on any of the others covered in this book. Don Juan reported that men were beaten and mutilated and hung up in trees by their wrists, even by their private parts, to make them reveal where they had hidden their silver. The President had a simple explanation of the privateers' brutality. 'They are fed up with the little prize they have.'[9] Don Francisco de Marichalar warned the Queen later in the year that, if the English should come again to Panamá, the whole population would immediately flee to the mountains, 'for the horror they have conceived of the cruelties and deaths that the pirates inflicted on them after they had surrendered and were prisoners'.[10] Such comments are unusual. The Spaniards were used to torture. What shocked them was that so many tortured men should die, and it is this that is the true measure of the privateers' frustration. Don Juan had told the Queen that, terrible though the disaster had been, he thought that the plunder would be very little, 'because the citizens had time to put all they had in a safe place'.[11] Some of these places did not prove as safe as the citizens had hoped, but the President's comment is substantially true. The Spaniards, forewarned of Morgan's advance, had sent their treasure away. 'This, together with their firing the Citty of Panama, made us return so empty home.'[12] This also made them more than usually unpleasant to their prisoners, even by their own nasty standards.

One way in which the privateers might have increased their prize would have been to do what the Spaniards expected them to do and sail south. Exquemelin said that a hundred of Morgan's men did make some plans to desert their Admiral and take the shipping which they had captured in the bay on a raid into the South Sea. 'They intended to capture a big ship, load it with their plunder, and get back to Europe by way of the East Indies.'[13] Such an exercise would become commonplace in the raids across the isthmus which were carried out in the 1680s, but Morgan himself never seems to have considered it. He wanted to go home to Jamaica, not England, and what he had done so far could just conceivably be justified by a very lax interpretation of his commission, always supposing that people believed the depositions collected at Isla Vaca. He had no intention of building a South American empire, nor had anyone else in Jamaica, even if a few dreamers might speculate on the treasures that might be collected by a full-scale expedition from England. He ordered the masts of the captured shipping to be cut down and burned. There would be no deserters to give him a bad name. Those who had come with him must go back with him. There might still be opposition on the way back across the isthmus, when the time came to return to the ships in the mouth of the River Chagres.

By the end of February, Morgan thought that that time had come. There was nothing left to loot on the Pacific side of the isthmus. He completed the destruction of the defences of Panamá by spiking the few remaining guns and prepared for departure. Scouts were sent ahead to check that there were no ambushes on the road and mules brought into the city to load the treasure. On 24 February, after an occupation that had lasted just four weeks, Henry Morgan left the shambles that once had been the proud city of Panamá and set off past the battlefield towards Venta de Cruces. His plunder followed in his wake. According to Exquemelin, there were 175 mules laden with silver plate and coin and five or six hundred prisoners. Some of these were Spaniards and other citizens who had yet to pay the 150 pesos a head that Morgan demanded in ransom,[14] but most of them were slaves – or, rather, blacks, for the privateers made little distinction between slave and free negro, and many a respectable black citizen of Panamá found himself reduced to the status of slave when he reached Jamaica.[15]

On the afternoon of the second day, the long procession had reached Venta de Cruces with no disturbance from the forces of Don Juan. Here the privateers spent nine days 'refreshing ourselves', which seems to have meant collecting food for the voyage home. It also meant waiting for the ransoms of the Panamá citizens to be delivered and passing the time by capturing another 150 fugitives from the mountains of the centre of the isthmus. Prisoners were told that they had three days to produce their 150 pesos ransom money or else they would be taken back to Jamaica. This was not all that much for a man of moderate substance to raise, about £35, and the threat seems to have been sufficient to produce the ransoms. Most of the white prisoners had been released by the time that Morgan reached San Lorenzo. This last part of the journey down the Chagres must have been sheer joy after their last experience of the river seven weeks previously. Rain had fallen in the meantime, and the water was now sufficiently high for them to travel the whole way by boat, a journey that was completed in two days.

The privateers who had been left as a guard for the ships and as a garrison for San Lorenzo Castle had not been idle in their Admiral's absence. They had looted the whole Caribbean coast of Panamá and Darien, leaving Portobello as the only place in the Audiencia where a Spaniard could still feel safe. Hunger had given an edge to their raids along the coast, for the provisions stocked up by Don Pedro de Elizalde had long since given out. 'There was not a man on the coast whom they did not take prisoner, nor a horse, a mule or a cow or any other kind of animal, grain or fruit which they did not kill or collect for their sustenance as a result of their great hunger and lack of provisions.'[16] The arrival of the main body of the privateers with rice and maize, which they had collected up-river, solved the immediate food problem, and Morgan decided to spend a few days at Chagres in a last attempt to increase his treasure. A ship was sent to Portobello to set the prisoners from Santa Catalina ashore and also to demand a ransom for the castle of San Lorenzo. The answer could surely have been predicted. The citizens of Portobello were still chafing over the ransom of their own city in 1668 and were certainly not going to pay for any more possessions of the Crown to be spared from destruction. So, when the ship returned from Portobello with the news that no ransom was to be paid, the castle of San Lorenzo was duly destroyed, its wooden walls put to the torch, its guns spiked and thrown down the cliff – one more job for the military engineers to attend to after Morgan's departure.

The time had now come for Henry Morgan's last and most audacious expedition to disperse and go home. It was decided to share the treasure there and then, according to Exquemelin because the men might well need money to buy food on the way home. But this seems unlikely. The privateers very rarely did buy food. It was more likely because everybody had by now heard of the peace and many were none too certain of their reception in Jamaica. Exquemelin tells us that Morgan had everyone, including himself, searched, lest anyone should have been so base as to retain some of the treasure of Panamá for himself. This was an unusual procedure – the custom of the privateers was to swear an oath that they had not concealed anything – and it caused some murmuring, especially from the

French, 'but they were in a minority and so had to keep quiet'.[17]

The division was then made. The results were predictably disappointing. Morgan said in his report that there was some £30,000 of plunder to be divided. This was only half what had been taken in Portobello and there were four or five times as many men to share it, so that the dividend, after allowing for deductions and bonuses, would have come to between £15 and £18 a head, depending on one's assumptions about the actual number of privateers. This figure agrees with one independent account which said that each man got £16, though two other accounts put the figure lower at £10 per head.[18] Something should be added for the four hundred or so slaves who were eventually either sold in Jamaica or redeemed by the Spaniards at eighty pieces of eight each. If this was shared fairly, it might perhaps have given each privateer another £4. But, whatever the exact figure, the rewards were very much less than had been received in the Portobello and Maracaibo campaigns and seemed desperately small to the men who had fought their way across the isthmus to earn them. Many refused to believe that all the treasure had been brought to the division. Others thought that an unfair price had been put on gemstones and bullion. 'The wrought silver was reckoned at only ten pieces of eight the pound,'* wrote Exquemelin. 'The price offered in exchange for various jewels was dirt cheap, and many jewels were missing – for which Morgan was publicly accused.'[19] Even Surgeon Browne, normally a great admirer of the Admiral, said that he 'cheated the soldjer of a very vast summe'.[20] There is no way that we can ascertain the truth after three hundred years, but these angry complaints sound today like the wild accusations of disappointed men. What little we know of the character of Morgan does not indicate that he was the sort of man who would cheat his own comrades. Browne's claim that the treasure brought home across the isthmus was worth £70,000, over twice what Morgan stated, seems to be a bad case of wishful thinking. Don Juan was surely right when he reported to the Queen that there would be little plunder. The sack of Panamá may have set the seal on Morgan's reputation, but it was not a very good investment.

That sense of brotherhood that made the privateers so formidable

---

* A piece of eight was approximately the same weight as an ounce of silver.

an enemy, that enabled them to undergo such intolerable hardship and danger, had disappeared. They were now just an ugly crowd of bitter, disappointed men, grumbling at the smallness of their pay on the Caribbean shores of Panamá, more dangerous to their captains than to their former enemy. Morgan did not like the mood of his men and he made haste to depart, not even signalling to the rest of the fleet to follow him. The game was over, and he wanted to be the first to get home, to make sure that his story was the one to be believed in Jamaica. He sailed on 16 March, just eight days after the Viceroy of Peru had first heard of the loss of Panamá and over five weeks before the relief force of South Americans arrived to drive him from the isthmus. Communications really were rather difficult in the Spanish empire of the Indies.

Most of the privateers did not follow their Admiral home to Jamaica. The game was over for them, too. Some sailed to leeward, some to windward, some went to search for more plunder, some for food, for supplies were now very short. Morgan sailed straight for home in company with just three or four ships, but he had outsailed all but one of them by the time that Sir James Modyford reported his arrival in Jamaica. 'Our Admirall is returned, onely with one shippe in his companie, ye rest a-coming in.'[21] When Morgan made his own report on 30 April, over two weeks after his arrival, he said of the rest of his fleet that 'some are arrived and the rest dayly expected'.

Many of the privateers never did come back to Jamaica, for a large number of Morgan's ships were wrecked on the Central American coast where they had gone to raid and look for food. One account says that nineteen were wrecked,[22] over half the fleet, but this seems to have been a gross exaggeration. All but one of the remainder had appeared in Jamaica by early July, where they continued to grumble at their small pay and their Admiral's duplicity.[23] Most of them did not stay in Jamaica long, too restless to enjoy a settled life in an island that was now at peace with the Spaniards. Some of the Englishmen followed the Frenchmen back to Tortuga and Hispaniola, where an approximation to the old privateering life was to continue for many years into the future. One or two privateers set up as independent pirates off the south coast of Cuba or in the Cayman Islands, surreptitiously selling their prizes to their brethren in Jamaica. Others sailed out of the West Indies to begin a new life elsewhere in the world. The biggest single concentration of former privateers was in Nicaragua and Honduras, where the men sailed to take up a new profession, the cutting of logwood for its dye. There were to be endless debates about whether this was a legal occupation, whether in fact much of the Central American coast was Spanish at all, since it had long been settled by Englishmen and so, by the terms of the Treaty of Madrid, should belong to its occupiers. The Spaniards never accepted this *de facto* English sovereignty, but the descendants of Morgan's privateers live in places like the Bay Islands of Honduras to this day, still speaking a weird seventeenth-century English patois.

Maybe a fifth, maybe even less of the Jamaican privateers who sailed with Morgan to Panamá ever settled permanently in Jamaica again. Some of these men had already salted away their previous plunder and could now make a living as planters or artisans. Some joined the crews of fishing or trading sloops, spending much of their time away from the island catching turtle or trading illegally with the Spanish colonists and often tempted to engage in their old raiding and robbing activities. Some just formed part of that riffraff who congregated in Port Royal as in any other large port. But all of them found the Jamaica to which they returned to be a rather different place from the island they had left in the autumn of 1670 when they answered Morgan's call for men. Jamaica was to remain a home for every sort of rogue; even pirates could usually hope to find a clandestine welcome there. But never again would the island's economy and defence depend on that 'old pleasing account of No purchase, No pay'. The days of the Jamaican privateers were over and the island was to try, not too successfully, to become a more respectable place.

Henry Morgan and Sir Thomas Modyford could at first congratulate themselves on their successful defence of the island against the Spanish threat. The plunder might be disappointing, but the Spaniards had been cowed, a piece of news that was welcomed by the great majority who would have agreed with the comment of the Governor's brother. 'I thinke we are prettie well revenged for their burning our houses on ye north and south side of this island and threatning more when we intended and had proclaimed peace.'[24] Others might think that the revenge was rather excessive and look forward to a different kind of relationship with the Spaniards, but as yet such talk was muted. At a meeting of the Council of Jamaica on 10 June 1671, Morgan's own report of his voyage to Panamá was read out and he was publicly thanked for 'ye execution of his last commission'. The Council 'approved very well of his acting therein'.[25]

Meanwhile, Sir Thomas Modyford could think about the implementation of the new peace treaty, now that Morgan was safely returned. In May, he wrote to the Governor of Puerto Rico, thanking him for sending a copy of the articles of peace between the two crowns. He said, quite truthfully, that he had not yet received a copy from England, nor any orders relating to the peace, but that he had been given news of the treaty from private hands. His masters in England still maintained their silence. Modyford agreed to publish the treaty in June, as the Governor of Puerto Rico suggested, unless he had different instructions from England. He had a similar correspondence with the Governor of Hispaniola, assuring him that 'all his master's subjects under his command rejoice much in this peace, and will contend with the Spaniards in all points of civility and friendship'. He probably meant it, just as he had probably meant it when he talked about peace and friendship in May 1669, but as usual he could not refrain from pointing out that this latest expedition to Panamá was not his fault but that of the Spaniards. Had it not been for the Queen of Spain's *cedula* of 20 April 1669 and the raids of the Spanish corsairs there would have been no need for Jamaica to go to war again. All of which was probably true, but it did not really help to heal the breach. Sir Thomas Modyford simply could not help annoying the Spaniards.[26]

This fact was only too well known in London and, as we have seen, it had long been decided to replace this awkward Governor of Jamaica as a sop to the Spaniards, whose continuous protests were not only very annoying, but might even spoil Sir William Godolphin's treaty at the last moment. But there is a strange delay between the issue of Sir Thomas Lynch's commission as Lieutenant-Governor early in January and his actual arrival in Jamaica on 1 July. The lack of instructions to Sir Thomas Modyford during his last year as Governor is also rather strange, especially the failure to give him official notification of the Treaty of Madrid. Could it be that London deliberately left Modyford and Morgan the scope to make one last great coup against the Spaniards before the publication of the treaty, knowing that, in the absence of royal or ministerial instructions, all the blame could be piled on the principal actors? This is what many commentators believe, and there seems to be no good reason to disagree with them. Such a policy accords only too well with the cynical attitude towards the Spaniards in the Indies of the whole decade since the Restoration. If this is the true interpretation, London was determined to see the farce out to the end. Lynch carried among his papers not only the revocation of Sir Thomas Modyford's commission but also a warrant for his arrest, issued long before the news of Panamá could conceivably have arrived in England.[27] He was instructed to carry out the arrest in the most circumspect manner possible, for it was felt that Modyford's friends, and especially the privateers, might rebel against such a high-handed action.

Lynch did his best to comply with his awkward instructions, not doing his own reputation much good in the process. He arrived in Jamaica on 1 July with two royal ships, *Assistance* and *Welcome*, the first that had been seen in the island since *Oxford* blew up. He was greeted with full honours by Sir Thomas Modyford and Morgan and invited to a formal dinner at the Governor's house. When they had finished eating, the revocation of Modyford's commission was read out. 'The people seemed not much pleased,' noted Lynch in a letter to England.[28]

Sir Thomas Modyford may have guessed that something more was in the wind, but he gave no sign of his fears. For the next six weeks he gave Lynch every assistance in his new duties, acting for him when he was sick with the gout and even providing him with accommodation in his own house; all of which must have made the unfortunate Lynch feel like a very treacherous guest. Meanwhile, Lynch tried hard to build up a party of his own in the island by distributing honours and by passing the word that privateering was now considered rather disreputable in England and that people such as Modyford and Morgan no longer enjoyed any royal favour. All this was not really necessary. There was no one in Jamaica who would have attempted to oppose the execution of a royal order. It was a very loyal island. But Lynch seems to have been pathologically suspicious and was afraid to carry out the arrest until the circumstances seemed favourable. Eventually, his hand was forced by news from London. Sir Thomas Modyford's son, Charles, had been arrested to stand hostage for his father's good behaviour and was now in the Tower. Lynch feared that, if his father should hear the news, he might flee the island and so decided to make the arrest immediately.

Modyford was inveigled aboard *Assistance* on the pretext that Lynch had 'something to import to him from the King'. There, in the presence of four members of the Council, 'that I had by contrivance gott there', Modyford was shown the royal warrant for his arrest on the charge that he 'hath, contrary to the King's express commands, made many depredations and hostilities against the subjects of his Majesty's brother, the Catholic King'. Modyford behaved with great dignity, objecting only to the underhand method of his arrest and wishing that 'hee might have shown his obedience by his voluntary submission to his Majesty's pleasure'. Lynch, who seems to have been very embarrassed by the whole business, did his best to cheer Modyford up, assuring him that Lord Arlington had told him that 'his life and estate was not in danger, but there was a necessity of making some resentments for such unseasonable irruptions'.[29]

It was the English Government's intention that Modyford alone should suffer for the sack of Panamá; one man whose 'life and estate was not in danger' would stay in the Tower for a while until Spanish anger subsided. Lynch was instructed to issue a general pardon to all the privateers, not excepting Henry Morgan, as long as they returned to Jamaica and submitted to him within a certain time. It was accepted that the privateers had acted perfectly legally within the terms of a proper commission and no action would be taken against them. The people of Panamá might have rather different views on the legality of the invasion by Henry Morgan and the privateers, but nobody in England was very interested in them. They were merely victims.

CHAPTER TWENTY-ONE

Peace in the Indies

NEWS travelled very slowly in the seventeenth-century world, and nowhere did it travel slower than between America and Spain. On the same day that Henry Morgan sailed fast away from Chagres to escape the anger of his disappointed men, Captain Sebastian Duran was at last ready to sail from Cartagena to Spain with the information that Pedro de Ulloa had been able to assemble about Morgan's invasion of the isthmus.[1] His voyage through the Bahama Channel and across the Atlantic took very nearly twelve weeks, and it was not until 5 June that he dropped anchor in Lisbon and so brought the first official report to the Iberian peninsula of what 'the English under the command of one Morgan' had done in the Indies. There had been rumours for weeks of some great coup, but this was the first properly documented information on the sack of Panamá. The Portuguese were delighted to hear that their old enemy and neighbour had been further humbled by their favourite allies, the English. 'They say the King of England may conquer the whole world,' reported the English consul in Lisbon, 'for nothing can be too difficult for Inglishmen to undertake.'[2] The reaction in Madrid, where the messenger arrived on 11 June, was very different.

The Queen was said to be 'in such a distemper and excess of weeping and violent passion as those about her feared it might shorten her life'. The seventy-year-old Conde de Peñaranda was also in tears, bitterly ashamed and remorseful that his treaty, 'upon which the ink is scarcely dry', should thus be slighted by the cynical and shameless English. Both the Queen and Peñaranda, and indeed everyone else at the Spanish Court, felt certain that this latest outrage had occurred, if not by the order, at least with the consent of the King of England.[3] Sir William Godolphin, who had just recovered from a serious illness, found himself in the most embarrassing situation, the central target of a Spanish fury whose justice he was the first to acknowledge. He wrote an angry letter to Lord Arlington, complaining bitterly of this appalling breach of the terms of the peace, and then settled down to spend the rest of the summer trying to heal that breach with soft words and protestations of his master's innocence of any responsibility for 'ye late accident in America'. The privateers were out of hand. They had acted entirely contrary to His Majesty's express command, but the King himself could not restrain them or set limits to their voyages. However, the guilty Governor had been arrested and was now on his way home to the punishment that he so richly deserved. The King, his master, had so much tenderness towards Her Majesty, the Queen of Spain, that he resented the scandalous depredations made by Morgan and Modyford just 'as if they had been committed on his own territories'.[4]

The blandishments of Sir William Godolphin had little effect at first. Spain was too angry and too bitter, desperate to avenge this latest and greatest humiliation of all. Wild propositions for huge expeditions to the Indies were seriously considered. Wily projectors besieged the Court with ingenious schemes to defeat the English, schemes which on consideration seemed more likely to fill the projectors' pockets than to humble the English in Jamaica.[5] But in the Council of the Indies, once the ministers had dried their tears and recovered from the initial shock, more serious plans were unfolded. The advice from Cartagena had reported that the privateers were fortifying Panamá and planned to maintain themselves there in permanence. The first priority, therefore, was an expedition to recover the city and open once again the lines of communication within the Spanish Empire.

The Queen suggested that an expedition of some three or four thousand picked men should sail to Cartagena in the seven ships of the Armada del Mar Oceano which were then in Cadiz and nearly ready to go to sea. This was generally agreed. The Prince of Montesarcho was chosen to command the fleet and the Duke of Medina Celi to command the expeditionary force. By mid-July, the Duke reported that he had selected the three thousand infantry and three companies of horse that were to accompany him and that they were already on their way to Cadiz. The men had been chosen from the very finest regiments. This time it seemed as though there really would be a full-scale Spanish expedition to avenge the fifteen years of humiliation from Jamaica.[6]

Simultaneous preparations were being made for a smaller expedition. Domingo Grillo, the Genoese holder of the slave *asiento*, had recently had his contract revoked, after accusations of trading with foreigners, and was eager to curry favour with the Spanish Court. As soon as he heard of the loss of Panamá, he came to Peñaranda and offered to provide a galleon at his own expense for the royal service. Spain did not often get a ship for nothing, and it was quickly decided to use the galleon to send some immediate reinforcements to Cartagena, 'considering the poor quality of the people in the Indies and how much encouragement it will give to them if some small help can be promptly sent'. Eventually, this 'immediate' reinforcement grew to three ships and 550 soldiers. Command was given to Don Antonio de Córdoba, Lieutenant-General of Horse in the Army of Flanders, who had already been chosen to replace Don Juan Perez de Guzmán as President of Panamá, not, it should be stressed, because of any failing on the part of Don Juan, but because Spain did not like any man to hold an independent position of power for too long. Córdoba got his orders on 6 July. He was to sail immediately to Cartagena, confer with the Governor and then take his men wherever their presence would be most valuable.[7]

In the end, Don Antonio de Córdoba did not sail with his three ships until 12 August, and the Duke of Medina Celi never sailed at all. It was, of course, inevitable that the news that Morgan had marched out of Panamá back in February would eventually trickle through to the Spanish Court, and that hasty and expensive preparations for the recovery of the city and for revenge would have to be reconsidered. Many people thought that Medina Celi should still sail, even though Panamá had been abandoned by its invaders. Since the English themselves claimed that the corsairs were out of hand, they need feel no misgivings, as the expedition would be 'merely to suppress piracy and to sweep the sea'.[8] But practical considerations soon ruled out such an exhilarating prospect. There was, as always, the question of money. There was also another consideration. Sir William Godolphin had been instructed by the King to be very conciliatory towards the Spanish Court and he certainly was, his messages of sympathy and sorrow culminating in a special audience with the Queen on 19 August, in which he expressed the deep regret with which His Majesty had heard of 'the accident that has happened in the Indies in the surprise of Panamá'. But Sir William's message from the King of England held a concealed threat. Lord Arlington had instructed him that, 'as His Majesty thinks fit thus to purge himself, he also requires you to add likewise that, if any of the preparations now making for the Indies shall invade Jamaica . . . he shall hold himself oblig'd to resent it'. This was something that Spain could not afford to face, a fresh beginning to that process of Spanish revenge and enormously inflated English reprisals that had been the history of the last ten years. The Queen had to swallow her pride and tell Godolphin that she was now satisfied that the King of England had no responsibility for the sack of Panamá.[9]

The Duke of Medina Celi's expedition was quietly forgotten. The English, in their turn, offered a fresh hostage to Spanish displeasure. Orders were sent to Sir Thomas Lynch in Jamaica to send Henry Morgan home as a prisoner. There was much delay. Morgan was sick, no doubt of some fever picked up in the isthmus, and Lynch was frightened of the effect of their leader's arrest on the other privateers. They might no longer believe in the pardon that he had been instructed to give them. It was not till April 1672 that Henry Morgan was taken aboard HMS *Welcome* 'as His Majesty's prisoner'.[10] By then the Spaniards were no longer insisting on punishment even for Modyford,[11] let alone for Morgan whom they seem to have considered as a mere agent and whom they rarely singled out for their displeasure. By then the humiliation of the sack of Panamá was little more than a bitter memory in a Spain which had known so many other humiliations.

The horrors of Morgan's invasion were not so easily forgotten in Panamá itself. The Queen had sent instructions to Don Francisco de Marichalar, an *oydor* from Peru, to act as interim governor until Córdoba's arrival. He had already spent a long time in Panamá, conducting a *visitá* or general enquiry into the government of the Audiencia, and had been in the city right up to the eve of the battle, when he had fled to Lima with his papers. It was therefore a man who knew Panamá well who returned to take over the duties of President on 9 October 1671.[12] He was horrified by what he found and wrote a long letter to the Queen describing the appalling conditions in which those citizens who had survived Morgan's attentions were now living.[13]

Every wooden house in the city had been burned to the ground and the fire had raged with such violence that, even in the few stone buildings, wooden beams had burned through so that walls and roofs that looked safe sometimes fell on their unfortunate occupants. What had once been a fine city was now just a heap of rubble and charred timbers in which it was impossible to rebuild. Those citizens who were most privileged now lived in some unburned shanties in the slave quarter, but most people were living in straw huts in the fields outside the city, suffering dreadfully from the constant rains and the terribly hot and humid climate. Many of the citizens had, of course, died in the battle or from the tortures inflicted on them afterwards, but more were now dying every day from sicknesses they had contracted while living in the open in the mountains. The insanitary conditions in their present straw huts and the very great shortage of decent food, for they had no money to pay for imports, had swelled the sickness to epidemic proportions. 'In short, Your Highness, this kingdom is in the most lamentable condition that you could possibly imagine, the citizens naked, poor, without food and all sick. There have been so many deaths since the invasion that they assure me that more than three thousand people have died.' This figure was later confirmed from the parish books. Nearly a quarter of the entire population of the Audiencia of Panamá died either in the course of Morgan's invasion or in the epidemic that was its almost inevitable aftermath.

Royal business must still continue, whatever the miserable condition of the city. The offices of the Audiencia still stood, and justice could still be administered, even though the buildings were badly damaged and hardly decent for the transaction of judicial affairs. Marichalar's immediate task was to conduct a *residencia* on his predecessor, Don Juan Perez de Guzmán. This was a normal procedure when a man left office and involved a full-scale investigation of the former Governor's performance of his duties, always an alarming and unpleasant occasion when a man's enemies had full opportunity to vent their spite in petty accusations.

The *residencia* began just three days after Marichalar's return to Panamá. In the circumstances, there was naturally considerable interest in the twenty-first of the fifty questions in the interrogatory that Marichalar drew up. 'Does the witness know whether the President has been negligent in the guard of this city . . . or whether he has, by his negligence, lost any forts or other places?'[14] Don Juan, like all colonial governors, had many enemies. There were also many men in Panamá who feared that they might find themselves accused of negligence, if nothing worse, during the recent campaign and they now hastened to give evidence against the former President in the hope that he might become the scapegoat for the whole disaster. So damning were some of the answers given to question 21 that Don Francisco de Valle, Procurator-General of Panamá and himself a well-known enemy of Don Juan, felt sufficiently confident to draw up an indictment, composed of thirteen charges, accusing Don Juan of the loss and ruin of the city of Panamá.[15] Marichalar, who seems to have been very sympathetic to his predecessor as President, had no choice but to hear these charges, and what amounts to a full-scale trial of the former President of Panamá began in the ruins of the city on 17 November 1671.[16]

The prosecution concentrated its attack on three main issues: the conduct of the campaign on the River Chagres, the conduct of the battle, and the orders to burn the city and thus cause losses to property-owners which were variously estimated at between eleven and eighteen million pesos,[17] a colossal sum when we compare it with the 120,000 pesos which was all that Morgan and his men got from their sack of Panamá. Witnesses claimed that Don Juan weakened the defences of the river by withdrawing men for the abortive attempt to recover San Lorenzo and also that he should have gone down to the river with his army to fight the enemy. He was blamed for fighting on the plain and not on the hill by which Morgan outflanked him. He was also blamed for not taking the city's artillery to the battlefield. Thirty witnesses gave evidence for the prosecution and, it must be admitted, they made a fairly convincing case against their former President.

Don Juan was, however, skilfully defended by a lawyer called Don Francisco Jaymes, who, in a very short time, had destroyed the credibility of several key prosecution witnesses, such as Francisco Gonzalez, the captain of the river, and his lieutenant, Luis de Castillo, as well as completely undermining the authority of the

Procurator-General by demonstrating that he was too young to have any real understanding of such matters, was totally ignorant of military and political affairs and had a well-known grudge against Don Juan to boot. Each of the prosecution's thirteen charges was destroyed in turn and then a fresh interrogatory of thirty-two questions was put to another thirty witnesses, many of whom had already given evidence for the prosecution. A very different picture emerges, very much the one presented in this book, a picture in which Don Juan did everything that could reasonably be done with the resources at his command, but was continuously let down by his subordinates' fear of the enemy. Don Juan's defence was sustained not only by the cross-examination of witnesses, but also by a mass of supporting documentary evidence which has been invaluable in the writing of this book. Jaymes produced character references, doctors' certificates, copies of Don Juan's letters to the Queen and the Viceroy asking for more men, and several scores of pages of evidence demonstrating the President's piety and his efforts to obtain divine assistance by the dedication of his person and the gift of his personal fortune to the Virgin and the Saints. When Marichalar had considered all this evidence, he had no doubt of his verdict. On 20 February 1672, Don Juan was acquitted on all thirteen charges and the prosecution was ordered to pay his costs.[18] Don Juan was to die three years later in Madrid, heartbroken and defeated but not, I think, dishonoured.[19]

A certain amount of judicial blood-letting was inevitable after so great a disaster, but for most people it was far more important that the city should be rebuilt so that business could get started again and the citizens of Panamá begin to live some semblance of a civilized life. It was quickly appreciated that some advantage could be gained from the catastrophe by moving the city to a more suitable situation. Nearly everyone was agreed that the peninsula of Ancon, some six miles from the old city and the site of the modern Panamá City, would be healthier, more easily defensible and much more convenient as a port for large ships. The decision to build at Ancon was confirmed in a *junta* of 22 January 1672 attended by Don Juan, Marichalar and Don Antonio de Córdoba, who had now arrived in Panamá to take up his new office as President and Captain-General.[20]

Don Antonio was an energetic man and he did much to get things started in the city, planning its defences and beginning their construction, giving out sites for the new cathedral, the convents and the public buildings, and generally encouraging the citizens to work hard to build a new life for themselves. Streets were laid out and private builders began work. Labour was in very short supply – many of the city's slaves were still in Jamaica – and progress was slow, but a start was made in what would be a very long process of recovery from the English invasion. The arrival of the Peruvian silver fleet in August 1672 was another sign of the return to normality. The fleet was carrying twenty million pesos of treasure, a million less than expected because of the huge cost of the Viceroy's relief force,[21] but still a very handsome sum. Panamá was indeed a prize worth taking, but only when the Armada del Sur was in port.

Don Antonio de Córdoba died in April 1673, and Marichalar, who replaced him, reported that his death had caused great disconsolation because it was believed 'that with his intelligence he would shortly place the city in a state of defence'.[22] Marichalar himself died soon after Córdoba, and the building programme slowed up until another energetic man, the Bishop of Panamá, became interim governor in January 1674. He it was who had the pleasure of dedicating the new cathedral, a matter of great joy since no one had expected it to be completed so soon and Mass could now be celebrated with decency. By April, he was able to report that the city had all its government buildings, the Sisters of the Conception were in as good a building as their poverty could afford and the rest of the religious people were building their churches and convents as quickly as possible. Already there were 113 private houses in the city and others were being built.[23] The quicker more houses were built the better, for the Bishop had discovered an appalling state of morals among the poor people still living in straw huts in the fields, 'many illicit cohabitations, adulteries, incests, failure to confess for many years, no knowledge of God or human subjection, from which arises many robberies'.[24] Jamaica and Henry Morgan still had much to answer for, even if Panamá had nearly recovered from its sack after three years of death and misery.

There were few signs of remorse in Jamaica. Sir Thomas Lynch, the new Lieutenant-Governor and the leader of the peace party, might refer to Morgan's last expedition as that 'disastrous voyage' or that 'unlucky designe', but it is clear that the adjectives do not describe the poor people of Panamá. It is the unlucky investors and the disastrous setback to friendly relations between England and Spain that he is thinking about. The truth is that even the hispanophile Lynch found it difficult to hide his pride at the stupendous success for English arms, while most Jamaicans simply gloried in the way their Admiral had humbled the old enemy and would have been only too happy if he had had the chance to do it again. When word got to Jamaica that the Spaniards were preparing an expeditionary force to the West Indies, Lynch had to report that 'the people gladly heare talk of warr', so keen were they to see the privateers at sea again.[25]

They were to be disappointed. The Spaniards forgot about revenge in the Indies, as we have seen, and the English Government stood by a fairly elastic interpretation of the Treaty of Madrid. There were to be no more private wars by the English in the Caribbean and no more privateering commissions, except in time of full-scale European warfare. Never again would an admiral of the privateers be commissioned to defend Jamaica from a real or imaginary threat. From now onwards, there was to be a continuous naval presence in the West Indies and, if there was an admiral in Jamaica, he would be a regular officer of the Royal Navy. This is not to say that privateering, let alone piracy, came to a sudden end. The trade was far too attractive for that. The buccaneers and *flibustiers* operated legally from Tortuga until 1684 and illegally thereafter, and many Jamaicans could be found among them. Other Jamaicans sailed surreptitiously from their own island and could usually expect to encounter few problems in disposing of their prize-goods in their old market of Port Royal. By the 1680s, rovers based on Jamaica were regularly crossing the isthmus to raid in the South Sea with varying degrees of success.[26] Such men still called themselves privateers, though the commissions which they kept carefully locked up in their cabins would hardly have borne close scrutiny and the word 'buccaneer' was coming into fairly general usage as a polite euphemism for the pirates that they really were. The new city of Panamá, now fortified and peopled and with a garrison four times as big as in 1670, was safe from the attentions of these small bands who mainly attacked shipping, but one of the rovers with an eye for the curious went to have a look at the ruins of old Panamá. 'Nothing now remains of it, besides rubbish and a few houses of poor people.'[27] The jungle was already creeping back to obliterate a century and a half of Spanish occupation.

The official attitude in Jamaica towards the latter-day privateers and buccaneers was, of course, that they were pirates and should be hanged if caught and found guilty. Actual policy varied considerably. The old concept that such men were the backbone of Jamaican defence died very slowly, and much piracy was condoned, if not actually encouraged. It was, in any case, extremely difficult to catch pirates, and when they were caught it was difficult to get evidence to convict them. There were never enough ships of the Royal Navy to sweep the seas, and those ships which were sent out to the West Indies were rarely a match in speed or manoeuvrability for the pirate vessels. In such circumstances, a policy of live and let live with the occasional sensational capture and hanging of a pirate was the usual situation.

Sir Thomas Lynch himself made great efforts to bring in all the privateers and to suppress those who refused to accept his pardon and turned pirate. He was to have moderate, but never total success. His voluminous correspondence, now self-congratulatory, now self-pitying, alternates between optimism and pessimism on the subject. Now there are only two pirates left at sea and he soon hopes to catch them. A few weeks later, a whole new crop of rovers has turned up. 'The cursed trade has been so long followed and there is so many of it that like weeds or Hydras they spring up as fast as you can cutt them down.'[28] It really was a rather hopeless business. Piracy and privateering were endemic to the West Indies, and the best that any colonial governor, English, French or Spanish, could do was to try to keep the evil at an acceptably low level.

A new Jamaica developed in the 1670s and 1680s which owed more to planting and less to privateering, but it was not until the eighteenth century that Jamaica fully developed the sugar plantations for which the island's colonial economy is best known. In this new world, piracy might be frowned on as bad for business, but illegal trading with the Spaniards remained one of the island's major occupations and the flow of pieces of eight through the hands of Port

Royal merchants was as active as in the heyday of the privateers. Despite the loophole offered by the 'wood and water' clause of the Treaty of Madrid, illegal trading remained illegal and the sloops which engaged in it had to be heavily manned, often with former privateers, to prevent seizure by Spaniards who still looked forward to opportunities of getting their own back on the Jamaicans. In such circumstances, there were frequent clashes between Englishman and Spaniard. Any hopes that there would ever be really friendly relationships between the two nations in the Indies were probably doomed from the start. They were certainly doomed from the day that Morgan set foot on the isthmus to march towards Panamá. There are some things that are difficult to forget.

Former privateers could live well in the new Jamaica and had no need to feel ashamed of their past. It was they who had enabled Jamaica to be what it was. It was they who had protected the island from its enemies for the first fifteen years of English rule and who had provided much of the capital which enabled the economy to thrive as well as it did. Now they could enjoy the fruits of their labours. Many of the more fortunate privateers had already bought plantations and could settle down to a bucolic, heavy-drinking life in which the cutlass and the musket on the wall and the silver chalice which looked suspiciously as if it came from some Spanish church were a reminder that this man who spoke so bitterly of the price of slaves and sugar had once led his company into the plaza of Portobello or Panamá. Many of these men were quick to make their peace with the new regime. Lawrence Prince, the man who sacked Granada and led Morgan's vanguard in the battle before Panamá, 'one of the great privateers' according to Lynch, was made the new Lieutenant-Governor's lieutenant. 'Hee's a sober man, very brave and an exact pilot. I thought it not amisse for that reason to employ him, and to lett the Spanyards see the privateers are subjects to the King's orders, and have not all left the island, but take it as an honour to serve the King in any capacity.'[29] Other men could serve their King in other capacities. John Morris, who served throughout with Morgan and was the man who put an end to the short career of Manoel Rivero Pardal, became the captain of the old privateer ship, the frigate *Lilly*, which was taken into the King's service. He was sent 'to take up the stragling privateers that are to leeward', a classic poacher turned gamekeeper. He 'is a very stout fellow, good pilot, and wee knowe will not turne pyrat', Lynch assured his masters in London.[30]

Most of the former privateers were stout fellows and good pilots. That was, after all, their trade. And there was no doubt who was the stoutest fellow of all, that 'honest, brave fellow' Henry Morgan, who had carried on his trade so well that 'they gave him public approbation and thanks which is recorded in the Councell booke'. When Lynch sent the famous privateer home to London as a prisoner, he wrote to Lord Arlington beseeching him to favour Morgan 'in all you may with Honour and Justice'.[31] England did favour Morgan. Indeed, they liked him so much that, in 1675, he returned to Jamaica with a knighthood and a commission as Deputy Governor in place of Lynch. He was preceded by Sir Thomas Modyford who, after two years' confinement in the Tower without trial, had apparently done sufficient penance for his seven years as Governor of Jamaica and was sent back to the island as Chief Justice. The Spaniards might not like it, but that was all the recompense they got for the sack of Panamá, Portobello and innumerable other places in the Indies.

Sir Henry Morgan was to live another thirteen years in Jamaica, drinking heavily, growing fatter and getting embroiled in the cut and thrust of local politics. He died of dropsy in 1688, the result of being 'much given to drinking and sitting up late', according to his physician.[32] The greatest of all the Jamaican privateers was given a rousing send-off with a 22-gun salute from the royal ships in Port Royal harbour and the colonial equivalent of a state funeral. He died a very wealthy man by colonial standards, with several plantations and a personal estate of over £5000, not bad for a man who came out to the Indies as a soldier of reasonable birth but very little fortune. Privateering could give an audacious young man a fine start in life. There are only a few signs in his probate inventory[33] that he had ever been other than the planter he was when he died: a few nautical instruments, a parcel of old charts and maps, rather more guns and pistols than one needed to defend a plantation, but no chest full of jewellery and doubloons. It is possible that some of his 109 negro slaves spoke Spanish and had once walked the streets of Panamá. It is possible that some of his personal jewellery had been taken off the fingers of unwilling Spaniards, but it is unlikely. Privateers did not usually keep what they took as prize. They sold it. Privateering was a business.

It was also, of course, rather more than that; a life of adventure and danger for the men who engaged in it; a means of imposing the diplomatic will of the dominant English on an impoverished Spanish Court. For the men who lived in the Spanish Indies, it was a curse. These wretched men and women lived every day in fear of the privateers and, in their weakness, relied for their main defence on the intercession of a God who saw fit to punish them over and over again for their sins. How often must they have prayed, as Don Juan did when he heard the news of the fall of San Lorenzo? 'God, who watches us with eyes of pity, give me victory over these heretical dogs.' And how often did they pray in vain.

A Note on Sources

THE MOST interesting and certainly the most original sources which I
have used for this book are those from the Archivo General de Indias
in Seville. This is the main depository of all Spanish colonial papers
and is a mine of information. But it suffers from the usual problems
of mines in that one has to dig and sift through an enormous pile of
useless material to find the gems one seeks. The collection is catalo-
gued and there is a cross-referencing system available to researchers
by consultation with the archivists, but these aids to researchers are
by no means totally reliable and certainly not comprehensive. Very
often the only way a researcher can find what he is looking for is by
thinking himself into the minds of the seventeenth-century Spanish
clerks who made up the *legajos* or bundles in which the documents
are stored. Thus the records of the court of enquiry into the loss of
Portobello are not under 'Portobello' or 'Panamá' or anything obvious like that. They form, instead, part of the defence offered by Don
Agustin de Bracamonte against charges that he was partly responsible for the city's loss and are therefore amongst the papers of his
residencia in the section Escribania de Cámara of the archives. This
section was in fact much the most useful for me, providing partial or
complete *averiguaciones* for nearly every one of the privateering
campaigns with which this book is concerned.

The documents which I have used fall into three main groups.
First, there are isolated letters and reports which may turn up in the
most unlikely places. Finding such material involves turning over,
folio by folio, as many *legajos* as possible whose catalogue titles look
fairly relevant. Then there are consolidated bodies of documents,
often bound together, which relate to the problems or events with
which one is concerned. Several of the most useful of these were the
records of a *junta* – for instance, to discuss the defences of Cartagena – and a mass of supporting papers such as *autos*, letters,

reports, depositions and various types of necessary legal documents. Finally, and most valuable of all, were *averiguaciones*. An *averiguación* had a formal legal procedure, involving the issuing of a commission to the investigating authority, *autos* stating the substance of the matter to be investigated, interrogatories and then page after page of evidence taken from witnesses under oath. If charges were brought as a result of the preliminary investigation, then these will be listed and there will then be a statement by the defence, followed by another interrogatory and the evidence of defence witnesses. Finally, if one is lucky, there may be the sentence, though very often cases were referred back to Spain and the sentences therefore were not included in the *legajos* made up by the colonial authorities. The procedure used in investigating a charge brought against an official in a *residencia* was very much the same. Both types of enquiry very often include supporting evidence, such as depositions made in the past relevant to the matter. Sometimes, as in the case of Agustin de Bracamonte mentioned above, the supporting evidence is much fatter than the papers of the *residencia* itself.

The historian's task is to make up his mind what value he can place on such evidence. He has to remember that most of these enquiries were the result of special pleading and that the witnesses were often obviously hand-picked. But, as long as he can locate the likely direction of bias, he can use the material in an intelligent way. The best situation is, of course, when there are witnesses on both sides of an argument and therefore a fairly clearly defined middle ground where the truth must lie. Much of the material is, in any case, non-contentious and in such cases it would be unnecessarily carping not to believe it. In general, there is not much difficulty in getting a very good idea of the actual course of events from the evidence available and, in addition, the labour of sifting through the material is constantly enlivened by little stories and scraps of dialogue which make research in these Spanish archives an attractive, if tiring, occupation.

The English material for the history of the Jamaican privateers is very well known to historians and I have managed to find nothing very original, except a few interesting pieces in Spanish which do not seem to have been used before. Nearly all the documents are either letters, depositions or reports. The English unfortunately did not go in for courts of enquiry in the way that the Spaniards did. The most important sources are the letters of the Governor of Jamaica and the reports of Morgan, both of which tell somewhat less than the truth but are amusing to read. One type of document which one finds quite often amongst the English colonial papers, but very rarely in the Archivo General de Indias, is correspondence by private individuals rather than by officials. Such letters, especially those of careful and interested observers such as the surgeon, Richard Browne, provide a very valuable counterpart to the official view of things.

One unique and rather extraordinary source needs also to be considered. This is the book, first published in English in 1684 as *Bucaniers of America* by the surgeon and buccaneer, Alexander Exquemelin. Different editions and different translations vary considerably in detail, but I have used the Penguin Classics edition of 1969, which is a new translation of the original Dutch, *De Americaensche Zee-Roovers*, published in 1678, only a few years after the events it describes. The introduction to the Penguin edition has some interesting speculation on just who Exquemelin was which there is no need to repeat here. The main point of interest here is the reliability of Exquemelin as a source, a judgement which is easier to make after considering the Spanish evidence. My feeling is that he is almost never totally and utterly wrong and sometimes is remarkably right, repeating stories which one can find in Spanish evidence but in no other English sources. I do not think he can have gone on every campaign he describes. He makes too many elementary mistakes in naming people and places and he very often gets a story just a little bit wrong, as if he had heard it in a tavern rather than experienced the events himself. A good example of this is the way that he describes the famous incident in which the prisoners at Portobello were used to help in the assault on Santiago Castle. Exquemelin says that they carried the scaling-ladders for the privateers, but the Spanish evidence makes it absolutely clear that they were used as a human shield to enable the privateers to fire the main gate. It seems very unlikely that an eyewitness would make such a mistake and incidentally get the geography of Portobello very wrong. The privateers were there for a month and must have known the place backwards. My impression is that Exquemelin was not at Portobello, but spoke to people who were, which makes him an important source but not as important as Morgan or the three or four dozen Spaniards who later gave evidence on the events in their city.

It seems much more likely that he went on the Panamá campaign, where there was a large buccaneer contingent. It is interesting, for instance, that Exquemelin gets all the Spanish names right for the forts in Santa Catalina and, although he makes a few mistakes in the nomenclature of the barricades on the River Chagres, his general account is very accurate. He gets nearly all the dates wrong, which is forgivable considering he must have written his account some time after the event. He is also guilty of some very tall stories which are normally quite easy to detect. The main general problem with his account is his assessment of Morgan. He goes out of his way to blacken the Admiral's name and to give him a reputation which is not sustained even by the Spanish evidence. The motive for this is quite clear. Exquemelin, like many of the privateers, thought that he had been cheated by Morgan after Panamá, and the book is a very good way of getting his own back. The English publishers of Exquemelin were forced to retract most of the defamatory material after a libel suit was settled out of court in 1685 and it seems probable that they were only doing Morgan justice in doing so.★ But subsequent editions have repeated Exquemelin's libels, and Morgan's name has suffered to this day as a result.

My approach to the use of Exquemelin in this book has been very cautious. Sometimes, he is the only source for a section of the story and I have been forced to make use of him. But wherever there are alternative sources I have used them in preference, employing quotations from Exquemelin simply as colour rather than to carry the story itself.

★ For details, see E. A. Cruikshank, *The Life of Sir Henry Morgan* (Toronto, 1935), ch. 12.

Sources and Bibliography

ABBREVIATIONS

Add	Additional Manuscripts, BL
ADM	Admiralty Papers, PRO
AGI	Archivo General de Indias, Seville
BL	British Library
CO	Colonial Office Papers, PRO
CSPAWI	*Calendar of State Papers, America and the West Indies*
CSPD	*Calendar of State Papers, Domestic*
CSPV	*Calendar of State Papers, Venetian*
Ct	Contratación section, AGI
EC	Escribania de Cámara section, AGI
Exquemelin	Alexander Exquemelin, *The Buccaneers of America*, Penguin Classics (1969)
HAHR	*Hispanic American Historical Review*
Harl	Harleian Manuscripts, BL
IG	Indiferente General section, AGI
Lima	Lima section, AGI
Mexico	Mexico section, AGI
NS	New Style
OS	Old Style
Panamá	Panamá section, AGI
PRO	Public Record Office
pza	*pieza*
SD	Santo Domingo section, AGI
SF	Santa Fé section, AGI
Slo	Sloane Manuscripts, BL
SP	State Papers, PRO

MANUSCRIPT SOURCES

Seville: Archivo General de Indias
Ct 3147: Papeles de armada de Manuel de Banuelos, 1669–70.
Ct 3161: Papeles de armada de Don Agustin de Diostegui.

Ct 3164: Papeles de armada de Henrique Henriquez, 1669 – includes 'Autos fechos . . . sobre las prisiones de D. Alonso de Campos', the main source for Chapter 9.
Ct 5102: Cartas de generales de armadas.
EC 455B: 'Causa de oficio de la Real Justicia seguida contra Don Estevan de Ocampo . . . y otros . . . sobre la perdida de Santa Catalina', the main source for Chapter 1.
EC 461A: Residencia . . . a . . . Don Juan Perez de Guzmán, *piezas* 1–4.
EC 461B: Residencia a Don Juan Perez de Guzmán, *piezas* 5–11. *Piezas* 10 and 11 include all the evidence for Don Juan's trial for the loss of Panamá. This is the most important *legajo* for the second half of the book.
EC 462A: Residencia a Don Agustin de Bracamonte. Includes in the first *quaderno* 'Autos y diligencias fechas contra los Castellanos . . . sobre la perdida de Porttovelo' and in the second *quaderno* the 'sumaria averiguación sobre la perdida de la ciudad de Portovelo'. Main source for Chapters 4 and 5.
EC 577A: Cartagena. Pleitos. 1668. This *legajo* is made up of *piezas* relating to the Portobello campaign and the defences of Cartagena. See, in particular, *pieza* 3, 'Informaciones hechas en la forma que el enemigo coxio la ciudad de San Felipe de Puerto Bello', and *pieza* 4, 'Autos y acuerdos . . . sobre la recuperación de Puertovelo'. This *legajo* duplicates some of the material in EC 462A and Panamá 81.
EC 660A: 'El señor Fiscal con Don Diego del Barrio . . . sobre la perdida de la Fregata La Soledad, 1669'. The preliminary court-martial proceedings against the Sergeant-Major of the Armada de Barlovento.
EC 699A: Residencia a Don Fernando de Villegas. Includes 'Autos originales fechos . . . para averiguación de la entrada del enemigo en la ciudad de maracaybo'. This is mainly about the relief force sent by the Governor of Venezuela.
IG 430: Libro generalismo de Reales Ordenes, etc., 1667–86.
IG 781: Consultas de Consejo y Cámara, 1668–70.
IG 782: Ditto, 1671–2.
IG 1600: Expediente de la Junta de Guerra y represaliás de Franceses e Ingleses, 1671–6. Includes Morgan's Articles of Agreement for 1668.
IG 1877: Junta de Guerra. Consultas originales, 1664–74. Invaluable for the Spanish reaction to events in the Indies.
IG 2516: Registros, reales ordenes y resoluciones sobre la Armada de Barlovento, 1605–1716.
IG 2541: Decretos, consultas, cartas y expedientes de las Armadas de Barlovento, 1668–9.
IG 2542: Ditto, 1670–6.

Sources and Bibliography

IG 2696: Relaciones de bastimentos de la Armada de Barlovento, 1644–73.

Lima 72: Cartas y expedientes del Virrey del Perú, 1671–2.

Mexico 470: Cartas y expedientes del Virrey, 1665–76.

Panamá 24: Cartas y expedientes del Presidente y Oidores, 1668–71. Not as helpful as it sounds.

Panamá 25: Ditto, 1672–5.

Panamá 31: Cartas y expedientes del Cabildo Secular de Panamá, 1625–97. One or two useful letters.

Panamá 72: Expediente causado en razón de las visitas hechas a la Audiencia de Panamá y oficiales reales, 1660–88. Has some useful letters.

Panamá 78: Expediente que trata de la reconquista de la isla de Santa Catalina por el general Juan Perez de Guzmán, 1666–8. Invaluable for Chapter 2 in conjunction with SF 223.

Panamá 79: Expedientes sobre los arbitrios concedidos a la ciudad de Panamá . . . para atender a su reedificación, 1672–98.

Panamá 81: Expedientes sobre el emprestito de 100 mil pesos de los vecinos de Panamá para rescatar Portobelo a las piratas, 1669–78. Invaluable for Chapter 6 and for the Portobello chapters generally.

Panamá 87: Cartas y expedientes del Presidente y Oidores . . . vistos por la Junta de Guerra, 1616–76. Some useful material on the defences of the Audiencia of Panamá.

Panamá 89: Consultas, etc. . . . sobre las fortificaciones de los castillos de Panamá, Portovelo y Rio de Chagre, 1632–73.

Panamá 92: Expedientes y otros documentos respectivos a militares, 1646–99.

Panamá 93: Expediente sobre la residencia tomada por Don Miguel de Marichalar a Juan Perez de Guzmán. This very valuable *legajo* includes 'Testimonio de acuerdos fechos por los señores desta ciudad de Cartaxena' which contains much useful material on the Panamá campaign and the defences of Cartagena. The same *legajo* has important letters from Don Juan Perez de Guzmán and a mass of papers arising out of the Spanish reaction to the loss of Panamá. The *legajo* needs to be used in conjunction with EC 461B for a full picture of the Panamá campaign.

Panamá 101: Cartas y expedientes de Obispo de Panamá, 1649–1709. One or two letters of value.

Panamá 104: Cartas y expedientes de personas ecclesiasticas, 1614–89.

SD 178A: Documentos correspondentes a la perdida de Jamaica, 1634–78. Very little relating to the period of this book.

SF 43: Cartas y expedientes del Gobernador de Cartagena vistos en el Consejo, 1656–72.

The Sack of Panamá

SF 223: Expedientes sobre la reconquista de la isla de Santa Catalina, 1635–96. Mainly about the 1641 expedition, but has much material on the 1660s.

Most of the English documents used are from the colonial papers in the Public Record Office. These are well known and are calendared in *CSPAWI*. I will not list them here. References will be found in the Notes. The following other sources were used:

London: British Library
Add 11268: Miscellaneous papers re West Indies, including Morgan's account of the capture of Panamá and captured Spanish papers.
Add 11410: Papers relating to the West Indies, 1654–82.
Add 13992: Miscellaneous Spanish papers, including papers relating to the galleons of 1669 and 1671 and measures for defending the colonies, 1671.
Harl 4034: Maps and charts of the Pacific coast . . . surveyed by order of the King of Spain and finished at Panamá, 1669.

London: Public Record Office
ADM 2/1734: Duke of York's instructions, 1668–72.
ADM 2/1746: Duke of York's letters, 1668–73.
ADM 2/1755: Letters relating to Admiralty and Vice-Admiralty Courts, 1663–84.
ADM 7/827: Orders and instructions, 1660–95.
SP 89/10–11: State Papers, Portugal, 1669–71.
SP 94/49–58: State Papers, Spain, 1665–71.
SP 103/66: Treaty Papers, Spain, 1667–1719.
SP 104/174B: Commissions and instructions, 1664–70.
SP 104/176: Minutes of Committee of Foreign Affairs, 1667–72.
SP 104/181: King's Letter Book, Spain and Portugal, 1670–4.

PRINTED SOURCES

Place of publication, unless otherwise stated, London
Philip Ayres (ed.), *Voyages and Adventures of Captain Bartholomew Sharp and Others* (1684). Includes a description of the Panamá campaign
T. Bebington (ed.), *Letters of the Earl of Arlington* (1701)
Richard Blome, *Description of the Island of Jamaica* (1672)
Breve epitome de la restauración de la isla de Santa Catalina (Seville, 1667)
Calendar of State Papers and Manuscripts Relating to English Affairs Existing in the Archives and Collections of Venice, xxxv–xxxvii (1935–9)
Colección Lugo, 'Recopilación diplomatica relativa a las colonias española y francesa de la isla de Santo Domingo', *Boletín del Archivo General de la Nación*, xiv–xix (Ciudad Trujillo, 1951–6)

Sources and Bibliography

William Dampier, *Dampier's Voyages* (1906)

F. G. Davenport, *European Treaties Bearing upon the History of the United States*, 4 vols (Washington, DC, 1917–37)

J.-B. du Tertre, *Histoire générale des Antilles*, 3 vols (Paris, 1667–71)

A. O. Exquemelin, *The History of the Bucaniers* (Thomas Malthus, 1684)

——, *Bucaniers of America* (W. Crooke, 1684)

——, *Histoire des aventuriers* (Paris, 1686)

——, *De Americaensche Zee-Roovers* (Amsterdam, 1678)

Thomas Gage, *The English-American* (1648)

Domingo Gonzalez Carranza, *Geographical Description of the Coasts, Harbours and Seaports of the Spanish West-Indies* (1740)

Edward Hickeringill, *Jamaica View'd* (1661)

Interesting Tracts Relating to the Island of Jamaica (Santiago de la Vega, 1800)

Jean-Baptiste Labat, *Nouveau voyage aux isles de l'Amérique*, 6 vols (Paris, 1722)

Jean-Baptiste Le Pers, 'Histoire civile, morale et naturelle de l'isle de St Domingue', *Boletín del Archivo General de la Nación*, x–xiii (Ciudad Trujillo, 1947–50)

Memorial del Capitan Sebastian Crespo (1670?)

Memorias de los virreyes que han gobernado el Perú (Lima, 1859)

Robert Ryal Miller (ed.), *Chronicle of Colonial Lima: the Diary of Josephe and Francisco Mugaburu, 1640–1697* (Norman, Okla., 1975)

Juan Perez de Guzmán, 'Relation of the Late Action There in the West-Indies', in Philip Ayres (ed.), *Voyages and Adventures* (1684)

Present State of Jamaica . . . to which is added an exact account of Sir Henry Morgan's voyage to . . . Panama (1683)

Arent Roggeveen, *The First Part of the Burning Fen Discovering the Whole West-Indies* (Amsterdam, 1675)

Manuel Serrano y Sanz, *Relaciones Históricas y Geográficas de América Central* (Madrid, 1908)

Antonio de Ulloa, *Relación histórica del viaje a la América Meridional*, 2 vols (Madrid, 1748)

Antonio Vázquez de Espinosa, *Compendium and Description of the West Indies* (Washington, DC, 1942)

Joseph de Veitia Linaje, *Norte de la Contratación de las Indias Occidentales* (Seville, 1672)

Lionel Wafer, *A New Voyage and Description of the Isthmus of America* (Oxford, 1934)

SECONDARY AUTHORITIES

C. L. G. Anderson, *Old Panamá and Castilla del Oro* (Washington, DC, 1911)

K. R. Andrews, *The Spanish Caribbean: Trade and Plunder, 1530–1630* (New Haven, Conn., 1978)

Violet Barbour, *Henry Bennet, Earl of Arlington* (Washington, DC, 1914)

——, 'Privateers and Pirates of the West Indies', *American Historical Review*, xvi (1911)

Jorge Basadre, *El Conde de Lemos y su tiempo* (Lima, 1948)

Bartolomé Bennassar, *The Spanish Character: Attitudes and Mentalities from the Sixteenth to the Nineteenth Century* (Berkeley, Calif., 1979)

F. P. Bowser, 'Colonial Spanish America', in D. W. Cohen and J. P. Greene (eds), *Neither Slave nor Free* (1972)

Carl and Roberta Bridenbaugh, *No Peace beyond the Line* (1972)

James Burney, *A Chronological History of the Discoveries in the South Seas or Pacific Ocean*, 5 vols (1803–17)

Ruben D. Carlos, *220 Años del periodo colonial en Panamá* (Panamá, 1969)

Guillermo Céspedes del Castillo, 'La defensa del istmo de Panamá', *Anuario de Estudios Americanos*, ix (1952)

P.-F.-X. de Charlevoix, *Histoire de l'Isle Espagnole*, 2 vols (Paris, 1730–1)

Huguette and Pierre Chaunu, *Séville et l'Atlantique*, 8 vols (Paris, 1955–6)

Germán Colmenares, *Historia económica y social de Colombia, 1537–1719* (Bogota, 1973)

W. F. Craven, *The Colonies in Transition, 1660–1713* (New York, 1968)

N. M. Crouse, *The French Struggle for the West Indies, 1665–1713* (New York, 1943)

E. A. Cruikshank, *The Life of Sir Henry Morgan* (Toronto, 1935)

Helen J. Crump, *Colonial Admiralty Jurisdiction in the Seventeenth Century* (1931)

Frank Cundall, *The Governors of Jamaica in the Seventeenth Century* (1936)

Enrique Marco Dorta, *Cartagena de Indias* (Seville, 1951)

J. H. Elliott, *Imperial Spain, 1469–1716* (1963)

Keith Feiling, *British Foreign Policy, 1660–1672* (1930)

C. Fernández Duro, *Armada española*, 9 vols (Madrid, 1895–1903)

Troy S. Floyd, *The Anglo-Spanish Struggle for Mosquitia* (Albuquerque, N. Mex., 1967)

Alfonso García Gallo, 'El servicio militar en Indias', *Anuario de Historia del Derecho Español*, xxvii (1956)

Peter Gerhard, *Pirates on the West Coast of New Spain, 1575–1742* (Glendale, Calif., 1960)

Sebastián Gonzaléz García, 'Notas sobre el gobierno y los gobernadores de Puerto Rico en el siglo xvii', *Historia (Puerto Rico)*, n.s., i (1962)

Sources and Bibliography

Cornelis Ch. Goslinga, *The Dutch in the Caribbean and on the Wild Coast, 1580–1680* (Gainesville, Fla, 1971)

C. H. Haring, *Buccaneers in the West Indies in the Seventeenth Century* (New York, 1910)

——, *Trade and Navigation between Spain and the Indies* (Cambridge, Mass., 1918)

F. R. Harris, *Life of Edward Montagu, Earl of Sandwich* (1912)

D. A. Howarth, *The Golden Isthmus* (1966)

R. D. Hussey, 'Spanish Reaction to Foreign Aggression in the Caribbean to about 1680', *HAHR*, ix (1929)

Juan Juarez, *Piratas y corsarios en Veracruz y Campeche* (Seville, 1972)

P. K. Kemp and Christopher Lloyd, *Brethren of the Coast* (1960)

Charles Leslie, *New History of Jamaica* (1740)

Samuel Lewis, 'The Cathedral of Old Panamá', *HAHR*, i (1918)

G. Lohmann Villena, *El Conde de Lemos, virrey del Perú* (Madrid, 1946)

Edward Long, *History of Jamaica* (1774)

Allyn C. Loosley, 'The Puerto Bello Fairs', *HAHR*, xiii (1933)

Angel Lopez Cantos, *Historia de Puerto Rico, 1650–1700* (Seville, 1975)

J. Lynch, *Spain under the Hapsburgs*, vol. ii, *Spain and America, 1598–1700* (Oxford, 1969)

Murdo J. MacLeod, *Spanish Central America: a Socioeconomic History, 1520–1720* (Berkeley, Calif., 1973)

John Masefield, *On the Spanish Main* (New York, 1906)

Gabriel Maura Gamazo, Duque de Maura, *Carlos II y su Corte*, 2 vols (Madrid, 1915)

——, *Vida y reinado de Carlos II*, 2 vols (Madrid, 1954)

G. A. Mejía Ricart, *Historia de Santo Domingo*, vol. vi, *1608–1801* (Ciudad Trujillo, 1953)

A. P. Newton, *Colonising Activities of the English Puritans* (New Haven, Conn., 1914)

——, *European Nations in the West Indies, 1493–1688* (1933)

F. N. Otis, *History of the Panamá Railroad* (New York, 1867)

J. H. Parry, *The Spanish Seaborne Empire* (1966)

Michael Pawson and David Buisseret, *Port Royal, Jamaica* (1975)

Pedro Perez Valenzuela, *Historia de los Piratas o los Aventureros del Mar en la América Central* (Guatemala, 1936)

Dudley Pope, *Harry Morgan's Way* (1977)

Benito Reyes Testa, *Panamá la Vieja y Panamá la Nueva* (Panamá, 1958)

A. Rubio, *Panamá; monumentos históricas y arqueológicas* (Mexico City, 1950)

W. A. Roberts, *Sir Henry Morgan, Buccaneer and Governor* (New York, 1933)

Donald Rowland, 'Spanish Occupation of the Island of Old Providence or Santa Catalina, 1641–70', *HAHR*, xv (1935)

Georges Scelle, *La Traite négrière aux Indes de Castille*, 2 vols (Paris, 1906)

Juan Bautista Sosa, *Panamá la Vieja* (Panamá, 1969)

T. Southey, *Chronological History of the West Indies*, 3 vols (1827)

S. A. G. Taylor, *The Western Design* (Kingston, 1965)

Manuel Tejardo Fernández, *Aspectos de la vida social en Cartagena de Indias durante el seiscientos* (Seville, 1954)

A. P. Thornton, 'The Modyfords and Morgan', *Jamaican Historical Review*, ii (1952)

——, *West-India Policy under the Restoration* (Oxford, 1956)

Pierre de Vaissière, *Saint-Domingue: la société et la vie créoles sous l'Ancien Régime* (Paris, 1909)

Geoffrey J. Walker, *Spanish Politics and Imperial Trade, 1700–1789* (1979)

J. Wanguemert y Poggio, *El Almirante D. Francisco Diaz Pimienta y su época* (Madrid, 1905)

Alexander Winston, *No Purchase, No Pay* (1970)

Justo Zaragoza, *Piraterías y agresiones de los ingleses, y de otros pueblos de Europa en la América española* (Madrid, 1883)

Notes

Works listed in the Bibliography are cited by short title

CHAPTER ONE: Santa Catalina

1. The main source for the English conquest of Santa Catalina is the *averiguación* carried out in Portobello on the orders of President Perez. This is in EC 455B. This material is too full to give references in detail. There is also a brief report of Mansfield's activities in CO 1/20, No. 100 (Modyford to Arlington, 16 June 1666), and a very inaccurate account in Exquemelin, pp. 119–20.

2. Labat, *Nouveau voyage*, ii, 254.

3. For Mansfield's activities, see *CSPAWI* 1661–8, Nos 1085, 1142, 1147, 1213 and 1216, and the evidence of his Spanish and Indian prisoners in EC 455B.

4. *CSPAWI* 1661–8, No. 1142.

5. CO 1/20, No. 24: Modyford to Albemarle, 8 June 1666. The dates of English documents in the Notes will be given in OS. All dates in the text are NS.

6. There is a good account of this action based on Spanish sources in Cruikshank, *Morgan*, pp. 66–9.

7. See, for what follows, Newton, *Colonising Activities*.

8. Ibid., pp. 298–304, and Wanguemert y Poggio, *El Almirante*, pp. 107–26.

9. For a collection of documents on the fortifications, condition and general morale of Santa Catalina, see SF 223. There is much information on the state of the island at the time of the invasion in EC 455B.

10. Such quotations are from the evidence given in EC 455B.

11. Dampier, *Voyages*, i, 58–9.

12. This sort of detail comes from the evidence of Mansfield's prisoners. See, for instance, the evidence of Francisco Gonzalez and Domingo de Soza in EC 455B, fos 16–20v.

13. This sort of biographical detail was given by Rodriguez in Portobello when he answered the charges against him. EC 455B, fos 95–100v.

14. CO 1/20, No. 100 (Modyford to Arlington, 16 June 1666).
15. For a good account of Modyford's activities, see Thornton, *West-India Policy*, and see below, Chapter 3, for more on this subject.
16. CO 1/20, No. 24(i): Council of Jamaica, 22 Feb 1665/6 OS.
17. Smith's commission was captured by the Spaniards and is in Panamá 78.
18. Also in Panamá 78.

CHAPTER TWO: A Spanish Triumph
1. The main Spanish sources for the recapture of Santa Catalina in 1666 are in Panamá 78 and SF 223. There is much duplication between these two *legajos*. See also *Breve epitome* and an English translation of this in Exquemelin, pp. 121–5, which seems to be accurate except for the date. In general, see Rowland, 'Spanish Occupation'.
2. This brief biography is based on Lopez Cantos, *Puerto Rico*, pp. 175–8, and Gonzaléz García, 'Notas sobre el gobierno'.
3. For the operation of this exchange, see Loosley, 'Puerto Bello Fairs'.
4. For the records of this, see EC 455B.
5. Exquemelin, p. 122. The records of the *junta* are in SF 223.
6. SF 223: Perez to Figueroa, 27 June 1666. Panamá 78: Perez to Queen, 11 Dec 1666.
7. These details regarding the expedition are in SF 223.
8. SF 223 for the papers of this *junta* and for what follows.
9. Panamá 78: Figueroa to Perez, 31 July 1666.
10. For the expedition, see Sanchez' report to Perez in Panamá 78, 23 Aug 1666, and Exquemelin, pp. 123–5.
11. Ibid., p. 124.
12. For Smith's account of the action, see CO 1/23, No. 42: Deposition of Samuel Smith, 19 Aug 1668.
13. *CSPAWI* 1661–8, No. 1851: Depositions of Robert Rawlinson, etc., 5 Oct 1668.
14. CO 1/23, No. 43: Deposition of Henry Wassey, 19 Aug 1668.
15. These letters, together with Spanish translations, are in Panamá 78.
16. *CSPAWI* 1661–8, No. 1851: Depositions of Robert Rawlinson, etc.
17. CO 1/21, No. 5: Modyford to Albemarle, 14 Jan 1666/7.
18. Panamá 78: Panamá, 3 Mar 1667. See also CO 1/23, No. 42: Smith's deposition.
19. Panamá 78: Perez to Queen, 24 June 1667.
20. Ibid.: Report of *junta*, 2 Sep 1666.
21. Ibid.: Perez to Figueroa, 8 Sep 1666.
22. Ibid.: Perez to Sanchez, 10 Sep 1666.
23. Ibid.: Evidence of Francesco Felix, 22 Aug 1668.

24. SF 223: Queen to Conde de Lemos, 20 Dec 1666.
25. The story of the row between Perez and Lemos is well told in Lohmann Villena, *Conde de Lemos*, ch. 3. The papers relating to this episode are in Panamá 93.

CHAPTER THREE: The Privateers

1. All these papers, together with Spanish translations, are in Panamá 78.
2. Sir Thomas Modyford's commission entitling him to issue 'commissions or letters of marque or reprizall' is in ADM 2/1755, 5 Feb 1663/4.
3. For what follows, see the instructions for the commissioners of the High Court of Admiralty in Jamaica issued in 1665 which are in Panamá 78 and, in general, Crump, *Colonial Admiralty Jurisdiction*.
4. *CSPAWI* 1669–74, No. 573, 28 June 1671.
5. Panamá 78: Perez to Queen, 24 June 1667. These papers were seen and discussed by the *junta de guerra* of the Council of the Indies in Feb 1669.
6. For general discussions of this subject, see Barbour, 'Privateers'; Haring, *Buccaneers*; Andrews, *Spanish Caribbean*.
7. The first use seems to have been by Exquemelin, whose book was translated as *Bucaniers of America* in 1684. The Dutch edition of 1678 used the word *Zee-Roovers* and the Spanish edition of 1681 was entitled *Piratas de la America*. Exquemelin's translators were almost certainly deliberately insulting the privateers of Jamaica by calling them buccaneers.
8. For this period, see Newton, *Colonising Activities*.
9. See Taylor, *Western Design*.
10. For the development of Port Royal, see Pawson and Buisseret, *Port Royal, Jamaica*.
11. For what follows, Thornton, *West-India Policy*, is a valuable authority.
12. IG 1877: Report by Don Ricardo Vhit discussed at a *junta* of 4 Dec 1671.
13. *CSPAWI* 1661–8, No. 753: King to Modyford, 15 June 1664.
14. Ibid., No. 767(i).
15. Ibid., No. 767: Modyford to Bennet, 30 June 1664.
16. CO 1/18, No. 113: Bennet to Modyford, 12 Nov 1664.
17. *CSPAWI* 1661–8, No. 942: Modyford to Bennet, 20 Feb 1665.
18. Ibid., No. 1076: Petition of Sebastian Crespo, Nov 1665. See also *Memorial* of Crespo, which gives many insights into the way that the Jamaican Court of Admiralty actually operated.
19. Not all this correspondence survives, but Modyford always noted the receipt of letters from Arlington in his own letters home.
20. *CSPAWI* 1661–8, No. 1264: Modyford to Arlington, 21 Aug 1666. The letter from Arlington referring Modyford to Albemarle does not sur-

vive, but Modyford refers to it in this letter and Arlington did not later deny the fact.

21. Ibid., No. 1142: Modyford to Albemarle, 1 Mar 1666.
22. This letter does not survive, but Modyford refers to it in ibid., Nos 1144 (Modyford to Albemarle, 1 Mar 1666) and 1264 (Modyford to Arlington, 21 Aug 1666).
23. CO 1/20, No. 24(i), 22 Feb 1665/6.
24. Ibid., No. 134: Modyford to Arlington, 21 Aug 1666.
25. Davenport, *European Treaties*, ii, 106.

CHAPTER FOUR: One Ship at Orange Island

1. The main source for this chapter and the description of Portobello contained in it is the *averiguación* carried out on the orders of Bracamonte. A copy of this appears as evidence in the *residencia* carried out on Bracamonte himself in 1671 and can be found in EC 462A.
2. The following description of Portobello rests partly on EC 462A, but also on the general accounts of travellers. See, in particular, Vázquez de Espinosa, *Compendium*, pp. 303–4; Gonzalez Carranza, *Geographical Description*, pp. 81, 130–2; Wafer, *New Voyage*, pp. 62–7; Gage, *English-American*. See also Chaunu, *Séville*, viii(i), 905–8, 927–55; Anderson, *Old Panamá*, pp. 286 ff; Loosley, 'Puerto Bello Fairs'.
3. There are numerous biographies of Henry Morgan, but I have relied mainly on Cruikshank, *Morgan*. Many writers have followed Exquemelin, p. 119, and given Morgan a rather lower status, but Exquemelin's description of Morgan was withdrawn after his English publishers were threatened with a libel suit, and it seems to me that Exquemelin was clearly malicious and so I have no hesitation in describing Morgan as a gentleman.
4. See the examinations of Captains Morris, Jackman and Morgan in CO 1/20, No. 21, 20 Nov 1665.
5. Such accounts rely on Exquemelin, p. 119.
6. CO 1/23, No. 43: Deposition of Henry Wassey, 19 Aug 1668. There are other accounts of Mansfield's death, but this seems the most likely. The date is uncertain.
7. Ibid.: The information of Admiral Henry Morgan, 7 Sep 1668. This is the main English source for the capture of Portobello.
8. CO 1/20, No. 24(i), 22 Feb 1665/6.
9. CO 1/24: Narrative of Sir Thomas Modyford, 23 Aug 1669. This sentence does not appear in the Calendar – a fact which has led many historians to underestimate the takings of the privateers by calculating their loot from the official figures of tenths and fifteenths.

10. This document, dated 8 Jan 1668, is in IG 1600. It was presumably taken in a captured ship, but there is no statement in the *legajo* as to its origin.
11. For an account of this exploit, see Morgan's relation in CO 1/23, 7 Sep 1668, and also Exquemelin, pp. 127–33.
12. Morgan's relation, CO 1/23, 7 Sep 1668.
13. Morgan's own account of his voyage to Portobello can be supplemented by information given by two of his Spanish prisoners and by an English-man who was captured outside Portobello. EC 462A, i, 320v–327.
14. Morgan's relation, CO 1/23, 7 Sep 1668, fo. 101.
15. Leslie, *New History*, p. 114.
16. EC 462A, i, 324: Evidence of Pasqual Garcia.
17. *CSPAWI* 1661–8, No. 1851: Depositions of Robert Rawlinson, etc., 5 Oct 1668.
18. Morgan's relation, CO 1/23, 7 Sep 1668, fo. 101.
19. EC 462A, i, 329.
20. IG 1600. See Note 10 above.
21. The evidence as to the composition of Morgan's invasion force comes from the source described in Note 13 above.
22. IG 2541: Viceroy of New Spain to Queen, 14 June 1669.
23. Most of what follows is based on Morgan's Articles of Association in IG 1600, but it is supplemented by information from Exquemelin, pp. 71–2, and Haring, *Buccaneers*, pp. 70–8.
24. IG 1877: Sir Richard White in a paper discussed at a *junta* of 4 Dec 1671.
25. Exquemelin, p. 75.

CHAPTER FIVE: The Capture of Portobello

1. The main source for this chapter is EC 462A (see Chapter 4, Note 1). This can be supplemented by information in EC 577A and Panamá 81. The main English source is Morgan's relation in CO 1/23, 7 Sep 1668. There is also a brief account in French in CO 1/24, 7/17 Jan 1669, by Jean Doglar or John Douglas, Morgan's Commissary-General. Exquemelin, as might be expected, has a field day with the capture of Portobello. His account is, however, very inaccurate, and I have made very little use of him.
2. For information on the defences of Tierra Firme, and particularly of Santa Catalina, which illustrate the role of Juan de Somovilla Tejada, see SF 223.
3. Many Spanish prisoners were told this story by their guards and report variants of Morgan's words. See EC 462A i, 138v (evidence of Rod-riguez); i, 127v (Arredondo), etc.

4. Panamá 81: Evidence of Alonzo Sanchez Randoli.
5. This famous incident which is reported, with considerable errors of fact, by Exquemelin, pp. 136–7, is very well covered in the evidence taken at the *averiguación*. EC 462A i, 249v (evidence of Astudillo); i, 258v (De la Parra), etc.
6. Exquemelin, p. 137.
7. EC 462A i, 149.
8. *CSPAWI* 1669–74, No. 138: John Style to the Principal Secretary of State, 4 Jan 1670.
9. EC 462A i, 125v–126: Interrogatory, which was supported by the evidence.
10. Ibid., i, 254v: Evidence of Saborino.
11. Ibid., i, 139v: Evidence of Rodriguez.
12. For Morgan's fleet, see EC 577A, pza 4, fo. 2v: Bracamonte to Figueroa, 17 July 1668.
13. EC 462A i, 329: Speech of Juan de Salina.
14. CO 1/23, fo. 103.
15. *Memorial del Capitan Sebastian Crespo*, p. 18. This interesting pamphlet is in the BL (1324 c.3(21)).

CHAPTER SIX: Ransom
1. The main sources for this chapter are EC 462A i, 318–49 (papers relating to the *junta de guerra* of 23 July 1668; ii, 161v–180 (evidence of Cristoval Garcia Niño); ii, 285–321 (evidence of officers from the Panamá army); and Panamá 81 (papers relating to the ransom of Portobello). The English sources have very little to say about the ransom. No doubt Morgan was ashamed of the poor terms he got.
2. EC 462A i, 318.
3. EC 577A, pza 4, fo. 2v: Bracamonte to Figueroa, 17 July 1668.
4. IG 2541: Viceroy of New Spain to Queen, 25 Mar 1669; Miller, *Chronicle*, p. 134.
5. For information on the Armada de Barlovento, see IG 2516; IG 2541; IG 2696: Ct 3161 and Ct 5102 (letters of 10 Dec 1667 and 4 Mar 1668). See also, below, Chapter 9.
6. Copies of this letter and the replies are in Panamá 81, bundle marked 1669 (III), fos 33v–39v.
7. EC 462A i, 347.
8. Ibid., ii, 176.
9. Ibid., i, 320–7.
10. Ibid., i, 328v–331.
11. All these papers are in ibid., i, 318–49.

12. Ibid., ii, 291v–299v: evidence of Aricaga.
13. For these ransom negotiations, see ibid., i, 178v–180 (evidence of Garcia Niño), and Panamá 81, bundle marked 1669 (III), fos 40–6 (capitulations, proposals and counter-proposals).
14. The records of this *junta* are in Panamá 81; duplicates are in the bundles marked 1669(I) and 1669(III).
15. Panamá 81, passim, but especially the bundles marked 1669(II) and 1669(IV).
16. Panamá 81, 1669(III), fo. 46: Inventory of treasure.
17. CO 1/23, fo. 102.

CHAPTER SEVEN: No Peace beyond the Line

1. *CSPV* 1667–8, p. 253: Piero Mocenigo to Doge, 31 Aug 1668.
2. Thornton, 'Modyfords and Morgan', p. 37. For an excellent general account of Anglo-Spanish relations during this period, see Thornton, *West-India Policy*, ch. 3.
3. For a guide to the diplomatic manoeuvres of this period, see Feiling, *British Foreign Policy*.
4. *CSPAWI* 1660–8, No. 1894.
5. The King's audience is reported by Lord Arlington in a letter to the Queen of Spain dated 23 Feb/5 Mar 1669 in IG 1877.
6. *CSPAWI* 1660–8, No. 1894.
7. *CSPV* 1669–70, p. 24: Piero Mocenigo to Doge, 8 Mar 1669.
8. IG 1877: Arlington to Queen of Spain, 23 Feb/5 Mar 1669.
9. SP 104/174b, fos 181–6: Instructions to Godolphin, 24 Feb 1668/9.
10. IG 1877: Molina to Queen of Spain, 8 Mar 1669; *CSPD* 1668–9, 20 July 1669.
11. IG 1877. This letter was commented on in a *consulta* of 9 Apr 1669.
12. Thornton, *West-India Policy*, p. 106.
13. There is a good account of the activities of these men in Basadre, *Conde de Lemos*, ch. 9. For the Clerque–Narborough expedition, see Clerque's statements, including his orders, in Lima 72 and Narborough's papers in Kent Archives Office and Slo 46–9, 819. Sir Richard White also reports on this expedition in IG 1877, which includes a Spanish translation of Narborough's journal.
14. Add 13992, fo. 103v: Spanish discourse of 1671.
15. For more about *Oxford*, see, pp. 107–9.
16. IG 1877: Letters from London considered by the Council of the Indies on 19 May 1670.
17. CO 1/23, 7 Sep 1668.
18. *CSPV* 1669–70, p. 63: Mocenigo to Doge, 7 June 1669.

19. For Peñaranda, see Maura Gamazo, *Carlos II y su Corte*, i, 150–5.
20. IG 1877: *junta de guerra* of Indies to Queen, 19 Feb 1669.
21. IG 430, fos 171v–172.
22. IG 1877: *consulta* of 16 Mar 1669.
23. IG 430, fos 176v–178v.
24. IG 1877: *consulta* of 9 Apr 1669.
25. Ibid.: *consultas* of 14 May, 23 May, 26 June, 20 Oct, 6 Nov 1669; 11 Jan, 22 Apr 1670.
26. Ibid.: Peñaranda to Queen, undated (22 Apr?) 1670.
27. SP 104/174b, fo. 181.
28. SP 94/55: Godolphin to Arlington, 8/18 Sep 1669.
29. Ibid.: Godolphin to Arlington, 5/15 Dec 1669.
30. SP 94/56: Godolphin to Arlington, 1/11 May 1670.

CHAPTER EIGHT: 'Our Portobello Men'
1. Leslie, *New History*, p. 106.
2. Thornton, 'Modyfords and Morgan', pp. 45, 52.
3. Leslie, *New History*, p. 100.
4. The best source of information on Port Royal is Pawson and Buisseret, *Port Royal, Jamaica*.
5. Leslie, *New History*, pp. 2, 21.
6. CO 1/23, 7 Sep 1668.
7. Ibid., fo. 115: Modyford to Albemarle, 1 Oct 1668.
8. Leslie, *New History*, p. 100.
9. Most of the information on *Oxford* comes from four letters written by the surgeon Richard Browne who sailed with her. *CSPAWI* 1660–8, No. 1867, 9 Nov 1668; ibid., No. 1892, 17 Dec 1668; *CSPAWI* 1674–6, Addenda No. 1207; *CSPAWI* 1669–74, No. 21, 18 Feb 1669. See also Beeston's journal in *Interesting Tracts*, p. 287.
10. Exquemelin, p. 142.
11. Dampier, *Voyages*, i, 72.
12. Thornton, 'Modyfords and Morgan', p. 54. Morgan's narrative, which is reprinted in this article, pp. 54–6, is the only English source for the Maracaibo campaign, apart from Exquemelin.
13. The captains signed a letter which Morgan wrote in the Laguna de Maracaibo and which is printed in his narrative, ibid. For the captains on the Portobello campaign, see IG 1600, Morgan's Articles of Association.
14. Chaunu, *Séville*, viii(i), 664–7.
15. For a Spanish source, see EG 699A, pza 1, fos 39v–40, 44, etc. For English sources, see Note 12 above.

16. Exquemelin, p. 146.
17. EC 699A, pza 1, fo. 45v.

CHAPTER NINE: A Bad Day for the Admiral

1. Mexico 470: Viceroy to Queen, 28 Mar 1669.
2. Ct 3164: Statement by Campos, 30 Oct 1669. This statement made in the *almirante*'s own defence is my main Spanish source for the Maracaibo campaign. I have not been able to find the papers for the full-scale enquiry which was held at Vera Cruz or for the later investigation in Spain.
3. For general information on the Armada de Barlovento, see Veitia Linaje, *Norte*, ii, 88–100; Haring, *Trade*, pp. 253–4; Hussey, 'Spanish Reaction'.
4. IG 2516. This *legajo* contains the orders and instructions for the Armada de Barlovento from 1665. It can be supplemented by IG 2541, which contains decrees, *consultas* and correspondence, and Ct 3161, which contains the administrative papers of Diostegui's fleet.
5. For the outward voyage and the campaign of 1667–8, see Diostegui's letters of 10 Dec 1667 and 4 Mar 1668 in Ct 5102.
6. IG 2516: orders dated 6 Apr 1668 and received by the Viceroy of New Spain by 14 Aug 1668; IG 2541: Viceroy to Queen, 14 Aug 1668.
7. *Magdalena*, Ct 3161; *San Luis*, IG 2541: Viceroy to Queen, 5 Apr 1669; *Soledad*, Ct 3161 and EC 660A: evidence of Varrio, fos 2–3.
8. For what follows, I have relied on Don Alonzo's statement in Ct 3164, 'Información fecha por partte de D. Alonço de Campos . . .', fos 1–4, and the supporting evidence attached to it.
9. For the response of the Governor-General of Venezuela to Don Alonzo's plea, see EC 699A. He sent two ships from La Guayra and a considerable body of infantry, but they arrived too late to affect the outcome.
10. Exquemelin, p. 154. There is another version of this letter reproduced in Morgan's report. Thornton, 'Modyfords and Morgan', pp. 54–5.
11. Exquemelin, p. 155.
12. Morgan's report: Thornton, 'Modyfords and Morgan', p. 55.
13. This and nearly all the evidence of the battle from the Spanish point of view comes from Don Alonzo's statement. See above, Note 8. There is further evidence from the court-martial of the captain of *Soledad* in EC 660A.
14. EC 660A: evidence of the castellan, Antonio Camarillo, fos 35v–6.
15. Ibid., passim.
16. Exquemelin, p. 161.

17. Ibid., p. 162. No other evidence mentions this stratagem, and the story may be apocryphal. The Spaniards merely said that the privateers sailed out by night and it was too dark to fire accurately at them.
18. Thornton, 'Modyfords and Morgan', p. 55; Exquemelin, p. 161; *CSPAWI* 1669–74, No. 103, 23 Aug 1669.
19. Thornton, 'Modyfords and Morgan', p. 55.
20. A copy of Modyford's proclamation is in IG 1877. It was discussed at a *junta* on 23 Nov 1669.
21. IG 430, fos 176v–178v.
22. EC 660A. The hearing started on 15 June.
23. For Don Alonzo's journey to Vera Cruz and his arrest, see his own statement and those of Don Enrique Enriquez and other officers of the Mexican silver fleet in Ct 3164.
24. Veitia Linaje, ii, 91.

CHAPTER TEN: Don Juan Returns to Panamá
1. There is a good account of this whole episode in Lohmann Villena, *Conde de Lemos*, ch. 3.
2. Panamá 93: *consulta* of 14 Jan 1668.
3. This description of Panamá is drawn from a wide assortment of sources, but particularly from Vázquez de Espinosa, *Compendium*, pp. 301–6; Gage, *English-American*, p. 195; Chaunu, *Séville*, viii(i), pp. 873–955; Anderson, *Old Panamá*, pp. 273–82; and the two descriptions of Panamá in Serrano y Sanz, *Relaciones Históricas*.
4. Gage, *English-American*, p. 195.
5. Panamá 31: Cabildo secular to King, 25 May 1646; Panamá 93: Marichalar to Queen, 25 Oct 1671.
6. Anderson, *Old Panamá*, p. 275.
7. Gage, *English-American*, p. 195.
8. Bowser, 'Colonial Spanish America'.
9. Gage, *English-American*, p. 195.
10. For this, see the *residencia* of Don Juan in EC 461A.
11. On the *doctrinas*, see Add 11268, fos 7–13; for the Indians' attitude to Don Juan, see EC 461B, pza x, fo. 581v.
12. Panamá 87: Bracamonte to Queen, 29 Oct 1668.
13. There are copies of twelve letters written by Don Juan to the Viceroy asking for men between 28 Apr 1669 and 6 Aug 1670 in EC 461B, pza xi, fos 620–48. Copies of the Viceroy's replies can be found in the same place.
14. See below, pp. 235–6.
15. Marichalar's commission and the investigation are in EC 462A, pza ii.

16. Referred to by Bracamonte's counsel in EC 462A, pza i, fo. 117.
17. Their imprisonment was a charge against Don Juan in his *residencia*. EC 461A.
18. Movements of the fleet are from the *papeles de armada* in Ct 3147.
19. Receipt in Panamá 87, 2 Nov 1669.
20. Ibid.; correspondence between Banuelos and Perez.
21. SP/94/56, fo. 518v: Godolphin to Arlington, 28 June/8 July 1670.
22. Letters from Perez to the Queen and the Viceroy of Peru in EC 461B, pza xi, and Panamá 87.
23. Add 11268, fo. 57v.
24. EC 461B, pza x, fo. 956v: evidence of the *alguacil mayor* of Panamá; cf. ibid., pza v, fo. 1317v.
25. Panamá 87: report of *junta*, 3 Nov 1669.
26. Don Antonio Fernandez de Córdoba, quoted in Basadre, *Conde de Lemos*, p. 202.
27. For Perez' reports on improvements to the fortifications, see Panamá 87 and EC 461B, pza xi, fos 562–5: Perez to Queen, 8 June 1670.
28. SF 43: report of 14 June 1669.
29. Panamá 93, fo. 65: report of Antonio de Quillana, captain of the coastguard.

CHAPTER ELEVEN: The Spanish Corsairs Attack

1. IG 1877. I can find no English copy of this proclamation. This is a retranslation of a Spanish translation which was discussed in the Council of the Indies on 23 Nov 1669.
2. IG 1877, loc. cit.
3. Spanish translation in IG 1877, loc. cit. English copy in CO 1/24, fo. 127: Modyford to Molina, 15 June 1669.
4. CO 138/1, pp. 42–3: Arlington to Modyford, 12 June 1670.
5. Charlevoix, *Espagnole*, ii, 80.
6. Le Pers, 'Histoire civile', p. 312.
7. *CSPAWI* 1669–74, Nos 103, 129, 138.
8. CO 1/25, fo. 129; *CSPAWI* 1669–74, No. 172(i).
9. Rivero's ship and papers were later captured. His commission is in CO 1/25, fos 128–129v, and the poem, which is very difficult to translate, is in ibid., fos 157–8. Further Spanish evidence of his exploits is in IG 2542: Ulloa to Queen, 24 Apr 1670.
10. CO 1/27, fos 65v–66: depositions of Boys and Cobino.
11. For the story of *Mary and Jane*, see *CSPAWI* 1669–74, No. 161; CO 1/25, fo. 51 (deposition of Cornelius Carstens), and ibid., fos 157–8 (Rivero's poem).

12. See Rivero's commission in CO 1/25, fos 128–129v, and IG 2542, loc. cit.
13. *CSPAWI* 1669–74, No. 161; CO 1/25, fo. 49: depositions of Coxend and Bursett.
14. CO 1/25, fo. 52: deposition of Lane.
15. *CSPAWI* 1669–74, No. 149.
16. Ibid., No. 162.
17. Ibid., No. 161.
18. Ibid., No. 172.
19. Panamá 93, fo. 54: evidence of Lao.
20. For the story of the capture of *La Gallardina*, see EC 577A, pza v.
21. CO 1/27, fos 64–5: depositions of Browne and Burnham.
22. Ibid., fo. 63v: deposition of Jenkins.
23. Ibid., fo. 63: deposition of Guy.
24. SP/94/57, fo. 5; another copy in *CSPAWI* 1669–74, No. 310(ii).
25. The record of the Council meeting is in Add 11268, fos 66–7; also in *CSPAWI* 1669–74, Nos 209–12.
26. CO 1/27, fo. 69v: Browne to Williamson, 21 Aug 1671.
27. CO 138/1, p. 50: Modyford to Ashley, 6 July 1670.
28. CO 1/25, fo. 92: Modyford to Arlington, 6 July 1670.

CHAPTER TWELVE: Rendezvous at Isla Vaca
1. See Morgan's commission, instructions and further instructions in Add 11268, fos 68–72, and also in *CSPAWI* 1669–74, Nos 211–12.
2. *CSPAWI* 1669–74, No. 222: Modyford to Arlington, 30 July 1670.
3. Ibid., No. 227: Browne to Williamson, 7 Aug 1670.
4. All information on tonnage, guns, numbers of men, etc., is from the list of Morgan's fleet in CO 138/1, p. 105.
5. Add 11268, fo. 73. This is Morgan's official relation. There is another copy in CO 1/26, fos 69 ff.
6. CO 138/1, pp. 42–3: Arlington to Modyford, 12 June 1670.
7. CO 1/25, fo. 116: Modyford to Arlington, 20 Aug 1670.
8. Ibid.
9. Ibid. This quotation is from the Calendar, *CSPAWI* 1669–74, No. 237.
10. *CSPAWI* 1669–74, No. 231: Browne to Williamson, 11 Aug 1670.
11. IG 1877: second paper of Sir Richard White.
12. *CSPAWI* 1669–74, No. 381. See also No. 367 for Lynch's instructions.
13. Morgan's movements from Add 11268, fo. 73, and Modyford's letters to Arlington, *CSPAWI*, Nos 237, 264, 270, 310, 359.
14. Add 11268, fo. 73.
15. Spanish descriptions of the capture of Rio de la Hacha are in EC 467B,

fos 7–8, and Panamá 93, fos 11–14, 19–21. The only English description is in Exquemelin, which is rather inaccurate. For further information on the town, I have used Chaunu, *Séville*, viii(i), 670–2, and Vázquez de Espinosa, *Compendium*, p. 314.

16. Panama 93, fo. 21: information of Don Manuel de Amos Costegui.
17. Add 11268, fo. 71.
18. Panamá 93, fo. 12v.
19. Add 11410, fo. 217v.
20. Panamá 93, fo. 21.
21. *CSPAWI* 1669–74, No. 227: Browne to Williamson, 7 Aug 1670.
22. CO 1/25, fos 159–159v. See also ibid., fo. 123, for a slightly different version.
23. Panamá 93, fos 54–54v.
24. CO 1/25, fo. 159.
25. Panamá 93: Ulloa to Queen, 16 Nov 1670.
26. *CSPAWI* 1669–74, No. 310: Modyford to Arlington, 31 Oct 1670. See also Panamá 93, loc. cit. and fos 133–4 for accounts of Prince's exploits.
27. Panamá 93: Ulloa to Queen, 16 Nov 1670.
28. CO 1/25, fo. 122: Modyford to Arlington, 20 Sep 1670.
29. IG 1877: letters from London considered by the Council of the Indies on 19 May 1670; Peñaranda to Queen (22 Apr?) 1670; SP/94/57: Godolphin to Williamson, 13/23 July 1670.
30. IG 1877: Paper by White [Vhit], 4 Dec 1671.
31. *CSPAWI* 1669–74, Nos 264, 264(iii).
32. CO 1/25, fo. 160: Browne to Williamson, 12 Oct 1670.

CHAPTER THIRTEEN: Bad News along the Main
1. Panamá 93, *quaderno* entitled 'Testimonio de acuerdos . . .', fo. 15: Juan de Ozeda to Barranco, 29 Oct 1670. Copies of the other letters to and from Barranco can all be found in this *quaderno*, fos 12–15 and 18–21.
2. Panamá 93, fos 1–4. All the actions of the government of Cartagena, together with the supporting papers, are recorded in this *quaderno*, and I will make no further reference to it.
3. Royal *cedula* of 30 Dec 1633. Copy in Panamá 93, fos 9–10.
4. Panamá 93: Ulloa to Queen, 16 Dec 1670.
5. Ibid., fo. 30: Lomellin to Ulloa, 21 Dec 1670.
6. For the negotiations, see SP/94/56–7; and, for the text of the treaty, see Davenport, *European Treaties*, ii, 183–96.
7. Queen's letter in IG 430, fo. 207v. Receipt of letter in Panamá 93, fo. 84.
8. Panamá 93, fo. 36: Ulloa to Perez, 7 Jan 1671.
9. Don Juan's preparations for the defence of Panamá can be found in

Panamá 93 and, especially, in EC 461B where all sixty witnesses testified to his actions, the only criticism being that he did not go to Portobello and Chagres himself but remained in Panamá to organize the defence from there.

10. Panamá 93, fos 66–8: report on the defences of Portobello, 1 Feb 1671.
11. EC 467B, pza viii, fos 7–9: Don Juan Lopez Cerrano to Perez, 18 Nov 1670.
12. EC 461B, pza x, fo. 222v.
13. For the defences of the river, see the evidence of Gonzalez Salado in EC 461B, pza x, fos 258–62.
14. Perez de Guzmán, 'Relation'. This contemporary translation of Don Juan's report to the Queen of Spain is an abbreviated and sometimes inaccurate version of the original Spanish, which is in Panamá 93: Perez to Queen, 19 Feb 1671.

CHAPTER FOURTEEN: The Privateers Sail
1. Add 11268, fo. 69.
2. Panamá 93, fo. 47v: evidence of Sabedra.
3. Ibid., fo. 55: evidence of Lao.
4. CO 1/25, fo. 225: Modyford to Arlington, 18 Dec 1670.
5. Panamá 93, fo. 30: Lomellin to Ulloa, 21 Dec 1670.
6. CO 1/27, fo. 69v: Browne to Williamson, 21 Aug 1671.
7. The two depositions are in Add 11268, fos 74–74v.
8. Panamá 93, fo. 64.
9. . A list of Morgan's ships with the number of guns and men can be found in CO 138/1, p. 105.
10. Ibid., and see CO 1/25, fo. 225: Modyford to Arlington, 18 Dec 1670.
11. Vaissière, *Saint-Domingue*, p. 19; Panamá 93, fo. 57.
12. Exquemelin, p. 172.
13. Add 11268, fo. 75.
14. CO 1/25, fo. 225: Modyford to Arlington, 18 Dec 1670.
15. Add 11268, fo. 75.
16. EC 592v, passim.
17. Estimates vary. Frogg said 300 (Add 11410, fo. 159); Ramirez 80 (SF 223: Ramirez to Queen, 13 Oct 1671); Exquemelin 190 (p. 177). The quotation is from Ramirez.
18. Add 11268, fo. 75.
19. Exquemelin, pp. 176–7.
20. EC 455B.
21. Exquemelin uses the alternative names of San Geronimo and Santa

Theresa for these two fortresses. I have stuck to the nomenclature that I have used in Chapters 1 and 2.
22. Panamá 93, fos 55v–58.
23. Add 11268, fo. 75.
24. Panamá 93, fo. 58.

CHAPTER FIFTEEN: San Lorenzo
1. Since the Spaniards considered that no one was to blame for the loss of San Lorenzo, there was no enquiry into the capture of the castle. Accounts of the action can be found in Panamá 93, fos 40–42v (Sabedra), fos 115v–118v (Castillo), n.p. Perez to Queen, 19 Feb 1671, n.p. Marichalar to Queen, 25 Oct 1671; EC 461B, pza x, fos 304–304v (Silva). The main English sources are Add 11268, fos 75–6 (Morgan); Add 11410, fo. 159 (Frogg); Exquemelin, pp. 180–5.
2. Panamá 93, fos 112v–113.
3. Ibid.: Perez to Queen, 19 Feb 1671.
4. Ibid., fo. 41v.
5. Exquemelin, p. 181.
6. Panamá 87: Bracamonte to Queen, 29 Oct 1668.
7. Panamá 93: Marichalar to Queen, 25 Oct 1671.
8. Ibid., fo. 115v.
9. Exquemelin, p. 183.
10. Details of Don Juan's illness are in EC 461B, pza x, fo. 517v: evidence of the surgeon, Antonio Delgado Carvasal.
11. Panamá 93, fos 111v–112: Perez to Ulloa, 9 Jan 1671.
12. Add 11268, fo. 76.
13. Panamá 93, fos 56v–57.

CHAPTER SIXTEEN: The River Campaign
1. The main sources for the Spanish defence of the river are in EC 461B. See, in particular, pza x, fos 7v–10, and pza xi, fos 791–794v, and the answers to the questions asked in these two interrogatories. See also Gonzalez' evidence in ibid., pza x, fos 258–72, and the reports of Perez and Sabedra in Panamá 93.
2. EC 461B, pza x, fo. 476: plea of Don Francisco Jaymes.
3. The English sources for this chapter are Exquemelin, pp. 186–93; Add 11268, fos 76–7 (Morgan); Add 11410, fo. 159v (Frogg). Exquemelin's dates and place-names are inaccurate, and I have relied on Morgan for fact and chronology and Exquemelin for colour.
4. Panamá 93: Perez to Queen, 19 Feb 1671, fo. 5.
5. EC 461B, pza x, fos 343v–346.

6. For my description of the river I have relied on travellers' accounts, especially Ulloa, *Relación histórica*, i, 145–50, and I have also used Otis, *Panamá Railroad*.
7. Panamá 93: Perez to Queen, 19 Feb 1671, fo. 5.
8. Otis, *Panamá Railroad*, p. 109.
9. Exquemelin, p. 187.
10. EC 461B, pza v, fo. 1318v.
11. Panamá 93: Perez to Queen, 19 Feb 1671.
12. EC 461B, pza x, fo. 271: evidence of Gonzalez.
13. Panamá 25: Córdoba to the Conde de Medellin, 9 Mar 1672.
14. Exquemelin, p. 189.
15. Ibid., p. 189.
16. Lima 72: Perez to Lemos, 9 Feb 1671.
17. Add 11268, fo. 76.
18. Exquemelin, p. 191.
19. Add 11268, fo. 77.
20. Ibid., fo. 177; Exquemelin, p. 193.
21. Exquemelin, p. 193.

CHAPTER SEVENTEEN: The Defence of the City
1. The main sources for this chapter are EC 461B; Panamá 93: Perez to Queen, 19 Feb 1671; ibid.: Marichalar to Queen, 25 Oct 1671.
2. For Don Juan's medical condition, see EC 461B, pza x, fos 517v–521.
3. Ibid., pza x, fo. 325v.
4. Panamá 93: Perez to Queen, 19 Feb 1671.
5. EC 461B, pza x, fo. 283.
6. Perez loc. cit.
7. Ibid. See also the contemporary English translation in Perez de Guzmán, 'Relation'.
8. The inventories are in EC 461B, pza x, fos 572–600.
9. Ibid., fo. 459v: plea of Don Francisco Jaymes.
10. Panamá 93: Perez to Queen, 19 Feb 1671.
11. EC 461B, pza x, fos 484v–485.
12. Ibid., pza v, fo. 1319.
13. Ibid., pza x, fos 462–3.

CHAPTER EIGHTEEN: The Battle for Panamá
1. The main Spanish sources for the battle are Perez de Guzmán, 'Relation'; Panamá 93: Perez to Queen, 19 Feb 1671; ibid., fos 45–45v (Sabedra); Lima 72: Perez to Lemos, 9 Feb 1671; Panamá 72: Marichalar to Queen, 19 Apr 1673; EC 461B, pza x, especially fos 347–9 (Salmon), 521

(Delgado). The English sources are Add 11268, fos 77–8 (Morgan); Add 11410, fos 159v–160 (Frogg); Exquemelin, pp. 194–6.

2. Add 11268, fo. 79: deposition of John Peeke.
3. Lima 72: Perez to Lemos, 9 Feb 1671.
4. Perez de Guzmán, 'Relation', p. 154.
5. Ibid.
6. EC 461B, pza x, fo. 486v.
7. Add 11268, fos 77–8 (Morgan).
8. Don Juan reported his exhortation rather differently in different places. This is a combination of his words from his 'Relation' and the letter to the Queen.
9. EC 461B, pza x, fo. 521 (Delgado).
10. Add 11268, fos 77–8 (Morgan).
11. Panamá 25: Córdoba to Conde de Medellin, 9 Mar 1672.
12. EC 461B, pza x, fo. 217v: evidence of Pau y Rocaberti. The evidence regarding the burning of Panamá is very confused, though nobody suggested, as Exquemelin did, that Morgan burned it himself. The main source is EC 461B, pza x. See the answers to question 13 in the interrogatory (fo. 19).
13. Ibid., fo. 312v.
14. Ibid., fos 312–14.
15. Ibid., fos 275–278v.

CHAPTER NINETEEN: No Help for Don Juan
1. EC 461B, pza v, fo. 1321. There are many testimonies as to what happened after the battle in ibid., pza x. See the answers to questions 10 and 11 in the prosecution's interrogatory, fos 15–17v.
2. Lima 72: Perez to Lemos, 9 Feb 1671.
3. Add 11268, fo. 47.
4. Ibid., fo. 38.
5. Perez de Guzmán, 'Relation', p. 156.
6. EC 461B, pza x, fo. 805.
7. Lima 72: Perez to Lemos, 9 Feb 1671.
8. Panamá 93: Lemos to Queen, 4 Apr 1671.
9. Panamá 93, fo. 129v: Olivares to Ulloa, 25 Feb 1671. This letter includes the gist of Don Juan's letter.
10. Ibid.: Perez to Queen, 19 Feb 1671.
11. Panamá 93, fo. 43v.
12. Ibid., fos 37–9.
13. Ibid., fo. 131v.
14. Ibid., fo. 84.

15. Ibid., fos 49–53: *acuerdo* of 12 Feb 1671 and fos 59v–60; statement by Ulloa, 14 Feb 1671.
16. Ibid., fos 82v–84v: Ulloa to Morgan, 19 Feb 1671.
17. EC 461B, pza x, fo. 316: declaration of Antonio de Silva.
18. Lima 72. This section is based mainly on three letters from the Viceroy to the Queen dated 24 Jan, 14 Feb and 28 Mar 1671. There is a mass of supporting material in the form of letters and declarations in this *legajo*. See also the accounts in Basadre, *Conde de Lemos*, pp. 175–99, and Lohmann Villena, *Conde de Lemos*, pp. 353–60.
19. Panamá 72: Marichalar to Council of the Indies, 19 Apr 1673.
20. There is a mass of information in Lima 72 on this incident with a useful summary in the Viceroy's letter of 28 Mar.
21. Some letters in English from these prisoners are preserved in Lima 72.
22. Lima 72: Lemos to Queen, 28 Mar 1671. See also Panamá 93: Lemos to Queen, 4 Apr 1671.
23. EC 461B, pza x, fo. 278.
24. Add 11268, fo. 61: Perez to Queen, 8 May 1671.

CHAPTER TWENTY: Henry Morgan Returns

1. Add 11268, fo. 78.
2. Exquemelin, p. 198; Add 11410, fo. 160.
3. EC 461B, pza x, fo. 484.
4. Ibid., fo. 314; Panamá 93, fo. 130v; Add 11268, fo. 57; Perez de Guzmán, 'Relation', pp. 156–7.
5. EC 461B, pza x, fo. 395v.
6. Exquemelin, pp. 198–9.
7. Panamá 93, fo. 130v.
8. CO 1/27, fo. 69v: Browne to Williamson, 21 Aug 1671.
9. Add 11268, fo. 58v: Perez to Queen, 31 Mar 1671.
10. Panamá 93: Marichalar to Queen, 25 Oct 1671.
11. Ibid.: Perez to Queen, 19 Feb 1671.
12. Ayres (ed.), *Voyages*, p. 144.
13. Exquemelin, p. 203.
14. Add 11268, fo. 58: Perez to Queen, 31 Mar 1671.
15. Panamá 25: Audiencia of Panamá to Queen, 16 Sep 1675.
16. Add 11268, fos 11v–12.
17. Exquemelin, pp. 205–6.
18. Add 11268, fo. 78 (Morgan); Panamá 93: report from London, 10 July 1671; Add 11410, fo. 160 (Frogg); CO 1/27, fo. 69 (Browne).
19. Exquemelin, p. 207.

20. CO 1/27, fo. 69: Browne to Williamson, 21 Aug 1671.
21. Thornton, 'Modyfords and Morgan', p. 56, dated 10 Apr 1671.
22. CO 1/27, fo. 69: Browne to Williamson, 21 Aug 1671. For various comments on the fate of the privateers after the Panamá campaign, see, in addition to this letter, *CSPAWI* 1669–74, Nos 552, 580, 588, 604, 638, 663, and Add 11410, fos 183–4, 196v, 207v, 215, 223–4.
23. Add 11410, fo. 183v: Lynch to Arlington, 27 June 1671.
24. Thornton, 'Modyfords and Morgan', p. 57, 10 Apr 1671.
25. Add 11268, fo. 79.
26. *CSPAWI* 1669–74, Nos 531, 544.
27. Ibid., Nos 405, 441.
28. Add 11410, fo. 181v: Lynch to Arlington, 27 June 1671.
29. Ibid., fos 185–91: Lynch to Sandwich, 20 Aug 1671; *CSPAWI* 1669–74, No. 604: Lynch to Arlington, 20 Aug 1671.

CHAPTER TWENTY-ONE: Peace in the Indies

1. Panamá 93, fo. 137.
2. SP/89/11, fo. 160: reports from Lisbon, including the examination of an Englishman who travelled in the ship from Cartagena.
3. SP/94/58: Godolphin to Arlington, letters of 14/24 June and 28 June/8 July; *CSPV* 1671–2: Contarini to Doge, 17 June 1671.
4. SP/94/58: Godolphin to Arlington, letters of 14/24 June, 28 June/8 July, 12/22 July; *CSPV* 1671–2: Contarini to Doge, 17 June 1671.
5. e.g. Add 13992, fos 87–106: scheme to reconquer all the English possessions with a fleet of corsairs from all over the Spanish dominions and then put the management of the Indies in the hands of a Spanish West India Company with private capital; IG 1877: scheme of Sir Richard White to bribe all English governors in the West Indies and to set up an elaborate information service. All would be done by White in return for a slaving concession.
6. Panamá 93: Queen to Peñaranda, 11 June 1671; *junta de guerra*, 13 June 1671; Queen to Medina Celi, 28 June; Medina Celi to Queen, 11 July.
7. Ibid.: Peñaranda to Queen, 14 June 1671; Córdoba's orders, 6 July.
8. *CSPV* 1671–2: Alberti to Doge, 14 Aug 1671.
9. Ibid.: Contarini to Doge, 12 Aug 1671; SP/94/58: Godolphin to Arlington, 9/19 Aug, 23 Aug/2 Sep 1671; Bebington, *Letters*, p. 328: Arlington to Godolphin, 6 July 1671.
10. *CSPAWI* 1669–74, No. 794: instructions to Capt. Keene, 4 Apr 1672.
11. *CSPV* 1671–2: Alberti to Doge, 4 and 18 Dec 1671.
12. Panamá 72: Marichalar to Queen, 2 June 1673. He reports that his *visitá* started on 5 May 1670.

13. Panamá 93: Marichalar to Queen, 25 Oct 1671. See also Panamá 89: Marichalar to Queen, 22 Jan 1672.
14. EC 461A, fos 31–4.
15. EC 461B, fos 4–23.
16. All the documents relating to this 'querella sibil y criminal' are in EC 461B, pzas x and xi.
17. See, in addition to the evidence in EC 461B, the letter from Córdoba to the Conde de Medellin in Panamá 25, 9 Mar 1672.
18. EC 461B, pza xi, fos 1110–11.
19. Ibid., pza viii, fo. 10.
20. Panamá 89: record of *junta*, 22 Jan 1672.
21. Lima 72: Lemos to Queen, 6 June 1672.
22. Panamá 72: Marichalar to Council of Indies, 19 Apr 1673.
23. Panamá 101: Bishop of Panamá to Queen, 24 Apr 1674.
24. Ibid.: report of 26 May 1675.
25. Add 11410, fos 183v, 189, 206.
26. See Burney, *Chronological History*; Céspedes del Castillo, 'La defensa'.
27. Wafer, *New Voyage*, p. 73.
28. Add 11410, fo. 224.
29. Ibid., fos 212v–213.
30. Ibid., fo. 235.
31. Ibid., fos 270–271v.
32. Quoted in Cruikshank, *Morgan*, p. 414.
33. Morgan's inventory is in the Jamaican Archives, Spanish Town: 1B/11/3. I am grateful to Mrs Nuala Zahedieh for getting me a copy.

Index

The Sack of Panamá

Index

Index

junta: described, 30; Perez de Guzmán, (1666) 30, (1670) 142, (1671) 211–12; Figueroa, (1666) 31, (1668) 82; Bracamonte (1668), 80, 81, 86, 88; Council of the Indies, (1669) 98, 100–1, 131, (1667) 119; Viceroy of New Spain (1669), 130–1; Ulloa (1671), 169; Castillo (1671), 201; Gonzalez Salado (1671), 203; Córdoba (1672), 256; records, 263

La Cortadura (fort), 18, 21, 34, 35, 184, 185
La Gloria, 70
La Guayra, 121, 127, 140
La Quebrada de las Lajas, 189
La Rancheria, 68, 70
La Rochelle, 108
La Tasca, 238
Ladron de Guevara, Don Pedro, 74
Laguna de Maracaibo, 110, 111, 112, 113, 114, 121, 123, 124, 128, 156
Laja Reef, 195
Lamb, 163
Lao, Juan de, 163, 180, 185, 196, 231 n
Lara, Sergeant-Major Antonio de, 83
Lemos, Conde de, Viceroy of Peru: arrives in Portobello (1666), 38; arrests Perez de Guzmán, 39, 80, 132, 143, 172; relief for Portobello, 82 and n; releases Perez (1669), 132–3; relations with Perez, 133, 138–9, 141, 228, 229, 232, 235, 256; alarm in Chile, 233–4; relief for Panamá, 235–6, 245
Leslie, Charles, 104
letters of marque, see commissions
Lilly, 109, 125, 156, 260
Lima, 27, 80, 132, 232, 233, 234, 235, 253
Lisbon, 250
Lomellin, Don Franco, 170, 172, 177
London, 37, 46, 49, 90, 91, 92, 130, 159, 160, 247, 248, 249, 261
Los Santos, 135, 175, 227
Louis XIV, King of France, 95
Luba, Marco de, 178, 179
Lynch, Sir Thomas, Governor of Jamaica, 159, 160, 247–9, 253, 257, 258, 259, 260, 261

Madrid, 31, 46, 59, 90, 91, 93, 97, 101, 105, 144, 157, 170, 250, 256
Madrid, Treaty of (1671), 101–2, 157, 158, 170–1, 172, 176, 177, 230, 246, 247–8, 250, 258, 260
Magdalena, 120, 122, 125, 126, 127, 129
Magellan, Straits of, 96, 233
Mallvegui, Sergeant Juan de, 76
Mansfield, Captain Edward: captures Santa Catalina (1666), 11–26, 33, 36, 51, 59, 64, 184; Cuba refuses supplies, 14; commission, 14; and Curaçao, 14–15
Manzanillo, 148
Mapoo, John, 65 and n
Maracaibo: L'Ollonais raids (1667), 110; Morgan raids (1669), 110–15, 120–30, 146, 180, 244
Margarita Island, 110
Maria Anna, Queen Regent of Spain: minority of Carlos II, 31 and n, 98; exonerates Perez de Guzmán, 39, 139; letter from Arlington, 94; and Charles II, 95; declares war in Indies (1669), 99–100, 130, 143, 145, 147–8, 150, 179, 247; and Godolphin, 101, 251, 252–3; reinforcements for Main, 139, 140; ends hostilities in Indies (1671), 171; and sack of Panamá, 250
Marichalar, Don Francisco de, 139, 241, 253, 254, 255, 256–7
maroons, 136
Martinique, 44
Mary and Jane, 148–9
Mata Asnillos, 214, 215, 222
Matapolo, 84
Maurice, Prince, 97
Mayflower, 156
mazamorra, see sickness
Medina Celi, Duke of, 251, 252, 253
Mercedarians, 56

Index

Nuestra Señora de Popa, 109, 169
Nuestra Señora del Buen Suçeso, 224

Ocampo, Don Estevan de, Governor of Santa Catalina, 20, 21–2, 24, 27, 185
oficiales reales, 30
Olivera, Manuel de, Constable of Artillery, 69, 71, 74
L'Ollonais, *see* Nau, Jean-David
Oxford, 97, 107–9, 111, 120, 156, 180, 248
oydores, 30, 38, 253

Panamá (city), 18, 24, 44, 54, 65, 72, 76, 77, 78, 79, 83, 84, 85, 88, 89, 105, 140, 163, 256, 258, 259;
    sack (1671), 26, 141, 171, 202, 204, 208, 217–25, 226, 228, 230, 235, 237, 239, 240, 243, 244, 245,
    246, 247, 248, 249, 250, 251, 252, 253, 260, 261, 266; mule-trains, 29, 55, 56, 81, 89, 135, 136,
    139, 173, 206; garrison, 30, 31, 86, 87, 106, 137, 138, 169, 174, 227; militia, 31, 81, 106; English
    prisoners in, 37; Royal Treasury, 89; Town Council, 134; conditions in, 134; population, 135,
    175; defence, 142, 175, 194, 197, 198, 199, 209–16, 229, 242; privateers' interest in, 163, 167, 172,
    173, 179, 182–3, 184, 186, 188; cathedral, 141, 175, 208, 212, 213; gaol, 198–9; plaza, 212–13,
    224; Convent of Our Lady of the Conception, 213; Matadero Bridge, 223; relief, 231–2, 235,
    236; privateers depart, 242; *residencia*, 254–5
Panamá, Audiencia of, 15, 27, 29, 38, 43, 132, 133, 134–5, 138, 140, 173, 225, 229, 245, 253, 254
Panamá, Bay of, 133, 238, 239
Panamá, Bishop of, 257
Panamá, Isthmus of, 27, 29, 55, 56, 80, 85, 88, 136, 137, 139, 141, 142, 172, 173, 174, 175, 182, 194,
    196, 197, 205, 207, 220, 222, 226, 227, 232, 237, 241, 242, 250, 253, 258
Panamá, Treasurer of, 211
Panamá Canal, 175, 200
Panamá City, 256
Panamá Railroad, 142
Parker, William, 62
Patagonia, 96, 233
Pau y Rocaberti, Castellan Alexandro Manuel, 75–8, 80, 81
Pau y Rocaberti, Don Balthasar, Captain of Artillery, 223
Payta, 235, 236
Peake, John, 178
Pearl Islands, 133, 224
Peña del Angel, 70, 71
Peñalosa, Don Diego de, 96
Peñaranda, Conde de, 98, 101, 165, 170, 250, 252
Penn, Admiral, 46
Pennant, Captain Jeffrey, 110 and n
Penonome, 137, 227, 228, 229
Pequen, 81
Perez, Lucas, 179
Perez, Pedro, 19
Perez de Guzmán, Don Juan, President of Audiencia of Panamá, 40, 43, 79, 135, 137, 178, 179,
    182, 188, 193, 197, 198, 203, 262; early career, 27; arrives in Panamá (1665), 27; duties, 29; Santa
    Catalina (1666), 29–38; *junta* (1666), 30; arrest, 39, 80; prison in Peru, 39, 80, 132, 143, 172;
    exonerated, 39, 132, 139; replaced in Panamá by Bracamonte, 80; returns to Panamá (1669), 133;
    relations with Lemos, 133, 138–9, 141, 228, 229, 232, 235, 256; wealth, 136, 212–13; defence of
    Panamá, 138–9, 140–1, 142, 172, 173, 174, 175, 186, 198–9, 204, 206, 209–16, 240; *junta* (1670),
    142; illness, 209–10, 226; *junta* (1671), 211–12; battle for Panamá, 217–24; flees city, 224, 226–7;
    rallies, 227–8; no relief for, 228–9, 231–2; house ruined, 238; and torture, 241; replaced by
    Córdoba, 252; *residencia*, 254–6; death (1675), 256
Perico, 133, 135, 207, 214, 223, 239
Peru, 37, 55, 89, 140, 209, 215, 229, 235, 238; riches, 27, 29, 62, 99, 134, 139, 237, 257; Perez de
    Guzmán imprisoned in, 39, 132–3, 138, 143, 172; weakness, 86, 96; possible invasion, 228, 232
Peru, Viceroy of, *see* Lemos, Conde de
Philip IV, King of Spain, 98
Pimienta, Captain-General Francisco Diaz de, 17, 18, 45
Pineda, Juan de, 87

Index